T0311781

The Political Economy of Special Economic Zones

Special Economic Zones (SEZs) have become a popular development policy throughout the world over the last half a century. These zones form designated areas where governments offer businesses lower taxes, tariffs, and often lighter regulations. Generally, SEZs aim to attract investments and raise a country's export and employment rates, but although success stories are often cited, there are numerous failed projects that have instead become burdens for their host countries.

This book examines SEZs from a political economy perspective, both to dissect the incentives of governments, zone developers, and exporters, and to uncover both the hidden costs and untapped potential of zone policies. Costs include misallocated resources, the encouragement of rent-seeking, and distraction of policy-makers from more effective reforms. However, the zones also have several unappreciated benefits. They can change the politics of a country, by generating a transition from a system of rent-seeking to one of liberalized open markets. In revealing the hidden promise of SEZs, this book shows how the SEZ model of development can succeed in the future.

Applying frameworks from various schools of political economy, this volume places SEZs in the context of their mixed past and promising future. It is essential reading for anyone with an interest in international economics, development economics, and political economy, including practitioners and consultants of SEZ policies.

Lotta Moberg is a Senior Macro Analyst on the Dynamic Allocation Strategies team at William Blair, USA.

Routledge Studies in the Modern World Economy

For a full list of titles in this series, please visit www.routledge.com/series/SE0432

The Political Economy of Special Economic Zones

Concentrating Economic Development

Lotta Moberg

Routledge
Taylor & Francis Group

LONDON AND NEW YORK

First published 2017
by Routledge

2 Park Square, Milton Park, Abingdon, Oxfordshire OX14 4RN
52 Vanderbilt Avenue, New York, NY 10017

Routledge is an imprint of the Taylor & Francis Group, an informa business

First issued in paperback 2018

British Library Cataloguing in Publication Data
A catalogue record for this book is available from the British Library

Library of Congress Cataloging in Publication Data
Names: Moberg, Lotta, author.
Title: The political economy of special economic zones : concentrating
economic development / Lotta Moberg.
Description: Abingdon, Oxon ; New York, NY : Routledge, [2017] |
Includes index.
Identifiers: LCCN 2016044661| ISBN 9781138237810 (hardback) |
ISBN 9781315298955 (ebook)
Subjects: LCSH: Enterprise zones. | Export processing zones. | Free ports
and zones. | Industrial sites. | Industrial promotion. | Economic
development.
Classification: LCC HC79.D5 .M623 2017 | DDC 338.9–dc23
LC record available at https://lccn.loc.gov/2016044661

ISBN: 978-1-138-23781-0 (hbk)
ISBN: 978-0-367-10926-4 (pbk)

Typeset in Times New Roman
by Taylor & Francis Books

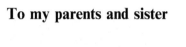

To my parents and sister

Contents

Illustrations

Figures

Tables

Preface

Henry Ford was more than the industrialist who built the first middle class car. He was also the founder of Fordlandia, a more than 14 square kilometers settlement in the Brazilian jungle. The Brazilian government granted tax breaks to Ford to start the production of rubber for the Ford Motor Company, and he transformed the area into a town with an American standard of living, with electricity, running water, American-style housing, and a cafeteria with American food. It was a bubble of modernity in an underdeveloped country, connected to the nearest city only by a river.

In Fordlandia, people would not only learn the American work ethic but also eat American food and enjoy American culture. As such, they were meant to become workers who both lived up to American standards and were exceptionally cheap to hire.

The project was ultimately unsuccessful. The rubber turned out to be unprofitable to extract, the American food rotted in the humidity, and the workers resented having the American way of life imposed on them. What looked like such a promising venture became the victim of unintended culture clashes, unexpected logistical problems, and unforeseen costs.

This was three decades before the first modern special economic zone (SEZ). Similar to Fordlandia, many SEZs aim to change the business environment in particular areas, and exploit tax breaks and cheap labor to promote investments. While Ford attempted to change the culture, more progressive SEZ planners aim similarly to change the rules in a particular area, often through different regulations or more efficient bureaucracies.

Alas, as Ford learned the hard way, what seems a straight path to spurring industrial plants is not all that smooth. Many SEZs have fallen prey to unintended costs, misdirected investments, and poorly functioning policies and institutions. Some SEZ schemes have, like Fordlandia, been deemed more as neocolonialism and cultural imperialism than mutually beneficial agreement between foreign investors and their employees. But just as Fordlandia told a useful lesson in the early 1930s, every mistake in the history of SEZs offers a lesson that can help enhance the SEZ model to promote real economic development. This book is about how to properly learn those lessons.

When I first came across the SEZ concept, I found it a promising development policy. This is unusual for a free-market economist like me. I am predisposed to be skeptical of development policies because of the government interventions they usually necessitate. However, SEZs do not require the government to set spending targets or to direct investments. By creating a space where companies find it attractive to invest, the zones can grow organically, with all the hallmarks of a free market, and create opportunities for workers and other companies in the host country.

SEZs are therefore different from other development policies. Foreign aid, infrastructure boosts, microlending institutions, and most other development policies rely on active and targeted government measures. Policy makers declare their vision of a country's development path and what steps the economy must take. They may, for instance, expect a particular bridge to boost trade between two localities, which in turn will raise income, make people spend more, and thereby develop the economy as a whole. They might aim foreign aid at boosting a country's spending on healthcare, which will help children stay in school and become more productive in adulthood.

Unfortunately, many conventional development policies have a disappointing record. It is difficult for governments to know what specific investments are the key to unleashing economic growth. Despite obvious deficiencies in health, for instance, several countries have failed to jump-start development with generous and targeted healthcare spending programs.

Because specific development investments are often misguided, broader approaches to development promotion, such as enhancing a country's rule of law and promoting a functional system of governance, are more promising. They do not rely on policy makers predicting a country's path. Instead, they encourage productive economic activities by facilitating exchange and protecting property rights.

The problem with such broader kinds of reforms is that they are seldom politically popular. Because the results of these reforms are delayed and often hard to identify, policy makers cannot use any specific metric of the economy to claim credit for any success. Without the necessary political will behind them, such broad reforms tend not to happen.

SEZs both offer a better economic environment and allow policy makers to point to specific industrial clusters and claim to be their creators. It therefore seems to be the development policy that most people should support, regardless of whether they believe government should take targeted measures to spur growth or are skeptical of the government trying to do so.

As it turns out, economists have very divergent views on SEZs. One view is that SEZs by definition are a good policy because they increase the level of growth promoting policies in a country. The other is that the SEZ model is misguided and discriminatory because it limits economic reforms to narrow geographical spaces. In my research on SEZs, I have attempted to find out which view is right and whether the two views can somehow be reconciled.

Previous studies on SEZs focus on measurable macroeconomic data on exports, investments, production, and employment to determine whether the zones are beneficial. The untold story is the one connecting zone politics with economics – that is, the political economy of SEZs. In the absence of a political economy analysis of SEZs, their picture is only half-painted. This is the picture this book is meant to complete.

I will argue that the macroeconomic measurements that make SEZs seem so promising actually do not tell us much about their real benefits. By focusing on superficial data, we easily miss the distortionary effects the zones can have and their role in destructive rent-seeking. We can also overlook that SEZs' real promise lies in their political, rather than their economic, effects. By changing the political dynamics in a country, they can set it on a reform path that would have been politically impossible in their absence.

This book offers a highly contextual picture of SEZs, with a lot of grey and very little black and white. While there are many reasons to be skeptical of SEZs, they also have the potential to profoundly change an economy for the better. By applying political economy frameworks to SEZs, it is possible to gauge what circumstances can make SEZs truly beneficial.

I hope this will be an informative and thought-provoking read for anyone interested in understanding the political economy of this peculiar but promising development policy.

Acknowledgements

I am grateful for valuable advice and comments from Tyler Cowen, Thomas W. Bell, and Christopher Nisbet. Thank you for making this book so much better and for your time, patience, and creative suggestions.

I want to thank Thomas Farole, Michael Castel Miller, Christopher Limnios, and Mark Lutter for your comments on my early book draft. I am also grateful to Garett Jones, Richard E. Wagner, Christopher J. Coyne, Robert Haywood, Barbara Cole, Vlad Tarko, Patrik Tingvall, Art Carden, Mark Koyama, Ryan Safner, and Lisardo Bolaños, for discussions, support, and ideas that formed the research behind this book. A special thanks to Carlos Rodriquez, Daniel Morales, Harold Vasquez, Ebell De Castro, and all the heroes of the Dominican SEZs.

Introduction

Special economic zones (SEZs) hold great promise for economic development. Several SEZ countries have diversified their economy's production, promoted exports, and attracted foreign investors that have hired thousands of domestic workers. Numerous studies have shown how businesses in an SEZ perform better than those in other parts of a country, and that countries can use SEZs to promote manufacturing exports and transform themselves from agrarian to industrialized economies.[1]

SEZs are, in essence, particular areas that abide by different rules than the country as a whole. At a minimum, this means certain tax and tariff exemptions for SEZ investors. Many SEZs also offer different rules, such as exemptions from certain labor and environmental regulations and minimized government bureaucracy for investors to navigate. The explicit goal is to attract investors, both foreign and domestic, in an effort to increase production, exports, and employment.

Often, SEZs are part of a broader agenda of economic diversification and industrialization. Countries dependent on agriculture for export may see their growth held back by the sector's limited economies of scale.[2] This is not a problem with manufacturing, which SEZs tend to promote.

The use of SEZs has been linked to the success of Asian tiger economies, in particular China and South Korea. These countries became internationally competitive exporters and grew at a remarkable rate when they opened up their economies. Their SEZs played prominent roles in this transformation.[3] As a British territory, Hong Kong has also functioned as an SEZ within China, with an unusual level of autonomy. Now a Chinese "Special Administrative Region" rather than an SEZ, Hong Kong nevertheless exemplifies the power of SEZs. In Africa, Mauritius stands out as an agricultural economy using SEZs to develop manufacturing and tourism industries.[4] In Latin America, the SEZs in Honduras and the Dominican Republic have made those countries important textile exporters to the United States. Mexico, with its "maquiladora" zones, along its US border, stands out as the largest Latin American apparel exporter to the United States.[5]

Successful SEZs have encouraged more countries to introduce zones in the expectation of similar fortunes. Governments have experimented with SEZs for more than half a century, and there are now thousands of SEZs in the world. It therefore seems that SEZ practitioners would have found some sort of blueprint for how to create successful SEZs.

Nevertheless, SEZs still often fail to attract many investors. As a result, they do not generate jobs or increase exports. A government may pronounce a new SEZ with great fanfare, build impressive infrastructure, and present the juicy fiscal incentives that await businesses that enter. Still, only a handful of companies may show up, far from enough to substantially contribute to the economy. The new infrastructure is left abandoned. Prospective SEZ firms complain that the facilities are not good enough, that the location is inconvenient, or that the fiscal incentives are inferior to those of SEZs in neighboring countries. A common conclusion from such alleged failures is that the government needs to be more committed to make SEZs successful. It should coordinate the infrastructure better, make incentives more attractive, and promote more linkages between SEZs and the rest of the economy.

Although superficially persuasive, such explanations for SEZ failure and such policy prescriptions are often mistaken and misguided. To understand the ways SEZs can benefit an economy and how they might fail to do so, one must look beyond the growth of SEZs themselves and apply a broader political economy perspective. As Chapter 1 will explain in depth, political economy frameworks take into account that motivations other than social welfare often lie behind policy making. Such frameworks can also account for governance problems and information deficiencies that may stand in the way of a policy's successful implementation.

A political economy approach also helps identify what SEZ success actually entails. The standard view is that SEZ success means a zone that attracts many firms and generates a lot of economic activity. Governments often introduce targets for the value of exports or investments, or how many jobs a zone is meant to generate, which serve as benchmarks for judging success or failure. The political economy approach to SEZs is very different. A zone that attracts a lot of firms may not be successful and can even be harmful for an economy. On the other hand, SEZs bring many benefits, both economic and political, that are not revealed by export and employment data.

Rather than looking for an SEZ blueprint or a zone manual, the political economy approach to SEZs requires an understanding of how different political and institutional contexts promote the success or failure of SEZs. Sometimes, a government must change fundamental parts of its administration for SEZs to become successful. Other countries may not benefit at all from adopting SEZs.

Numerous SEZs have brought more harm than good to their host countries because governments have tried to promote the symptoms of SEZ success, rather than its causes. An understanding of the political economy of SEZs is a step toward avoiding such mistakes in the future.

The rise of the zones

The zone concept is far from novel. In ancient Greece, the holy island of Delos was designated a free harbor. This special status was meant to encourage imports to the holy sanctuary, which lacked the agriculture, building material, and objects of worship to accommodate its many visitors.[6] More recently, the zone concept has developed in various ways, offering a variety of combinations of fiscal and regulatory incentives.

Several of the countries that introduced SEZs in the early 20th century were developed countries. Spain attracted one of the early Ford Motor plants in Europe to a zone in the 1920s, and the United States sought to spur international trade through its 1930s "foreign trade zones."

The first modern SEZ was the export processing zone (EPZ). EPZs are a simpler form of SEZ that is best described as an industrial park. These zones are generally limited, fenced-in areas focused on production for export and lack residential property. They traditionally focus on manufacturing and, as the name suggests, have in many cases been a part of a country's export-promotion agenda. The first EPZ appeared in Ireland in 1956 at Shannon International Airport. Since then, primarily developing countries have combined their low labor costs with fiscal and other incentives, using EPZs to convince foreign manufacturers to offshore their labor-intensive production.[7]

The 1980s brought a great breakthrough for the zone concept, mainly as a result of two developments. One was the SEZs in China. The previously isolated socialist economy took a radical turn when it started launching its reforms in 1978. With only a handful of SEZs in the early 1980s, the Chinese SEZ scheme expanded with tens of zones along the coast, and later spread into the Chinese interior. The SEZs attracted a large share of the country's FDI and stood for a large share of its exports. They played a visible role in the country's economic progress and soon became the example that many other countries would attempt to emulate.

Another reason for the growing popularity of SEZs in the 1980s was the necessity many countries faced to change their trade regimes. After decades of experience with import substitution, it was increasingly clear that high trade barriers had not helped developing countries but had rather turned them into economic laggards. Economic crises made it obvious that things had to change and created momentum for reform. Sometimes pressed by the lending conditions of the International Monetary Fund (IMF), many developing countries therefore abandoned their import-substitution policies and turned to economic liberalization and export promotion.[8]

SEZs became a popular policy in pursuit of this change. Investors were seeking to employ developing countries' abundant labor in manufacturing for export. However, because the domestic raw material and other inputs were too costly, of insufficient quality, or simply non-existent, investors often stayed away. With SEZs, governments could offer investors exemptions from tariffs and taxes, which made the country sufficiently investor friendly. To ensure that production focused on exports, many host countries imposed export requirements. Although such schemes resemble export subsidies, the SEZ setup made the export promotion acceptable in the context of international trade politics.

In recent decades, the number of SEZs has surged. The International Labor Organization (ILO) lists 79 SEZs in the world in 1975.[9] In 1986, as the Chinese SEZs began to show impressive performance, there were 176 zones in 47 countries. By 1995, 93 countries had adopted 845 zones in total. The ILO estimated the number of zones in 2006 to around 3,500, spread over 130 countries.[10] Bell counts the current number of zones as 3,337.[11] No number will ever remain accurate, as new SEZs keep emerging. Counting the world's SEZs is also sensitive to the definition one chooses for SEZs, and in particular whether single-factory zones are included. This point brings us to the issue of how to define SEZs.

What makes for an SEZ?

While SEZs come in many shapes and sizes, they have some features in common that I will assume throughout this book. For one, they offer businesses tariff exemptions on imported inputs for SEZ production. Tariff exemptions are generally aimed at attracting investors in manufacturing that use local labor while importing primary material and other inputs. In a small country in particular, SEZ investors are unlikely to find the material that they need on the domestic market. And even if the material is produced in the host country, tariffs might inflate its price to such an extent that investors find it unprofitable to pay for it.

Another fiscal incentive involves tax breaks. These often aim to be generous enough to attract investors while not depriving the government of all tax revenues from SEZ businesses. Zone investors may, for instance, pay no or very little business tax while their workers still pay income tax. Rather than depriving the government of tax revenues, SEZs that increase the level of local employment can thus boost government revenues through the income tax.

Different rules from the country as a whole often prevail in SEZs. These include more investment-friendly regulations, such as relaxed labor-market rules or environmental regulations. SEZ benefits also often include streamlined government administrative services, such as business registration and customs clearance. This may not sound like a great improvement, but it can be significant in a country with messy bureaucracies that delay production and complicate business processes. For instance, it normally takes about a month to start a business in Latin America, the Caribbean, and Africa. Shortening that time can attract investors seeking to avoid onerous government bureaucracies.[12]

Many governments also boost the attractiveness of SEZs by investing in their infrastructure and utility services, such as electric power and water. If the country as a whole experiences daily power cuts, such services can make SEZs attractive for investors demanding a secure electricity supply.

Zone benefits sometimes come with stringent conditions, such as minimum investments requirements and demands that the companies hire mostly local workers. Another common requirement is for SEZ companies to export all or some of what they produce. This is primarily the case with so-called export processing zones (EPZs), which are often introduced to increase a country's exports. Export requirements are also a way to prevent SEZ firms from competing on unfair terms with domestic companies. While previously common, export requirements are increasingly falling out of favor. This is partly due to agreements of the World Trade Organization (WTO), which I will discuss in Chapter 9.

While these are all common features of SEZs, in this book I will assume only the fiscal incentives to be a necessary condition for an area to function as an SEZ. While regulatory and bureaucracy exemptions may be the more promising reforms, many SEZ schemes still rely primarily on fiscal incentives.

What's in a name?

SEZs have been given a variety of labels. The World Bank's Facility for Investment Climate Advisory Services (FIAS) lists several different forms of SEZs. It distinguishes them based on features such as their various development objectives, size, target markets, and types of economic activities.[13] When ranked roughly in order of size, the list includes the following zone definitions:

- *Freeports* are generally large and host various activities and production aimed both at exports and the domestic market. They can encompass whole cities, and therefore also allow residential properties. Some of China's earliest zones were freeports, such as the Shenzhen SEZ, which borders Hong Kong and has over 10 million residents. While generating much of the country's exports, the businesses in the Shenzhen SEZ also produce for domestic and local consumption. The world's largest freeport is the Jebel Ali Free Zone in Dubai, introduced in 1985.[14] Its port is also the world's ninth busiest and the largest man-made port.
- *Export processing zones (EPZs)* are much smaller. They take the form of industrial parks and generally do not host residential property. These have been the most popular form of SEZs, as developing countries throughout Asia, Latin America, Europe, and Africa introduced them to promote their manufacturing industries. In Latin America, for instance, Mexico, Honduras, and others used EPZs as they went from exporters of agricultural crops to exporters of clothes to the American market. While businesses in EPZs usually focus on manufacturing for export, the nature of EPZ production has evolved and diversified. Textile manufacturing

still dominates in many EPZs, but services such as warehousing and call centers have become an increasingly important part of EPZ activity. While most EPZ firms are exporters, they do not have to be. So-called hybrid EPZs are explicitly divided into areas for export production and production for the domestic market.

- *Free trade zones* tend to be even smaller than EPZs, and are generally located in ports. Like EPZs, they tend to be fenced in and do not host any residents. They focus on trade-promoting activities such as warehousing, storage, and trans-shipment. The United States has 250 such zones, called foreign trade zones.[15] Companies operating in the American zones are taxed as if they are on foreign soil. Equipped with facilities for handling and shipping as well as warehousing, they are meant to attract US trading activity, employment, and value added.[16] The Colón Free Zone in Panama may also count as a free trade zone, although, with its 4.5 square kilometers, it is unusually large. Located at the entrance of the crucial Panama Canal, this free trade zone is a central location for imports and re-exports for the Americas.[17]

- *Single-factory zones* are the smallest SEZs. They include only one company, which is generally not required to locate in any particular area. Single-factory zones are thus quite different from other SEZs in that they resemble simple tax-break arrangements given to individual companies. For this reason, single-factory zones could have been excluded from this study altogether. Yet since the mainstream view is that they are indeed SEZs, and since their peculiar features serve as extreme examples of some of the main weaknesses of SEZs, I will include the single-factory zone nevertheless.

  Many countries allow single-factory zones in addition to their larger SEZs. Ghana, for instance, has its main EPZ at the port in Tema, while the bulk of zone activity takes place in single-factory zones. In 2008, such individual companies accounted for 80 percent of official zone exports.[18]

- *Enterprise zones* are also included in the FIAS list of SEZs. These are usually urban residential areas, deemed in need of revitalization. Enterprise zones stand out from SEZs in the important aspect that their aim is to lessen unemployment and boost the economy in particular depressed areas that lag behind the rest of the country. Rather than a way to increase investments and employment in the country as a whole, enterprise zones are a regional policy aimed at geographical equality and poverty alleviation.

  The policy emerged in the United Kingdom at the beginning of the 1980s and later spread to the United States and France, the latter of which has introduced several zones in the poor suburbs of its main cities.[19] In the United States, these kinds of zones have been part of the federal government's assistance to state and local governments in their poverty reduction efforts.[20] A newer version of this concept is the American "Promise Zones" introduced in 2014. This federal program targets particular areas in some of the country's largest cities, and aims at economic revitalization through a variety of different targeted policies.[21]

While some enterprise zones clearly fail to achieve their goals, there is no objective way to judge whether enterprise zones are successful.[22] Most of them likely impose net costs for the country as a whole by redistributing economic activities from one location to another. However, whether they are successful depends on the improvements for poorer people in the zones being worth the costs in the economy as a whole. This is a philosophical, more than an economic, question. Because of their peculiar characteristics, enterprise zones will not be included in the SEZ concept of this book.

There are other ways to classify SEZs. Farole and Moberg divide zones based on their use, such as trade, manufacturing, services, or mixed use.[23] Haywood suggests dividing SEZs into small, wide-area, industry-specific, and performance-specific zones. By this categorization, small zones would include EPZs. An industry-specific zone may focus on banking, insurance, gambling, tourism, textiles, or other specific forms of production. By performance-based zones, Haywood refers to such things as employment, technology, and investment-based performance.[24]

Classifying SEZs may be useful when comparing the macroeconomic performance of various zones. If a government wants to promote tourism, for instance, it should study the features of tourism-specific zones and not freeports. For the purpose of this book, though, using several different SEZ categories would confuse rather than clarify. In discussing the political economy dynamics of SEZs, I will exploit angles that are more general and do not depend on what types of industries a zone may host. The only zones I will single out under special labels are the smaller EPZs and the even-smaller single-factory zones. As will be clear throughout this book, zone size matters through its effect on incentives of policy makers and businesses. Distinguishing between smaller and larger zones will therefore be useful when discussing this aspect. Otherwise, "SEZ" will serve as a generic term that includes EPZs and single-factory zones.

The unhelpful mainstream view of SEZ success

SEZs are generally described as successful if they attract companies and generate jobs. On the face of it, gauging the extent of such success is an easy task. You can walk into an SEZ and look at occupied structures. You can enter these structures and see hundreds of workers busy making jeans or electronic gear. To add additional certainty to such vivid signs of success, you may leave the SEZ to verify that the government has contributed with a road from the zone to the port and upgraded the port to serve the SEZ.

With these observations at hand, you may conclude that the SEZ is a successful project. Thanks to a reliable pledge of commitment by the government, the success story seems likely to continue. On your way from the SEZ, you may note that the surrounding villages and countryside are devastatingly poor and idle looking, in contrast to the bustling industrial activity in the zone. The striking contrast convinces you of the SEZ's contribution to the area and of the prosperity the country could enjoy if more zones were built and similarly connected to the country's roads and harbors.

As a final verification, you may go downtown and meet the people at the zone regulator to look at their export data. Seeing in black and white that the SEZ indeed generates a large share of the country's exports confirms your on-the-ground observations. You therefore conclude that the zone must be important. The official at the agency confirms your beliefs, explaining with authority that the increased exports enhance the country's trade balance. More exports relative to imports, he explains, generates more jobs and thus creates more prosperity in the country as a whole. At the end of the day, you confidently conclude that you have observed a great SEZ success.

Alas, such observations are often deceptive. As a spectator on the ground, you have seen only the benefits of the zone, not its costs. This one-sidedness is the main problem with the common definition of SEZ success. With enough spending and fiscal incentives, any zone can look successful. However, merely moving resources from one project to another does not mean wealth is being created. If the aim of the SEZ is to promote economic development by creating locomotives for growth, one cannot focus merely on what is created within the zones but must also assess what the project costs for the rest of the economy. What matters is whether an SEZ benefits the economy as a whole, not only the zone companies and workers.

It is misguided to compare a zone with its neighboring areas. SEZs that offer fiscal and regulatory incentives along with higher-than-average government spending will likely have an upper hand compared to the rest of the economy. The question is whether this happens to the benefit or at the expense of other areas. If other areas become poorer as a result of an expanding SEZ, the contrast will deceivingly make it look as though the SEZ is particularly successful. It is similarly misguided to assess a zone based on its fulfillment of certain export or investment goals since such performance may also come at the expense of other areas.

We need to recognize that a "successful" SEZ does not necessarily come for free. A government that pays for zone infrastructure, roads, and an adjacent port has to take this money from somewhere. Somehow, the people of the country must pay for it. It thus matters how much the whole project costs.

Equating the amount of workers employed with newly created jobs is misleading for a similar reason. Workers entering an SEZ factory come from somewhere. While some SEZ workers may previously have been unemployed, many have left a job to work in an SEZ factory that, thanks to its fiscal benefits, can offer better conditions or higher pay.

SEZ companies compete with domestic firms for both workers and material resources, thus raising the costs of both for the domestic businesses. While a trend of pay rises and better working conditions is a positive development, it inevitably means a loss of jobs in the rest of the country. Investment can similarly be depressed in the rest of the economy when domestic firms must scale down or shut down altogether because of higher costs of capital for their production.

Setting up goals for a zone in isolation will therefore cause unnecessary distraction. As SEZ exports grow and salaries increase thanks to fiscal and other benefits, zones frequently become the most vibrant part of an economy.[25] When a country with SEZs is ready to industrialize, it is no surprise that this happens first in the zones. However, this does not necessarily mean the country could not have industrialized without them. Foreign investors can enter the country in other ways, and foreign technology can spread through other means than foreign direct investments.

Besides simply attracting resources from the rest of the country, SEZs bring an additional complication. Resources moving into SEZs do not mean just a reallocation, but fundamentally also a misallocation, of resources. Capital and labor can presumably generate more value when subjected to lower taxes and less stringent regulations. However, firms entering SEZs are moving to an implicitly inferior location, since this is not the area they chose in the absence of the differential treatment. If the SEZ location were superior, the companies would have been there already. The zone location may eventually be optimal, as roads are extended around it, workers move to the vicinity and set up communities, and the economy at large adapts to the change. However, this is a protracted process the cost of which we can never fully estimate.

Companies will only choose to move to a zone if the SEZ benefits are large enough to compensate for both a potentially inferior location and the cost of relocating. Tariffs and tax breaks in SEZs thus work as subsidies that encourage costly reallocation of resources in the economy. If SEZs only attract existing production, without encouraging more of it, SEZ growth likely comes about at the expense of the government, and thus at a cost to taxpayers. This is because, in the absence of new investments, lower taxes mean less revenue to the government. To compensate, the government must eventually recoup those funds from elsewhere, either by taxing domestic businesses or making the people poorer by taxing them or cutting down on government expenditures.

Crowding out economic activity elsewhere in the country is less severe when companies from other countries, instead of domestic firms, invest in the SEZs. This is because multinationals tend to bring some of their own capital and a share of their workforce, as well as their own technology.

Whether this is actually a benefit is not always clear, however. When foreign companies import both capital and labor, they become isolated from the rest of the economy and are also less likely to impact it in a positive way. Although they may bring technological skills, they will hardly spread technological know-how if they also bring their own workers and inputs. Such dynamic effects are more likely to come about when multinational companies integrate with the local economy by employing local workers and by buying inputs from domestic firms. These are long-term effects, since the knowledge diffusion comes about only as the workers leave the multinational investor to work in the domestic economy.[26]

Foreign companies that bring their own work force thus only contribute to the economy through their modest tax contributions. While they produce enhanced GDP and export statistics, these say nothing about whether the foreign SEZ companies benefit the economy.

The implication is that SEZ goals should be set to country aggregates rather than just zone performance. When they are, though, such goals often have narrow and biased focus. A common goal is that SEZs should increase a country's exports. The problem is that steering resources toward exports instead of domestic consumption may be inefficient. If a government simply subsidizes an exporting industry, the loss to the government and to the people in the form of higher domestic prices will be higher than the benefits to the exporting firms.

Similarly, with SEZs, the government may provide incentives, infrastructure, and facilities for SEZ investors, which are then obliged to export all they produce. Thanks to the SEZ incentives, their production costs are likely lower than they would otherwise be. While this lowers the price on the goods produced by the SEZ exporters, it only benefits consumers in other countries. Meanwhile, by discouraging production for the domestic market, domestic prices will rise. The increase in exports thus imposes a misallocation of resources that can hardly benefit the economy as a whole.

Incentivizing exports can enhance a country's trade balance, a metric governments often point to as a barometer of productivity. In the case of SEZs, however, the trade balance increases only because the country's residents cannot afford to buy imported consumer goods to compensate for the fact that more of the country's resources are devoted to exports. Therefore, the fact that an SEZ scheme has boosted the trade balance says little about whether it has increased domestic welfare.

A more credible argument for SEZ export requirements is that they prevent distortions on the domestic market. SEZ businesses that enjoy lower costs thanks to tariff and tax breaks may compete with domestic firms outside SEZs that face higher import costs. Non-SEZ firms may then go out of business despite being more productive than their SEZ competitors.

Although this is a valid point, export requirements may still cause more distortions than they avoid. Celebrating the progress of a particular indicator such as exports may therefore deceive people into believing the SEZs are promoting prosperity. Other narrow targets, such as amount of investments and zone employment, are similarly misleading as they also fail to capture the whole picture.

This discussion implies that to assess whether an SEZ scheme is successful, a government should focus on broader economic measures, such as GDP growth in the country as a whole. However, no macroeconomic statistic can really capture the full impact of an SEZ. Many of the zone-related costs do not appear in the government budget, for instance. It is also hard to know the value of the alternative use of capital and labor that an SEZ may attract from the rest of the country, or to measure such dynamic benefits of SEZs as technology transfers, changes in business climate, and political effects.

Attempting the cost-benefit analysis

A few scholars have nevertheless attempted cost-benefit calculations of SEZs by making macroeconomic calculations. Warr presented his framework in 1989, in which he included foreign exchange earnings, employment, domestic raw materials, domestic capital goods, electricity, domestic borrowing, taxes, development costs, and recurrent costs of the zone area.[27] To estimate net benefits, Warr compared the net revenue from each component to its social value, or shadow price, in different countries. For example, if an Indonesian worker is paid one dollar per hour in the SEZ and the shadow price of labor in Indonesia is 90 cents, then the SEZ has an added benefit of 10 cents per worker.

Warr recognized that such calculations come with a good amount of arbitrariness. He noted, for instance, that he could account for neither skill transfers to employees nor technology transfers to domestic businesses. Using a single shadow price for such resources as "labor" also fails to reflect assets such as human capital. To be fair, Warr considered only export processing zones, which are small and have no residents. Thanks to their simplicity, they lend themselves better to cost-benefit analyses than larger and more complex zones. The analysis is also closer to the truth for developing countries, where one might assume that labor in the zones is low skilled and that all production is exported. This also means, however, that the calculations can only tell us something about the simplest forms of SEZs in particular parts of the world.

Both Warr and, later, Jayanthakumaran applied the cost-benefit framework to assess the net national benefit of EPZs in Asia.[28] Taken together, their calculations indicate that the schemes in South Korea, Indonesia, Malaysia, Sri Lanka, and China had positive net present values, while the SEZs in the Philippines were a net negative.

As with so many SEZ programs, whether the Philippine SEZs were successful depends on which benchmark you use. Some have noted the scheme's improved investment climate,[29] successful SEZ authorities,[30] and the commitment of the people to the project.[31] The scheme looks successful if one considers that it employed almost 1.3 million people by June 2016. Also, the SEZs generated as much as 78 percent of the country's exports in 2011. While the SEZs kept increasing their level of export, this share fell to a still impressive 59 percent by 2015.[32] Yet Jayanthakumaran points out that the cost of the Philippine SEZs, in the form of infrastructure and government-subsidized loans to SEZ investors, surpasses these gains.[33]

Which SEZs to measure

If cost-benefit analyses can be used at all, they only apply to smaller and simpler SEZs. The single-factory zone, which can be as small as the floor of a building, lends itself best to cost-benefit analysis. A single company's income statement reveals how much it produces and sells and the cost of its inputs and workers. With a simple survey, one can compare the salaries of its employees with what they were previously making. The executives can even declare whether the company would have been located in the country in the absence of the SEZ privileges.

In this way, one can plausibly estimate the net effect on the country of giving the company SEZ status. If the company would not have located in the country in the absence of SEZ status, and it is hiring domestically and paying higher wages to workers than they would have earned otherwise, the company is probably bringing some benefits. For the zone to be a net gain for the country, though, these benefits must also be larger than the government's infrastructure and administration costs.

While single-factory zones are easiest to assess in this way, they are also the most dubious SEZ model. In many ways, single-factory zones work like targeted tax-break schemes. A casual observer would hardly be able to tell a single-factory zone from a regular company receiving tax benefits. The only practical difference may be that some single-factory zones, like most EPZs, need to meet certain export requirements. In that case, however, these companies are not receiving production subsidies but export subsidies, which impose an even greater cost on the economy as a whole.

Because EPZs include several companies, they are more readily recognized as SEZs. The smaller and simpler EPZs can also lend themselves to cost-benefit analyses. Like single-factory zones, they predominantly have static effects, which are easier to measure than dynamic ones. Data on employment, investments, exports, and tax revenues are more readily available than technology transfers and political change, for instance. As Chapter 3 will explain at length, such dynamic effects tend to be rare in the EPZ case.

Net effects are hardest to measure for large SEZs that host a diversity of activities and residential property. The Shenzhen SEZ in China is a good example. Founded in 1979, the SEZ was extended in 2010 to span the whole city of 10 million people. There are good reasons to believe this giant SEZ is good for the country of China. Although it enjoyed fiscal benefits and government infrastructure spending, it also benefited from more political autonomy and fiscal decentralization than other Chinese SEZs. Better local rules, which impose smaller, if any, costs on the rest of the economy, were a more important part of Shenzhen's success than any central government infusion of resources.[34]

Unfortunately, we cannot possibly measure the costs and benefits of such grand and long-term SEZ projects as that in Shenzhen. They are so numerous, complicated, dynamic, and variable that a workable cost-benefit framework could not possibly capture them all. Also, as soon as people become zone residents, they derive most of their utility from the zones from sources other than merely their wages. Any assessment of an SEZ's effects then becomes inherently unreliable. How can we possibly evaluate the change in quality of life in an SEZ compared to outside it? We can presume that the SEZ residents prefer life in the zone to living elsewhere, but we cannot say by how much just by looking at their income.

It is thus in the nature of SEZs that the more interesting and promising they are, the harder it is to measure their effects. There are several reasons why it is more interesting to study zones with more regulatory rather than fiscal incentives, as well as larger and more diversified zones. With regulatory benefits, SEZs have greater potential to grow independently rather than at the expense of the country as a whole. In contrast to fiscal incentives, regulatory incentives are, if anything, more likely to save money for the government. Simplifying rules generally means less need for public administration and policing.

Larger and more diversified SEZs are interesting because they can more readily generate positive external effects, thanks to their integration with the country as a whole. Large SEZs often have no fences around them. People both live and work in them, and there is no point in isolating their economic activities from the rest of the country. Larger zones are also interesting to study because they are increasingly popular. India and Pakistan have had SEZ laws for decades that let investors set up smaller and simpler export processing zones. Both countries have now introduced new SEZ laws meant to pave the way for larger and more inclusive SEZs. Japan is also introducing SEZs with different regulations from the rest of the country. The plan is for the zones to be large enough to include significant parts of some of the country's main cities, including Tokyo, Osaka, and Fukuoka.[35]

In conclusion, cost-benefit analyses of SEZs of the kind Warr proposed in the 1980s cannot say much of relevance about the economic impact of modern and more promising SEZs. One can only try to calculate the effects of smaller zones, where the political and other dynamic effects are less prominent. As I will discuss later in this book, the main benefits of SEZs are political and dynamic rather than economic and static. Cost-benefit analyses therefore overlook the most important benefits with SEZs. Fortunately, the political economy approach is better at capturing both the political benefits and the political costs of SEZs.

The difficulty with regional and country analyses

Some studies on the macroeconomic impact of SEZs take account of changes both inside and outside the zone borders.[36] One way to do that is to compare economic outcomes between countries or provinces that have SEZs and those that do not. In contrast to comparing an SEZ with its surrounding areas, this approach is less likely to overlook the investment diversion SEZs cause, simply because it is less likely to occur between larger areas than between SEZs and their immediate surroundings.

Wang compares Chinese municipalities with and without SEZs and includes the decrease of investments in neighboring municipalities in the analysis.[37] The study implies that, while an area adjacent to an SEZ munici-pality does lose out on some investment, this is less than what is gained by the municipality introducing an SEZ program. It therefore looks as though the SEZs are a net positive. However, this kind of analysis does not account for the rate at which SEZs lure investments from non-adjacent areas and from provinces far away.

China may still be the country most likely to produce useful statistics about SEZs since there are so many of them spread across so many municipalities. The problem is that Chinese municipal data are famously unreliable. These kinds of studies could therefore be interesting primarily for their possible application to SEZ schemes in other countries. Alas, no other country may be vast enough and have a large enough SEZ program to provide meaningful statistical tests of the effect of SEZs.[38]

To avoid such country-specific shortcomings, it may seem that simply comparing countries with and without SEZs would be a better approach. On a cross-country level, diversion is not an issue since countries need not factor in the loss of investments in other countries as a cost. To capture the full effect of SEZs, one should look at a welfare proxy such as GDP and not a narrow indicator such as exports or employment.

However, there are two main problems with looking at the impact of SEZs on GDP. For one, there are myriad other factors contributing to GDP growth, so discerning the marginal contribution of SEZs is difficult. Controlling for all other factors makes the data analysis uncertain, if not impossible. If a country grows faster than another after introducing SEZs, this may still be due to other policies or external factors.

To capture the full effect of an SEZ scheme, any study of this kind needs to take a long-term perspective to account for the delayed effects of SEZ intro-duction. This is because the zones often do not become a significant part of a country's economic activity until a few years into the program. Another reason to take a long-term view is to capture the dynamic effects that proponents of SEZs stress. One of these is technology transfers, which happen as inter-national companies educate their workers and when they trade with domestic companies. As I will discuss in Chapter 3, SEZs can also have political effects that are at least as important as the economic ones. All these dynamic effects take a long time to translate into higher economic growth and other macro-economic aggregates. To capture the main part of an SEZ's contribution to growth, studies must therefore be long-term, perhaps spanning decades.

The problem with having to look at effects over a long time is that too many other factors play a part in causing the difference in economic progress between countries. Regimes change, conflicts emerge, and trade patterns shift. It also becomes increasingly hard to discern the direction of causality. SEZs may lead to economic growth, but growth inevitably also allows SEZs to attract investors.

It is also not clear how one should define an SEZ country. Some countries have an SEZ law but no zones. Some have one SEZ, others have many, and some have numerous registered but inactive SEZs. Ranking countries by the number of their operative SEZs is also dubious, since one country may have many small zones and another country one large zone. Cross-country studies that make an SEZ country a binary variable are therefore highly unreliable.

Because of the shortcomings of macroeconomic studies on SEZ performance, most of the best SEZ work consists of case studies. These allow for the consideration of many vital nuances about an SEZ's development, dynamic effects, and long-term political impacts.

As this book will make clear, the best approach to assess SEZ performance is through a political economy analysis. In Chapter 1, I will lay the foundations of the main theories in political economy. As the subsequent chapters will make clear, these foundations can be applied in different ways to conclude whether or not SEZs are successful.

Defining SEZ success

By SEZ "success," people generally mean that a zone has attracted investors, generated jobs and exports, and become an important part of a country's economy. A zone that has "taken off" has captured momentum of growth and is therefore considered successful. As we know, though, such an image of success does not account for SEZs' costs, and therefore fails to address the relevant question of whether SEZs are on net beneficial to the host country as a whole. These aspects are best captured through a political economy lens.

In considering a country's political economy, there are two different ways to define SEZ success. One is to compare the SEZ policy to the status quo, which is the country in the absence of SEZs but with all other prevailing policies in place. On the one hand, SEZs provide incentives for more production in the country. On the other hand, they can cause several problems, including resource misallocations and opportunities for rent-seeking. These problems will be the focus of Chapter 2.

The other way to define SEZ success is to compare the zones with their political alternative. If the political alternative is the status quo, comparing them to the status quo is still correct. However, a government might have put other policies in place that are preferable to the country as a whole if it did not have the SEZ policy. This can happen if the government uses SEZs to avoid broader and more radical reforms. In that case, the SEZs cannot be seen as beneficial even if they are superior to the status quo. When studying SEZs, we therefore need to ask what the political development would be like in the absence of SEZs. This is the topic of Chapter 4. Before this discussion, Chapter 3 will discuss how SEZs may contribute to countrywide reforms, in which case they are truly valuable.

The book thus deals with three central questions regarding the political economy of SEZs:

1   When is an SEZ regime better than the status quo (Chapter 2)?
2   How can SEZs promote political reform (Chapter 3)?
3   When are SEZs better than their likely political alternatives (Chapter 4)?

Each question has a chapter devoted to it in the first part of this book, which is primarily theoretical. The following part contains case studies that address the same questions on the basis of the theoretical discussion. The last part of the book derives some policy implications and looks ahead to the future of SEZs.

The political economy approach to an SEZ analysis accounts for the costs of market distortions, miscalculations by SEZ planners, wasteful rent-seeking, and corruption. It therefore offers a more critical view of SEZ policy than a purely economic approach, which might simply be counting the number of jobs created. This perspective also recognizes political benefits of SEZs that mainstream economic analyses overlook. A political economy analysis can thus both be more positive and more critical of SEZs than macroeconomic analyses, and can come to more extreme conclusions about their benefits and costs. The result is a more nuanced and realistic picture of the role SEZs can play in a country's economy, politics, and international relations.

Combined with the case studies, the theoretical frameworks show how many considerations go into determining SEZ success. The main finding is that while no SEZ scheme is perfect and none is completely detrimental to an economy, we can say quite a lot about the performance and potential of SEZ schemes around the world by understanding the interactions between knowledge, incentives, and institutions in the SEZ context. So far, the world has produced a wide range of SEZ performances, from the dismally wasteful and stagnant to the politically beneficial. By learning about the importance of the political economy of SEZs, we can make sure more SEZs are created in the future with potential for success.

Notes

1 Basile and Germidis 1984; FIAS 2008: 32; Haywood 2000; Farole and Akinci 2011; Wang 2013. Several SEZ researchers and practitioners are however often careful also to point to some of the problems with the SEZ model.
2 Myint 1973: 77.
3 Amirahmadi and Wu 1995.
4 Sobhee 2009; Baissac 2011: 229; Frankel 2014.
5 International Trade Administration 2016.
6 Farole 2011: 31.
7 Wong and Chu 1985: 2; FIAS 2008.
8 Rodrik 1994; Frieden 2006: 351.
9 ILO 2007.
10 Id.
11 Bell 2017: Annex 1. This figure excludes bonded warehouses in Bangladesh, which, if counted, would increase the number to 9,695 zones.
12 *Doing Business* 2016.
13 FIAS 2008: 10. FIAS (2008: 11) also lists SEZs based on their specific functions. This list includes technology or science parks, logistic parks or cargo villages, and zones focused on petrochemicals, financial services, software and Internet, airports, and tourism.

14 *Economist* 2015.
15 Foreign-Trade Zones Board 2016.
16 Foreign-Trade Zones Board 2014.
17 FIAS 2008: 10; Sigler 2014.
18 Farole 2010.
19 Zenou 2012.
20 HUD 2016.
21 White House 2014.
22 For an example of an admitted failure, *see* Korte 2003.
23 Farole and Moberg 2014.
24 Haywood 2000.
25 One example of many is the Dominican Republic (Schrank 2005: 48; Oppenheimer 1999).
26 Farole et al. 2014: 28.
27 Warr 1989.
28 Id.; Jayanthakumaran 2003.
29 Makabenta 2002.
30 Booz Allen Hamilton 2008.
31 Gordon 2002.
32 Malapad 2016.
33 Jayanthakumaran 2003: 62.
34 Yeung et al. 2009.
35 *Economist* 2014; HSBC 2014; Foster 2015.
36 See, e.g., FIAS 2008; Farole and Akinci 2011; Wang 2013.
37 Wang 2013.
38 India has recently introduced hundreds of new SEZs. As these SEZs become operational and produce reliable local data, one might make a similar study of India in the future.

References

Amirahmadi, Hooshang, and Weiping Wu. 1995. "Export Processing Zones in Asia." *Asian Survey* 35(9): 828–849.
Baissac, Claude. 2011. "Planned Obsolescence? Export Processing Zones and Structural Reform in Mauritius." In: Thomas Farole and Gokhan Akinci (Eds.), *Special Economic Zones: Progress, Emerging Challenges, and Future Directions*. The World Bank, Washington, D.C., pp. 227–244.
Basile, Antoine, and Dimitrios A. Germidis. 1984. *Investing in Free Export Processing Zones*. Paris: OECD Publishing.
Bell, Tom W. 2017 (Forthcoming). *"Your Next Government: From Nation State to Stateless Association."* Cambridge University Press. Data available at: goo.gl/ju7IfQ (accessed 29 October 2016).
Booz Allen Hamilton. 2008. "Enhancing Cross-Border Trade Flows: Tariffs, Trade Zones, Customs Currency, and Community." In: *SEA CLIR Trade, Advancing a Regional Agenda for Shared Growth*. Report for the United States Agency for International Development, Ch. 2.
Doing Business, The World Bank. 2016. Data available at http://www.doingbusiness. org/rankings (accessed 29 October 2016).
Economist, The. 2014. " Economic Zones for Japan: Some More Special than Others." *The Economist*Mar. 31, 2014. Available at: http://www.economist.com/blogs/banyan/ 2014/03/economic-zones-japan (accessed 29 October 2016).

Economist, The. 2015. "Dubai's Economy: Growing Up. " From the print edition, Jun. 6, 2015. Available at http://www.economist.com/news/middle-east-and-africa/21653621-gulf-states-expansion-more-sustainable-its-previous-boom-growing-up (accessed 29 October 2016).

Farole, Thomas. 2010. "Case Studies of Special Economic Zones: Ghana." *World Bank memo*, Washington, D.C.

Farole, Thomas. 2011. *Special Economic Zones in Africa: Comparing Performance and Learning from Global Experience.* The World Bank, Washington, D.C.

Farole, Thomas, and Gokhan Akinci (Eds.). 2011. *Special Economic Zones: Progress, Emerging Challenges, and Future Directions.* The World Bank, Washington, D.C.

Farole, Thomas, and Lotta Moberg. 2014. "It Worked in China, so Why not in Africa? The Political Economy Challenge of Special Economic Zones." *UNU-WIDER Working Paper* 152/2014. Available at https://www.wider.unu.edu/publication/it-worked-china-so-why-not-africa (accessed 29 October 2016).

Farole, Thomas, Cornelia Staritz, and Deborah Winkler. 2014. "Conceptual Framework." In: *Making Foreign DirectInvestment Work for Sub-Saharan Africa: Local Spillovers and Competitiveness in Global Value Chains.* (Thomas Farole and Deborah Winkler eds.). The World Bank, Washington, D.C., pp. 23–55.

FIAS (The World Bank's Facility for Investment Climate Advisory Services). 2008. *Special Economic Zones: Performance, Lessons Learned, and Implications for Zone Development.* World Bank Group, Washington, D.C.

Foreign-Trade Zones Board. 2014. "76th Annual Report of the Foreign-Trade Zones Board to the Congress of the United States." Available at: http://enforcement.trade.gov/ftzpage/annualreport/ar-2014.pdf (accessed 29 October 2016).

Foreign-Trade Zones Board. 2016. "Frequently Asked Questions." *Foreign-Trade Zones Board* Available at: http://enforcement.trade.gov/ftzpage/info/ftzstart.html (accessed 29 October 2016).

Foster, Martin. 2015. "Is Japan Losing Focus on Special Economic Zones?" *Japan Today*, Aug. 11, 2015. Available at: http://www.japantoday.com/category/business/view/is-japan-losing-focus-on-special-economic-zones (accessed 29 October 2016).

Frankel, Jeffrey. 2014. "Mauritius: African Success Story." *African Successes: Sustainable Growth* 4. University of Chicago Press, Chicago.

Frieden, Jeffry A. 2006. *Global Capitalism.* W.W. Norton, New York.

Gordon, Richard J. 2002. "The Subic Story: One Community's Response to the Challenge of Change and Development." *Address of Hon. Philippine Secretary of Tourism in the International Colloquium on Regional Governance and Sustainable Development in Tourism-driven Economies*, Cancun, Mexico, Feb. 21, 2002. Available at: https://www.hitpages.com/doc/5227601459150848/1#pageTop (accessed 29 October 2016).

Haywood, Robert. 2000. "Free Zones in the Modern World." *World Economic Processing Zones Association Publication*, CFATF Meeting, Aruba, October 18, 2000.

HSBC. 2014. "Japan Economics Comment: Abe's Trojan Horse Takes Another Step." *HSBC: Global Research – Economics*, Mar. 31, 2014.

HUD (U.S. Department of Housing and Urban Development). 2016. "Welcome to the Community Renewal Initiative." *HUD Homepage.* Available at: http://portal.hud.gov/hudportal/HUD?src=/program_offices/comm_planning/economicdevelopment/programs/rc (accessed 29 October 2016).

ILO (International Labor Organization). 2007. "Database on Export Processing Zones (Revised)." *Working Paper* 251, Geneva, Switzerland: International Labour Office.

International Trade Administration. 2016. Homepage, National trade data, Global Patterns of U.S. Merchandise Trade. Available at: http://tse.export.gov/ (accessed 29 October 2016).

Jayanthakumaran, K. 2003. "Benefit–cost Appraisals of Export Processing Zones: A Survey of the Literature." *Development Policy Review* 21(1): 51–65.

Korte, Gregory. 2003. "Audit Says Cincinnati Wasted Much of Empowerment Grant." *The Cincinnati Enquirer*, Feb. 4, 2003. Available at: http://enquirer.com/editions/2003/02/04/loc_empower04.html (accessed 29 October 2016).

Makabenta, Maria Peregrina. 2002. "FDI Location and Special Economic Zones in the Phillipines." *Review of Urban and Regional Development Studies* 14(1): 59–77.

Malapad, Anna Rose R. 2016Personal correspondence with Anna Rose R. Malapad, Philippine Economic Zone Authority, Aug. 23, 2016.

Myint, Hla. 1973. *The Economics of the Developing Countries, 4th Ed.* Praeger Publishers, New York.

Oppenheimer, Andres. 1999. "Dominican Republic Seen as Role Model." *The Miami Herald*, Nov. 28, 1999.

Rodrik, Dani. 1994. "The Rush to Free Trade in the Developing World: Why So Late? Why Now? Will It Last?" *National Bureau of Economic Research Working Paper* No. 3947.

Schrank, Andrew. 2005. "Entrepreneurship, Export Diversification, and Economic Reform: The Birth of a Developmental Community in the Dominican Republic." *Comparative Politics*, 38(1): 43–62.

Sigler, Thomas J. 2014. "Panama's Special Economic Zones: Balancing Growth and Development." *Bulletin of Latin American Research*, 33(1): 1–15.

Sobhee, Sanjeev K. 2009. "The Economic Success of Mauritius: Lessons and Policy Options for Africa." *Journal of Economic Policy Reform* 12(1): 29–42.

Wang, Jin. 2013. "The Economic Impact of Special Economic Zones: Evidence from Chinese Municipalities." *Journal of Development Economics* 101: 133–147.

Warr, Peter G. 1989. "Export Processing Zones: The Economics of Enclave Manufacturing." *The World Bank: Research Observer* 4(1): 65–88.

White House, The. 2014. "Fact Sheet: President Obama's Promise Zones Initiative." Statements and Releases of the Office of the Press Secretary. Available at: https://www.whitehouse.gov/the-press-office/2014/01/08/fact-sheet-president-obama-s-prom ise- zones-initiative (accessed 29 October 2016).

Wong, Kwan-Yiu, and David K.Y. Chu. 1985. *Modernization in China: the case of the Shenzhen special economic zone.* Oxford University Press, Hong Kong.

Yeung, Yue-man, Joanna Lee, and Gordon Kee. 2009. "China's Special Economic Zones at 30." *Eurasian Geography and Economics* 50(2): 222–240.

Zenou, Yves. 2012. "Nystartszoner – den ekonomiska synvinkeln". In: *Från utsatt till utmärkt område: Bortom ekonomiska frizoner*, Andreas Bergh (Ed.), Fores, Stockholm, pp. 25–38.

Part I

The theory of zone politics

1 The political economy context

To see why SEZs succeed or fail, we need to understand the capabilities and goals of the people who govern them. Mainstream economic analyses generally assume a government introduces SEZs to maximize the welfare of the people it represents. The government is also often presumed to have sufficient information and capacity to do so. A political economy approach, by contrast, does not assume such perfections. Instead, it incorporates the imperfect knowledge and self-interested motives of policy makers in the economic analysis.

The following three chapters will explore the three main questions about SEZs.

When will SEZs be better than the status quo? This question can be divided in two parts. First, when are people in government able to introduce beneficial SEZs? And second, when do they want to do so? The government's ability and incentive to introduce wealth-enhancing policies are the two pillars of the robust political economy framework, which is introduced in this chapter. I will assume that the government cares about the people's welfare when discussing whether it is actually able to promote it. Conversely, I will assume that the government is capable of promoting welfare when analyzing whether policy makers have the incentive to do so.

A comparison between a country's SEZ regime and the status quo implicitly assumes that, in the SEZs' absence, the country would pursue all its other current policies, so that the only difference is the SEZ regime. This is in a way the crudest form of assessing the effects of SEZs. Nevertheless, it is not a simple task, and therefore requires some theoretical deliberation, which is the focus of the next chapter. Chapter 2 then applies this framework to SEZs.

What kind of political economy environment allows SEZs to be at their best? This is the focus of Chapter 3. In the best-case scenario, SEZs generate significantly beneficial countrywide economic reforms. The analysis in this chapter will not assume people in government have any intention to promote welfare for its own sake. They are purely self-interested. Nevertheless, they may promote wealth-enhancing reforms if the right incentives are in place. These incentives depend on the payoffs policy makers enjoy from the different economic systems they can promote.

To analyze this dynamic, it is necessary to recognize that the government is not a monolithic unit with a coherent goal but a network of individuals who face different incentives. Therefore, the policies that ultimately emerge from the government depend on the dynamics among different people who can influence the government and who have different wills and tools at hand to push for particular policies. SEZs can then be a potent tool for those opting for economic reforms.

How can a government use SEZs to avoid broader reforms in its attempt to optimize its rents? This is the focus of Chapter 4, where the government is treated as an organization that tries to maximize its rents. To examine the government's incentive structure more closely, I simplify reality by treating the government as one coherent organization, rather than as comprising people with different preferences. While this may seem an unrealistic simplification, it is acceptable considering the government's ability to act as a coherent organization if most influential policy makers agree on their main goals. In this case, they want to pursue higher rents and are ready to impose uncompetitive policies to achieve that.

The government is thus modeled somewhat differently throughout this book depending on the question in focus. The most accurate depiction of the government is that of a complex network of individuals who are also influenced by outside forces and advocates. Emerging from their interactions are policies that, to some extent, reflect their relative bargaining positions, power, and advocacy tools. From the outside, the government may look like a unified organization, but that is only a result of one political faction having won the political battle and thus having the privilege to set the agenda.

Therefore, I refer to the government as the individuals constituting it whenever feasible, while simplifying the picture by treating the government as a unified organization when necessary. This simplification is needed in Chapter 4, which discusses how the government may use SEZs to optimize its rents.

A crucial theme throughout this book is that a government is ultimately comprised of self-interested individuals. It can therefore not be assumed to be a benevolent organization. Policies are endogenous in that they emerge out of political discussions, negotiations, and battles. These interactions among officials result from their personal considerations, which in turn depend on a system's institutional and policy environment.

Robust political economy

The two political economy aspects, what governments want and what they can do, have been combined in a framework labeled "robust political economy." This framework is a way to separate and analyze the two core components of the political economy approach – the capability of policy makers to pursue beneficial policies and their incentives to do so.

A robust political economy analysis treats people in government as both imperfect in their knowledge and self-interested. While economic models usually treat ordinary market actors this way, they generally assume policy makers to have perfect knowledge and benevolent intentions.

The ignorance and self-interest of policy makers cause two different categories of problems. The first category of problems pertains to the difficulty of improving on markets through government interventions. Policy makers have a "knowledge problem" in that the knowledge needed to rearrange economic activity in a more efficient way than that obtained through a market process is so immense and complex that they cannot possibly amass it. Their best chance in improving outcomes through intervention is therefore to make some wild guesses, which inevitably risks imposing higher costs on the economy than the benefits it yields. The general lesson from the knowledge problem is that policy makers should be cautious about trying to fine-tune the industrial composition of their economy or in other ways steer development in any particular direction.

A second category of problem results from public officials' incentive to serve their self-interest rather than the welfare of the people. These "incentive problems" come about as policy makers and bureaucrats do not benefit from increasing social welfare. The remedy to this problem is institutions that can align officials' self-interest with promoting socially beneficial policies. Absent such institutions, officials should at least be scrutinized in their work and perhaps be deprived of some of their power.

A robust political economy analysis helps identify these problems, detect the environments in which they tend to occur, and identify possible institutional solutions. A robust system contains institutions and policies that solve both the knowledge problem and the incentive problem. The knowledge problem can be solved by delegating decision-making to those with the most knowledge, and the incentive problem by providing the right incentives to policy makers and bureaucrats to introduce and execute beneficial policies.

The next sections take a closer look at the logic behind the knowledge problem and the incentive problem. They rely on fundamental political economy assumptions and extend common notions about people's imperfections to government officials. An important point is that these human weaknesses have more severe consequences when residing with people in the public sphere than with market actors. Readers familiar with political economy and its scholarship may want to skim or skip the rest of this chapter and jump to the next, which applies the robust political economy framework to SEZs.

A government with imperfect information

A political economy analysis extends assumptions about ordinary people's ignorance to people in government. While economists often model market actors as having complete information, many models do include components of uncertainty or imperfect information. To increase their knowledge, economic agents need to search for information or act on the basis of probabilities. A person looking for a job, for instance, does not know which job application will lead to a position. The job seeker can only assess the optimal search time, which depends on factors such as the probability of finding a job and the salaries on offer for different jobs.

When assumptions of ignorance are applied to government officials, they can no longer be seen as capable of stepping in and improving matters whenever ignorant ordinary people make mistakes. Because officials are just as likely to misjudge any situation, they may end up doing as much harm as good when trying to intervene.

The case for market interventions is often made by referring to market failures. Take, for example, a polluting industry. It will pollute more than is socially optimal when the costs to the people living nearby are not taken into account. An all-knowing government could then step in and force a reduction in the pollution. The problem is that the government does not know the optimal level of pollution for the area, and therefore risks aiming at an inefficient pollution target. It cannot weigh the benefits of production against the discomfort of the people, let alone the unknown heightened risk they face of lung diseases and cancer.

In essence, these kinds of market failures come about due to a lack of institutions that allow for trading of rights. If the industry could compensate the residents for polluting, they would essentially be buying their emission rights from them.[1] Still, the only recognized "solution" is generally for the government to limit the pollution through regulation.

Other situations of lack of trade are rarely identified as market failures but cause similar inefficiencies. People often lack the mechanism to transfer wealth that would make an exchange worthwhile. Peter may be willing to do the dishes one night for Paul, who is willing to part with 20 bucks to get the job done. Or he may want to sell his old candleholder for five dollars to Paul, who would love such a bargain. Instead, Peter throws his old stuff away and Paul does his own dishes, simply because it would be too costly and take too much time for Peter and Paul to find each other.

In situations like these, improvements are theoretically possible if people could abolish the transaction costs and perform the trade. In theory, the government could perform this task if it knew the optimal allocation of resources. Due to the knowledge problem, however, it does not know where the opportunities for improvements are or how a given situation should be altered. It cannot know who wants to sell old junk and who wants to buy it. The government also cannot know what institution could generate more efficient allocations. It may introduce an old-candleholders exchange, but the benefit of such an operation would not warrant the costs. The government is therefore not in a position to resolve the situation.

The knowledge problem implies that the government should be careful about intervening, even when a possible market failure is detected. One reason for this is that new policies can have negative unintended consequences that may overshadow the benefits. There might be some scope for policy makers to act by trial and error, just as a person looking for a job goes to several interviews that lead nowhere. In the context of policy making, though, the costs of failed attempts are unknown and millions of people may suffer if they go wrong. Policy makers cannot calculate these risks, even with policies that have been previously implemented. As Robert Lucas argued, governments cannot predict the effects of policies based on historical evidence of their effects. People will never react exactly the same way to a policy the second time it is executed. Their plans change from one period to another, and they also learn to expect the effects of various policies.[2]

Ludwig von Mises was similarly skeptical of the benefits of interventionism. Even though policy makers intervene with the best of intentions, he explained, they tend to do more harm than good. Not only do they often fail to solve the problem, but one intervention begets new problems, with more interventions being called for as a result.[3] For instance, in the case of pollution, the government may force the polluting factory to shut down, forcing people to drive far away to buy goods from another factory, with even higher emissions as a result. This, in turn, calls for higher taxes on gasoline, and so on.

If a market can be created economically when one is missing, non-government actors tend to figure this out. Previously unfulfilled exchanges come about thanks to innovations such as TaskRabbit, a marketplace where Peter can announce his willingness to do some extra dishes, and eBay or Craigslist, where he can sell his candleholders. Besides avoiding harmful actions, another reason for the government to refrain from solving market failures is therefore to leave the field open for market participants to find efficient solutions.

If regular people and companies can find the solution, why cannot people in government do so, given that they are made of the same stuff? Friedrich A. Hayek explained this best. Nobody in isolation can figure out solutions to problems like these because each person has limited knowledge. Knowledge is dispersed among millions of market participants, each holding only a tiny fraction of the total knowledge of society. Amassing all that knowledge is a tremendous task that is likely impossible for any organization. And even if somebody could amass all current information in a giant computer, the information pool would constantly need to change along with economic development. A government cannot possibly make all the trade-offs among different forms of production, technologies, and the like. Even if it could list all prevailing prices of inputs and goods in the economy, it would still not be able to keep up with the multiple price adjustments that constantly take place in the market.[4]

Competition in the marketplace not only mobilizes information, but also allows for the discovery of new information that public entities without competition seldom stumble upon.[5] The drivers of this market dynamic are profits and losses, which function as signals to businesses and help them navigate the market, constantly update their strategies, and make incremental improvements of their products. A non-profit seeking government lacks this feedback mechanism, which is crucial for the emergence of market solutions that lower the transactions costs of exchange.

There is another reason to believe the government is inferior to market participants in determining what should be produced and how. The information businesses use to make these decisions is not of the kind one can actually record and save on some massive computer server. Rather, it is "tacit" – intuitive for somebody practicing a trade but impossible to describe in words.[6] People with a gut feeling about such things as how much salt will make the recipe just right or how customer tastes will evolve are considered experts, but they often cannot state explicitly how they come to their conclusions because they follow intuition rather than explicit formulas.

Many insights about the knowledge problem sprang from the disputes about the validity of central planning during the time when the Soviet Union was practicing communism. This "calculation debate" pitted central-planning skeptics against the admirers of what they thought was the more efficient system: socialism. Ludwig von Mises was a prominent skeptic, and he argued that no market exchange meant no market prices. No prices, in turn, meant no economic calculation, thus rendering socialism impossible.[7] His arguments implied that even if a supercomputer could amass all the existing data in the market, building it would be futile, as no such data would exist in the absence of a market.

Hayek made a similar argument, while adding his insights on the importance of tacit knowledge.[8] Even if price data existed, and a computer could be built to collect and organize them, it would still lack all the tacit knowledge in the world, which is vital for efficient production. Without efficient production, there could be no functional economic planning.

Even though few governments of today are pursuing Soviet-type organization of the economy, the insights from the debates about extreme forms of central planning are still relevant for its less rigid forms. Such planning includes intervention in the form of industrial policy, including SEZs, as the next chapter will explore. In contrast to Soviet-type planning, industrial policy often uses market mechanisms to reorganize resources in an economy, and is thus a more indirect form of planning.[9] However, it can still lead to severe inefficiencies if policy-makers steer resources in the wrong directions.

While often carrying the label of a free-market or free trade policy, SEZs are a way for the government to reorganize economic activity. As policy makers use them to direct specific production to particular areas, they are a tool to redesign the market structure of their host economy.

A government of self-interest

The other imperfection policy makers share with ordinary people is their self-interest. Most economic models assume market actors are rational and aim to maximize their utility and profits. Market actors are generally assumed to be selfish, in that they do not spend resources on making strangers happy. Businesses, likewise, do not donate money to other companies unless it can increase their own profits.

While not a complete picture of human nature, such assumptions are useful in understanding the incentive effects of different policies. In the absence of self-interest, the economic analysis becomes both strange and uninteresting in its lack of realism. In a model where the government has created the perfect communist man, it can dictate how much people will work and how much vacation they will enjoy. In such a fictional model, people do not work less if taxes are raised, do not free ride on government welfare, and do not choose professions based on career prospects and salaries.

For economic models to be useful, we do not assume people belong to this non-existent type of human. Strangely enough though, government officials are mostly assumed to be completely altruistic and not responsive to incentives. A political economy analysis, by contrast, treats people in government as human, which means they too are self-interested when executing their duties as policy makers or executive bureaucrats.

As previously mentioned, the government may be modeled as a network of heterogeneous individuals or as a unified organization. These approaches also allow for different considerations about what motivates a government's actions. As a coherent organization, the government tries to maximize its revenues from official budget items or rent-seeking, depending on what it deems more profitable for its members. Official budget items include taxes, tariffs, and fees. Although a large share of this is returned to society through government spending, some of it also goes to government salaries, offices, and advertisement campaigns aimed to increase the popularity of the government. In a less transparent government system, officials might use regular government revenues for personal consumption as well. A government administration can also make itself more popular by means of its spending in order to prolong its stay in power.

The other source of government revenue consists of more informal contributions from particular industrial groups, businesses, and individuals in the form of rent-seeking. The government can offer favors, contracts, and direct subsidies in return for these various favors.[10] Illegal rent-seeking is generally referred to as corruption, while legal forms include items like campaign contributions and lobbying.

An analysis that treats government like a cluster of individuals rather than as a single actor allows for officials to pursue very different goals. Politicians seek popularity among voters and a solid legacy. Bureaucrats seek more power, larger offices, and lots of leisure time. They may all differ, though, in the extent to which they want to promote higher official budgets versus their own personal rents. While the latter may be a more direct revenue source, they also benefit from their organization's official budget.

Regardless of their position in the governing hierarchy, most people want high compensation, prestigious titles, and dinners and resort trips provided by their agency. They also want good relations with the business community, which may offer them lucrative positions in the future. Policies are the result of the interplay between people in government and between government officials and the agents in the private sector, such as companies or households.[11]

The incentive problem is best understood from the perspective of the government as a cluster of individuals. It is also useful, however, when analyzing the dynamics of distorted incentives when the government acts as a unified organization.

Instituting a robust political economy

A robust political economy is an economy with institutions and policies that prevent the damages from the knowledge problem and the incentive problem. A society cannot rely on benevolent and wise people being in power, primarily because such perfect people may not exist. And if they do, they tend not to be the ones who reach powerful positions.[12]

Furthermore, while purely benevolent people exist in theory, omniscient ones do not. Any system of governance therefore needs safeguards against self-interested and ignorant people in office. In a robust system, the people with the best knowledge make the decisions, which in many cases are market actors rather than government officials. The system also aligns the self-centered incentives of the people who make the decisions with the progress of the economy as a whole.

A robust political economy does not guarantee economic success for a country. It is rather a way to safeguard against the severe costs of misguided and distortive policies. It is also true that not all policies introduced under a non-robust regime are economically damaging. Very large spurts of economic success have happened in several autocratic societies, for instance. In most cases, they have occurred when a sufficiently benevolent leader enters power at a time of evident opportunities for economic growth, often as a result of previous dismal economic management. South Korea and Singapore provide good examples of this.

The success of some authoritarian regimes at generating some of the fastest growth spurts in history leads some to proclaim the preeminence of authoritarianism in promoting growth. However, authoritarian regimes have also overseen the greatest economic catastrophes.[13] Thus, while it is more likely that an economy grows quickly under autocracy, it is also more likely that it puts people in the direst situations, including devastation and famine.[14] Systems that rely on the character of a concentrated elite or a single person are thus more fragile. The idea of a robust political economy is to prevent the people in power from doing such damage.

When it comes to specific institutions and policies, there is often no single way to design them that fits all countries at all times. Take central banking, for instance. In several countries, this institution began as governments gave monopoly privileges to banks, which financed wars and other government activities in return.[15] As official central banks, these institutions gained autonomy from the government over time, to avoid political manipulation of monetary policy. Before, central bank independence might have constrained the government's war spending. In most countries today, central bank independence serves to safeguard against the government inducing short-term stimuli to the economy before elections by boosting the money supply.

There are, however, limits to how far central bank independence should go to prevent the central bank from being pressured by outside political lobbying. The most independent monetary policy may be that of a single central bank president determining monetary policy. One individual is more likely to be free of ties to various interests than a group of central bank governors. However, while such a system works well with the right person at the top, it is not robust since it relies on the qualities of that person. Most countries therefore have central bank committees determining interest rates. In Britain, a minority of committee members are government appointees while, in the United States, a majority is. This creates the risk of government interference but reduces the risk of relying on one individual. India currently has a single official in charge of monetary policy, but is moving towards giving that power to a committee instead.[16] Depending on the institutional context at large, central banks in different countries and times may have very different setups to minimize rent-seeking in the system.

As the institution of central banking exemplifies, there is no absolute case of a robust political economy, so robustness should rather be thought of as a spectrum. This is particularly true for the knowledge problem, which will never be perfectly solved in terms of distributing knowledge perfectly to the right actors. Where there is a role for the government to provide pubic goods, there will be risk of a knowledge problem. The relevant question is whether the costs the knowledge problem imposes are smaller than the benefits of centralized decision-making.

Because we will never find the perfectly robust system, the robust political economy framework may seem like an unhelpful tool. However, it is particularly useful to assess the introduction of new policies. Previous scholarship has analyzed policies such as foreign aid, welfare policies, and monetary policies from a robust political economy perspective.[17] In all cases, a policy cannot be deemed non-robust just because it does not make the system as a whole robust. Rather, it is a matter of assessing the risk of a particular policy, introduced in a system with all its particular knowledge and incentive problems, falling prey to these problems or even causing more problems on its own.

The rest of this part of the book will deal with knowledge and incentive problems in the SEZ context. The next chapter gives them equal weight, which also allows for discussion on how different policies may affect the incentive problem and the knowledge problem in different ways. The subsequent chapters will focus on the incentive problem with SEZs. This disproportionate focus is because the incentive problem encourages rent-seeking, which, unlike the knowledge problem, does more than make the SEZ scheme costly and wasteful. Rent-seeking also provides a reason for policy makers to change the political landscape in a way that benefits them. The incentive problem therefore has broader implications for policy making.

Notes

1 Coase 1960.
2 Lucas 1976.
3 Mises [1929] 1977.
4 Hayek 1937.
5 Boettke 1993: 206.
6 Hayek 1945.
7 Mises [1949] 1998: 694.
8 Hayek 1945.
9 Myint 1973: 144.
10 Buchanan 1980: 9.
11 Tullock 1965; Niskanen 1971; Wagner 2007.
12 Hayek [1944] 2001.
13 Alesina and Perotti 1994: 353.
14 Sen 1999; Sharma 2016: 87.
15 Smith 1990.
16 Indian Express 2016a; 2016b.
17 Beaulier and Subrick 2006; Pennington 2011; Salter 2016.

References

Alesina, Alberro, and Roberto Perotti. 1994. "The Political Economy of Growth: A Critical Survey of the Recent Literature." *The World Bank Economic Review* 8(3): 351–371.

Beaulier, Scott A., and J. Robert Subrick. 2006. "Poverty Traps and the Robust Political Economy of Development Assistance." *Review of Austrian Economics* 19(2–3): 217–226.

Boettke, Peter J. 1993. *Why Perestroika Failed: The Politics and Economics of Socialist Transformation.* Routledge, London and New York.

Buchanan, James M. 1980. "Rent Seeking and Profit Seeking." In: 1980. *Toward a Theory of the Rent-Seeking Society* (Buchanan, James M., Robert D. Tollison, and Gordon Tullock eds.). Texas A&M University Press, Texas, pp. 3–15.

Coase, Ronald H. 1960. "The Problem of Social Cost." *Journal of Law and Economics* 3: 1–44.

Hayek, Friedrich A. 1937. "Economics and Knowledge." *Economica* 4(13): 33–54.

Hayek, Friedrich A. [1944] 2001. *The Road to Serfdom*, Routledge, London and New York. Ch. 10: "Why the Worst Get on Top", p. 138.

Hayek, Friedrich A. 1945. "The Use of Knowledge in Society." *American Economic Review* 35(4): 519–530.

Indian Express, The. 2016a. "Budget 2016: RBI Act Will Be Amended to Set Up Monetary Policy Committee." *The Indian Express*, Feb. 29, 2016. Available at: http://indianexpress.com/article/business/budget/govt-to-amend-rbi-act-to-set-up-monetary-policy-committee/ (accessed 29 October 2016).

Indian Express, The. 2016b. "Govt to Nominate 3 Independent Members to Monetary Policy Committee Soon." *The Indian Express*, May 11, 2016. Available at: http://indianexpress.com/article/business/banking-and-finance/govt-to-nominate-3-independent-members-to-monetary-policy-committee-soon/ (accessed 29 October 2016).

Lucas, Robert E. Jr. 1976. "Econometric Policy Evaluation: A Critique." *Carnegie-Rochester Conference Series on Public Policy* 1: 19–46.

Mises, Ludwig von. [1929] 1977. *A Critique of Interventionism*. Translation copyright by Margit von Mises.

Mises, Ludwig von. [1949] 1998. *Human Action*. Ludwig von Mises Institute.

Myint, Hla. 1973. *The Economics of the Developing Countries, 4th Ed.* Praeger Publishers, New York.

Niskanen, William A. 1971. *Bureaucracy and Representative Government*. Aldine-Atherton, Chicago.

Pennington, M. 2011. *Robust Political Economy: Classical Liberalism and the Future of Public Policy*. Edward Elgar Publishing Limited, Cheltenham, UK, and Edward Elgar Inc., Northampton, MA, USA.

Salter, Alexander William. 2016. "Robust Political Economy and the Lender of Last Resort." *Journal of Financial Services Research* 50(1): 1–27.

Sen, Amartya K. 1999. *Development as Freedom*, Oxford University Press, New York.

Sharma, Ruchir. 2016. *The Rise and Fall of Nations: Forces of Change in the Post-Crisis World*. W.W. Norton, New York.

Smith, Vera C. 1990. *The Rationale of Central Banking: And the Free Banking Alternative*, Liberty Fund, Indianapolis, 2nd edition.

Tullock, Gordon. 1965. *The Politics of Bureaucracy*. Public Affairs Press, Washington, D.C.

Wagner, Richard E. 2007. *Fiscal Sociology and the Theory of Public Finance: An Exploratory Essay*. Edward Elgar Publishing Ltd, Cheltenham, UK, and Edward Elgar Inc., Northampton, MA, USA.

2 Are SEZs better than the status quo?

Knowledge and incentive problems with SEZs

SEZs have some obvious benefits. By liberalizing the economy, albeit only in a limited space, they encourage more economic activity, which benefits the country as a whole. They can also improve the government's finances by increasing production and employment. As a discriminatory policy, though, SEZs also lead to resource allocation that is not based on fundamentals but rather on a preferential fiscal and regulatory environment in the zones.

The government's knowledge problem is that it cannot know to what extent such damage will occur or how to prevent it. It will also not know how much foreign capital the zones may attract. The more the SEZs merely relocate domestic companies, the more they will deteriorate the government's finances. If, by contrast, all SEZ investors are foreign, the revenue loss for the government will be smaller.

The government must also consider the cost of government-financed zone infrastructure, such as roads, bridges, utilities, and buildings. In addition, governments are generally responsible for the surrounding infrastructure that provides SEZs with necessary connections to cities and ports. These are all considerations that are impossible to predict, and which therefore contribute to the government's knowledge problem.

SEZs cause incentive problems too, as they create opportunities for rent-seeking. This leads to waste and discourages productive activities. The question is therefore whether SEZs actually can benefit a country. Without them, the country may be plagued by protectionism that hampers the emergence of a manufacturing export sector that depends on imports. Yet with regard to the political economy problems it may cause, an SEZ regime can still inflict more harm than benefits.

If the public investments are well targeted and the location of an SEZ is attractive, a zone has great potential to benefit an economy. Whether that will be the case will depend on the robustness of the country's political economy. The robust political economy framework can suggest both why some SEZs succeed and others fail, and what changes in a country's policies and institutions may help SEZs benefit the economy.

Good institutions allow decisions to be made by the people possessing the best knowledge. They also channel the actions of government officials in a beneficial way, making them act as if they are in fact benevolent welfare maximizers. As with other policies, SEZs will never be completely robust or totally non-robust. The best we can do is to assess how severe the knowledge and incentive problems are in the different institutional contexts in which a government introduces SEZs.

The knowledge problem of SEZs

Let us postulate for a moment that the policy makers who introduce and plan an SEZ do their utmost to improve the lives of the people they govern. Assuming they are completely benevolent allows us to focus on the knowledge problem with SEZs. We will deal with the question about their incentives later.

The policy makers responsible for their economy's development discuss how to promote economic development. One of them recently read an article about the Chinese economic miracle, and how they used SEZs to spearhead development. "If China got so far with SEZs," he muses, "we will be happy to achieve half of their success." They immediately proceed to the planning stage of introducing an SEZ with generous fiscal benefits to make sure to attract investors.

Practical questions immediately emerge. Where should the SEZ be located? What shall be produced in it? How can they possibly know the ultimate result of reorganizing the production of their economy in the way they are about to do? The logic of the knowledge problem leaves them skeptical of the merit of the policy.

To improve the economy, the SEZ planners need superior knowledge and understanding about how the market works, why it fluctuates, and what opportunities exist for improvement. As the fiscal SEZ benefits will reallocate the country's resources, the planners should find locations that are better for investments than where businesses are currently located. Because of how knowledge is dispersed throughout the economy, however, government officials are instead even less likely than market actors to possess this knowledge.[1]

With the absence of the necessary knowledge, the policy makers risk unintended and damaging consequences with the new policy. When the government reallocates resources that market actors are already using in their production, this will almost inevitably be the case.[2] Whether by SEZs or other means, the government is therefore rarely able to promote an economy's technological progress by taking on the task of planning resource allocation and production.[3] The following sections will examine the important decisions policy makers make about location and the composition of production in SEZs.

Choice of zone location

The benevolent SEZ planners, hopeful they will find the recipe for market improvements, want to find a location that optimizes return on investment for businesses. They realize that failing in this pursuit will likely lead to the SEZ failing or requiring very generous, and hence expensive, incentives. However, any place where investors have not already gathered is likely to be inferior to more developed locations. There is thus a great risk that an SEZ will cause unfavorable distortions in the economy. This failure will not be obvious to an outsider. If incentives are great enough to attract investments, people will perceive it as an economic success and presume the location was a good pick. However, by causing economic distortions, the SEZ is likely a net cost for the country.

In addition to resource reallocation through fiscal incentives, governments also reallocate capital directly by supplying SEZ infrastructure. The problem with policy-driven resource reallocation may become evident only if government-financed infrastructure ends up as so-called white elephants, structures that cost more to maintain than the revenues they generate. Yet even if SEZ infrastructure is put to use and the zone attracts investments, the SEZ planners cannot conclude their spending was prudent.

If reasoning does not suffice to make the SEZ planners doubt their ability to choose good locations, some precedents might. In the past, there have been SEZs so poorly located that they failed to attract any investments. The Bataan EPZ in the Philippines serves as a painful reminder of the risks of misguided government spending. After the United States closed its military base at Bataan, the Philippine government decided to promote the spot as an export processing zone. It invested almost $200 million in the EPZ in the 1970s and 1980s, upgrading its port and supplying the zone with bridges, roads, and other infrastructure. Investors enjoyed lighter regulations and generous fiscal incentives, which included exemptions from customs duties and from provincial and municipal taxes.

Alas, the location of the Bataan zone proved to be too remote, and the zone failed to attract much investment. Sixteen years after its introduction, the zone's performance was so discouraging that the Bataan case challenged the positive view of zones internationally.[4]

In cases like these, people often blame insufficiently attractive incentives and poor infrastructure. Indeed, if they are both generous enough, any location might do for an investor. However, businesses tend to invest in good locations even in the absence of generous benefits. Governments therefore need to choose a good location to avoid having to incur high tax and infrastructure expenditures. While developing countries are the keenest on spurring growth by using SEZs, they are also the most vulnerable to such waste of public resources.

Nigeria's Calabar Free Trade Zone is a case in point. This is a multimillion-dollar project, spanning 220 hectares, with an estimated capacity of up to 30,000 workers. It was initially planned for 1992 but only became operational in 2001. The Nigerian government both developed and ran the zone. A decade later, it had only 16 fully operational companies, which was far from initial expectations. In 2014, it only employed around 1,000 people. As a result, much of the infrastructure the government provided remained unused. In 2015, people were complaining that the zone was still not operational.

The planners of the Calabar zone had reasons to believe they were choosing a good location close to Calabar Port. However, the port was later deemed insufficiently linked to the zone for this to be of great benefit. It also needed to be dredged, and when that did not happen, goods were instead shipped by truck to the port in Lagos. By 2015, the Calabar port was still dormant. Previous political conflicts had also made international investors generally cautious about Nigeria.[5]

The Calabar zone is nevertheless commonly cited as a partial success, in part thanks to some investment inflow. And the government did, after all, achieve its goal of replacing grazing herdsmen on the site with factories.[6]

Too often, governments believe that the success of one SEZ portends the success of another. In China, the Zhuhai SEZ was chosen for its proximity to Macao, the country's second special administrative region beside Hong Kong. The thinking was that, just as Shenzhen would receive investments from nearby Hong Kong, capital would flow from Macao to Zhuhai. Although the SEZ accomplished impressive growth, a decade after its 1980 inauguration, just over 20 percent of its investments came from Macao, with the bulk instead coming from Hong Kong. By 2009, some of the zone's infrastructure remained idle, and it was clear that the expected synergies with Macao had failed to materialize.[7]

These cases exemplify how SEZ locations are sometimes obviously miscalculated. In most cases of SEZ failure, however, this is not the case. Instead, SEZs fail because the resources they use would generate faster, better, or more sustainable development in other projects, whether by the government or the private sector. By this definition, the potential examples of SEZ failures become numerous.

Choice of zone production

Let us return to our imaginary SEZ planners. Having agreed on a location, they meet again to decide on SEZ production. Other countries have successfully boosted particular industries by singling them out as "strategic" and targeting them with special benefits.[8] The SEZ planners are now hoping to use the new zone for this purpose.

Alas, as with the choice of zone location, the knowledge problem implies that the SEZ planners have little hope of improving the economy by choosing the best form of production. Investors in the country have already targeted and exploited the country's most profitable industries. To improve on the composition of production, the policy makers must have a superior sense of unexploited market opportunities.

This is probably the biggest problem with industrial policy. Its whole premise is that the government can intervene to mitigate market failures, such as those stemming from imperfect information, which dissuade businesses from pursuing profitable projects.[9] Instead, governments are at an inherent disadvantage to market participants when it comes to finding unexploited opportunities.[10]

The SEZ planners may well succeed in developing a particular industry by offering SEZ status only to those companies with the desired form of production. However, boosting a particular industry is not the same as benefiting the economy as a whole. Any particular kind of production will likely grow faster than it otherwise would when granted special privileges. But this can only happen by extracting resources from other forms of production.

As with zone location, it is hard to tell in what instances a government succeeds in promoting the "right" industries. The only time their mistake is obvious is when the industry fails to take off despite generous incentives to promote it. Typically, this happens when governments try to promote industries the country does not already have. The objective is often to industrialize by weaning the economy off a dependency on raw material exports and instead promoting manufacturing.

A government may choose to support industries such as high tech that it sees as harbingers of the future for the economy. It might also look at other countries that have developed a particular industry and copy their approach. Historically, this has often meant betting on apparel manufacturing.

However, what made sense when Latin American countries, China, and other countries in Asia developed their SEZs in the 1980s no longer does. The last couple of decades have seen liberalization in international trade that made it hard for most countries to compete on price with factories in Asia. Today's Latin American apparel producers can primarily thank their geographical proximity to the United States for their survival. This gives them an advantage in speed and reliability of product delivery, while they can no longer compete on being the cheapest alternative.

What then, is the industry of the future for an SEZ starting up today? Many governments seem to believe that it lies in high-tech and IT businesses. This means new projects to build high-tech parks, sometimes connected to universities. Alas, since most developing countries cannot compete with more advanced economies on this front, such projects often end up wasting more resources than they create. When Bangladesh introduced SEZs in 1983, it was already an established apparel exporter. In an effort to steer the economy in a different direction, the authorities allowed SEZ investors only in high-tech industries. As a result, the SEZs failed to attract much investment. Only after an apparel company calling itself Hi-Tech Knitwear managed to enter the zone scheme did rules change to let in textile manufacturers. This development promoted the boom in textiles that Bangladesh has experienced since.[11]

It is not easy for government officials to find the right location and industry for an SEZ. Any choice of location can end up relocating business activity in an inefficient way. Whichever industry they choose for the SEZ may grow by stealing resources from other sectors. Even when the SEZ is up and running, the officials will not know whether it is actually a net contributor to the economy, regardless of how many companies it attracts. The relative growth of an SEZ is merely a sign that businesses find the SEZ incentives valuable enough to relocate and adjust their investments to match the SEZ criteria.

It might seem that policy makers can simply copy models from other countries that seem to host successful SEZs. However, in the world of international trade, what was the best strategy yesterday will not be so tomorrow. This is the great challenge of change. Perhaps the best example of this is the end of an international trade agreement that completely redrew the map of international apparel trade. It is worth a discussion.

The Multi-Fibre Arrangement and other harbingers of change

Technological and political changes in the economy make the difficult task of economic planning even harder. Often, the most disruptive changes result from political changes, rather than unforeseeable natural catastrophes. A major policy change that affected many of the world's SEZs was the decade long phase-out of the Multi-Fibre Arrangement (MFA) between 1995 and 2005. The MFA was a system of quotas for international trade in apparel. From its inauguration in 1974, this system made trade in the apparel sector the most heavily regulated trade in the world. Within the arrangement, countries negotiated textile export quotas bilaterally, thus imposing restrictions on trade in apparel.

The MFA's abolishment changed the rules of the game in the world of textiles. With the lifting of quotas, China and India, in particular, gained significant access to international markets. Many other countries, previously shielded from Asian competition, saw much of their apparel production vanish within a few years. Apparel manufacturing based on cheap labor, which had previously been such a promising model, quickly became obsolete in many places.

The reaction of policy makers to such sudden changes is often to preserve the old model rather than to look for a new one. While the developments in the Dominican Republic will be discussed later, it is worth noting here how the Dominican government reacted to the end of the MFA. Like several other countries in Latin America, the Dominican Republic enjoyed an artificial comparative advantage for apparel thanks to the MFA, with secure access to the US market. Within a few years after 2004, with the MFA finally ending, the country's SEZs lost 60 percent of their textile producers, with the number employed in the sector dropping from 120,000 in 2004 to 41,000 in 2009. What used to be a source of job creation became the greatest cause of rapidly increasing unemployment in some parts of the country.[12]

The Dominican government reacted to the change by giving the apparel investors new privileges. In 2007, it helped textile firms remain in business by offering them subsidized loans. The same year, the government began a period of wage subsidies to all SEZ firms. For every worker, the firms received $50 per month, a sum equivalent to 30 percent of the country's minimum wage at the time. To further boost the textile industry and absorb laid-off textile workers, the government extended the same privileges that SEZ companies enjoyed to all firms in the textile, shoe, and leather businesses.[13]

Honduras was affected similarly by the MFA. It lost 34,000 of its 134,000 workers in the SEZ sector as US companies started outsourcing to Asia in the aftermath of the financial crisis.[14] Because people in countries like the Dominican Republic and Honduras enjoy higher wages than Chinese textile workers, they need to either refine their value added, by for example engaging more in design or capital-intensive weaving, or to pursue other economic sectors to specialize in. They can no longer compete with cheap labor alone.

When government officials try to determine what industries to promote in SEZs, they need to anticipate changes in their country's comparative advantage and guess what industries will prevail when the old ones are no longer around. Due to the knowledge problem, governments are best advised to stay out of that guessing game. It is an entrepreneurial challenge that can only be taken on by market actors through a process of trial and error.

The end of the MFA provides an important lesson for government officials trying to invest in the future. If they believe they can play it safe by investing in industries where the country already has a comparative advantage, they must concede the inevitability of change. Sometimes change comes fast, as with the end of the MFA, but often it is a gradual process. To adapt, entrepreneurs are constantly trying to navigate each new nuance in their respective markets and find new ways to be competitive in the developing environment. Because policy makers can only see that an industry is lucrative for the country once entrepreneurs are successfully developing it, it is particularly risky to trust policy makers with setting a country's industrial path.

Developing clusters

One objection to the skepticism of government planning of SEZs is that it does not matter that the government targets inferior locations or industries. If the government can cluster companies together, it can foster external economies of scale that make businesses more efficient regardless of location or industry. The development of economic clusters is thus a rationale for why a government should determine the locations of businesses in particular industries.

External economies of scale come about as similar firms can use the same labor pools and production factors, in addition to exchanging ideas and technologies and engendering social relationships.[15] Such integration between similar companies is commonly described as horizontal. Different firms in the same value chain can also benefit from geographical proximity, through so-called vertical integration. If several button makers are located near several apparel manufacturers, for instance, they both gain from the security of having a partner to trade with even if some firms go out of business.

The benefits of existing clusters, however, do not have clear policy implications. While many agglomeration industries are dynamic and prosperous, this may not be the result of clustering. Clusters tend to form organically as successful market actors discover their individual benefit from being close to particular businesses. Businesses thus coordinate into clusters on the basis of market opportunities, in various unpredictable ways.[16] Agglomeration looks more like the result of a successful industry than its cause.[17] Therefore, even though businesses can benefit from economies of scale, policies to promote clusters are vulnerable to the same kind of knowledge problem as other forms of government intervention.[18]

With clusters coming in many shapes and forms, they are hard to define, and it is even harder to predict how the process of cluster coordination evolves.[19] It is therefore inherently hard for economic planners to determine what nexus of business relations would be beneficial. Just as with business locations, they must find opportunities worth relocating for that firms have not already exploited. Clusters are therefore a weak argument for SEZs as a policy that concentrates businesses to particular areas.

One recent example of a misguided cluster policy is the industrial clusters in Ho Chi Minh City, Vietnam, which have had several problems attracting enough investments in their infrastructure. One designated industrial zone is surrounded by residential buildings, which are shrinking the zone by eating into its territory. There is clearly more demand for making this a residential area than an industrial cluster.[20]

One study looked at clusters in 66 different industries in India, to investigate the effects of the government's agglomeration policies. As it turns out, other factors, including labor market pooling, infrastructure, and closeness to the coast, drove the industry agglomeration, rather than government policy.[21]

In conclusion, SEZ planners face some tricky problems related to insufficient knowledge, which are only exacerbated by constant market changes. We can see how these problems are not solved by building SEZs into industrial clusters.

Solving the knowledge problem: delegation and decentralization

Are there any solutions we can offer SEZ planners to help them avoid the knowledge problem? If they are going to invest in infrastructure to attract investors, they should find ways to avoid wasting public resources. Because the knowledge problem is a result of the centralization of decision-making, some form of decentralization might help mitigate it.

One way to decentralize decision making is to delegate the determination of SEZ location and nature of production to officials closer to local markets. Local policy makers will have a better understanding of the market conditions in their particular jurisdictions. They can therefore better anticipate what effects an SEZ would have and what industry would be most successful. It is also easier for local policy makers and bureaucrats to spot changes in local markets and to amend SEZ policies accordingly. Because they can have conversations with SEZ businesses, they can more easily spot the opportunities for innovative, beneficial policy changes. If no approval for every policy change is needed from the central government, the local policy makers' reaction time will be shorter. Local governments can thus better avoid wasting money on unnecessary infrastructure. If they are planning a facility for textile production and observe that services are a more promising field, they can choose to erect an office building instead.

There are additional benefits to a system where local officials seek out the SEZ models that best suit their local conditions. As they try out new SEZ policies, they can learn from each other by observing and copying approaches that seem to work elsewhere. Decentralization thus safeguards against adopting bad policies on a national level. If a local leader introduces a poor SEZ model, others can avoid making the same mistake. In a centralized system, policies are more likely to be adopted across the board. A process of trial and error allows local policy makers to use SEZs more like policy entrepreneurs than central planners. When zones are adopted and governed by local initiatives, ideas that prove beneficial can more easily spread from the zones to the rest of the country as well.

There is some empirical support for the benefits of decentralization. Comparing the governance structures of SEZs in some Asian countries, Aggarwal found that Sri Lanka and Bangladesh had relatively decentralized forms of SEZ governance with more autonomous SEZ authorities. The zones in these countries also seemed to be outperforming those in India, which had a more centralized system.[22]

Local officials are better positioned to make decisions about SEZs because they are closer to the relevant market. Decentralized political decision making may therefore suffice to alleviate the knowledge problem, as long as the system functions well in other respects. However, the government may need to move decision-making even closer to those with relevant knowledge, which is possible by delegating to the private sector.

Solving the knowledge problem: private decision-making about SEZ industries

Another form of decentralization is to allow private investors to determine the appropriate kind of production in SEZs. While local policy makers are more likely to know what industries will be successful in the area, they may still get it wrong. And the more specific they are about the criteria for SEZ firms, the higher the risk that they will make a mistake.

Governments do not need to pick market winners to create successful zones, and instead leave decision-making about production to entrepreneurs.[23] A central government can still be in control of SEZ location. Many countries use SEZs to develop specific regions of the country, often with the goal of incentivizing investments outside of cities. In this pursuit, the SEZ planners might avoid the knowledge problem by simply not specifying which kind of firms should invest in SEZs.

There are almost no limits to the types of companies SEZs may include. The classical export processing zone often hosts manufacturing plants but has the capacity to host any kind of business. Even basic production such as farming and food processing are found in SEZs in many countries. Services such as call centers are also springing up as SEZ firms. By allowing investors of all industries to become SEZ firms, governments may be unable to predict what the development in their zones will look like. In this way, though, the SEZs are more likely to be beneficial for the country than if the government stakes out their development path.

Solving the knowledge problem: private decision-making about locations

The SEZ planners may experience too strong a political pressure to promote particular industries to avoid determining what kind of companies to support. In that case, they can choose the industry of an SEZ but allow the private sector to determine the SEZ location. If a particular industry can take hold somewhere in the country, it is more likely to do so if the government does not confine it to a particular spot. Private decision-making about zone location therefore increases the chance that the policy makers will avoid the knowledge problem while still determining the nature of SEZ production.

The zone model that offers the most flexible location for an SEZ company is the so-called single-factory zone. The government allows for a single plant, a building, or even just a floor in an office building to become a "zone." It can then grant SEZ privileges to a single company, which does not have to move to a suboptimal location to receive benefits. Countries that have adopted this model include Mexico, Mauritius, Fiji, Honduras, Ghana, and the Dominican Republic.[24]

There are some serious problems with the single-factory model, though. In most respects, as previously mentioned, single-factory zones do not even pass as SEZs. A better characterization would be a government tax break to a single company. This characterization matters, as SEZs carry the glow of a development policy, while tax breaks smack of an unfair corporate-welfare scheme. As I will discuss later, there are also some obvious incentive problems with single-factory zones.

The SEZ planners do not need to introduce single-factory zones to make SEZ locations flexible, however. Instead, they can allow private SEZ developers to purchase and develop the land they choose. The developers can then invite companies and charge them a fee for the services and infrastructure the developers provide. Private zone developers will invest in locations that they believe will attract SEZ businesses in the designated industry. They are more likely than the government officials to know which locations can provide the best business case for a zone. Countries that allow for private zone development tend also to allow the investors to propose the locations.

Solving the knowledge problem: private skin in the game

While private decision making about either SEZ industries or locations may alleviate the knowledge problem, the chance of SEZ success is the greatest if both location and type of industry can be determined on a market basis. If the SEZ planners face no political imperative to develop a particular area or industry, they should write a legal framework that discriminates against neither regions nor types of firms. They can then simply sit back and watch what kinds of SEZs emerge.

For seemingly successful SEZs to be genuinely beneficial, policy makers should also avoid the pitfall that comes with their spending on infrastructure. As previously noted, government spending on SEZ infrastructure can cause resource misallocation, and this is true regardless of who designs an SEZ. The government cannot know whether the resources it spends on the SEZ would have been better spent in other ways. Having SEZ production and location determined by the private sector may thus only save the SEZ planners from embarrassingly empty zones. They do not guarantee the SEZ scheme will actually be beneficial.

To fully overcome the knowledge problem, the government might therefore need to go one step further. In exchange for the freedom to determine zone locations and industries while enjoying SEZ benefits, the government can demand that private actors incur the costs of developing the zone infrastructure. Only if private investors have skin in the game can they be correctly guided by profits and losses to invest in the right projects.

Privately financed SEZs are generally called "private zones." In this model, governments determine the SEZ incentives but it is up to private entrepreneurs to rent or buy land and provide the zones with infrastructure, utilities, and services.

Private SEZ developers will only make this investment if they can earn more in rents from SEZ investors than their costs in infrastructure, land, and company services. If they can make a profit, this is a signal that the value of being located in a zone for a company is higher than the cost, which implies the SEZ is worthwhile. Private skin in the game helps prevent unprofitable SEZs from being developed. If a location is bad or access to water and electricity too costly, for instance, no SEZ developer will want to invest in the venture. It is therefore an effective way to avoid the knowledge problem of resource misallocation. Similarly, if the government fails to provide basic utilities that businesses demand, private investors can step in. India's IT-clusters, for instance, have generated a market in water supply, due to the unreliable quantity and quality of public water provision.[25]

It may seem that private zones, while low in cost, would have a limited impact on a country's employment and exports. In fact, there is much evidence to the contrary: In several countries, private zones constitute the main share of both SEZ exports and employment. In the 1980s, many of the rapidly growing SEZs in Central America did not receive much government support. The same has been true for many of the later Southeast Asian zones that sprung up since the 1990s.[26]

Private zones are thus becoming more numerous. The SEZ program in the Philippines, for instance, which started in 1972, hosted only public zones in its first two decades. The program then saw a surge in private zones with its industrialization in the early 1990s. By June 2016, the Philippines had an impressive 337 private and only 4 public SEZs.[27]

Honduras has also seen private zones overtaking public ones. Private participation in the program started to grow in 1987, when the government made the zones more accessible for foreign investors. By 2011, Honduras had only one publicly developed zone, which never expanded much beyond its development phase. This contrasts to the 24 private SEZs Honduras hosted by 2008.[28] The United States' foreign trade zones similarly rely on private investors for their development, supply of utilities, and even the provision of quarters of government officials present in the zones. After a slow start in the 1930s, since the 1970s, the US scheme has grown to over 200 zones today.[29]

SEZ planners can only introduce private zones if they are not too tempted by the political reward that comes with rapidly growing zones in the country. If no entrepreneur sees a profit opportunity in developing an SEZ, the zone will not come about, nor should it. Grand promises may thus result in disappointment as no zone developer step in to take up the government's offer of fiscal and regulatory incentives. In such cases, SEZ schemes are generally described as failures. If the government would provide more of the infrastructure, the argument goes, businesses would come. Firms confirm this assessment by attesting that the lack of facilities makes them reluctant to invest in the zones. However, when a government relies on private developers, empty zones signal the absence of a business case for zone development and hence no potential net benefits. In this light, it is a good thing that what would be a loss-making zone does not come about. There is a bigger risk of real failure when the government supplies zones with lots of infrastructure and services to attract investors.

The risks posed by the knowledge problem should give the SEZ planners pause. Despite their intention to promote economic development, they may end up investing tax revenues in projects that create less value than if the money had simply stayed with the people.

Private zone development is probably the best way to avoid such waste. However, privatization may not always be politically feasible if the SEZ planners are pressed to create zones that take off. If so, the officials may still avoid the knowledge problem by privatizing the choice of either location or industry. If they are uncomfortable leaving such decisions in private hands, they can at least delegate decision-making regarding location and SEZ policies to local policy makers. These are all more or less effective ways to move decision-making closer to the people with the relevant knowledge.

The incentive problem and SEZs

Solving the knowledge problem enables SEZ planners to introduce beneficial SEZs. The next question is whether they actually want to. Let us assume these policy makers are in fact not benevolent, but rather respond to incentives that appeal to their self-interest. If so, they might exploit the fact that SEZs, like other government privileges, offer a range of opportunities for government officials to benefit themselves. If this rent-seeking happens at the expense of the economy as a whole, the SEZ scheme falls prey to the incentive problem and may become more of a burden than a benefit for the country.

The rent-seeking government

Officials have several ways to exploit SEZs to extract rents. If the government finances the infrastructure, SEZ officials can use the procurement process to advance favors to their kin and cronies. They can demand bribes and favors from anyone benefiting from the SEZ, from construction companies to production-plant investors. If they do not find bidders for this kind of exchange, they have the power to increase the fiscal incentives until they do.

The development of the SEZ program in Poland has been described as driven by rent-seeking. Companies lobbied the government to obtain SEZ status, which expanded the program beyond what seemed to be its original purpose. Instead of pursuing healthy market competition, companies in Poland were competing with each other for SEZ privileges.[30]

In the Philippines, the government made the former U.S. naval base Subic Bay into an SEZ to attract private investment that would transform it into an industrial hub. As companies competed to be designated as the port terminal operator, the administration of President Fidel Ramos intervened to give the privilege to a company with government connections. While ultimately unsuccessful, this made the whole process longer and costlier.[31]

The opportunity to extract rents from SEZs incentivizes policy makers to introduce zones for this purpose. The main damage to the economy does not come about as people take advantage of rent-seeking opportunities, but as policy makers promote their proliferation. This happens when the same people exploiting rent-seeking opportunities also have the power to increase their prevalence. As John Joseph Wallis points out, a great worry for the designers of institutions in the Anglo-Saxon world in the 18th century was the incentive policy makers had to introduce policies that corrupted the economic system.[32] Unfortunately, SEZs are yet another policy with high potential to become vehicles for rent-seeking.

The most convenient way for government officials to trade SEZ incentives for rents is arguably the single-factory zone. With these, firms do not need to relocate to a new area. Policy makers must only make the criteria for SEZ businesses sufficiently lenient to generate a lot of zone-status applicants. With high demand for a limited supply of SEZ-status concessions, SEZ applicants can be made to pay higher rents to be chosen.

Single-factory zones are also attractive for policy makers because they can generate favorable statistics for an SEZ program without anything substantial happening on the ground. Senegal's SEZ scheme, for instance, may look decent for anyone just looking at its level of investments. The World Bank counts $228 million in cumulative investments since the opening of the first SEZ in Dakar. However, $178 million of these investments originated from single-factory zones, formed as domestic firms simply switched their status to obtain the SEZ benefits.[33]

The SEZs in Ghana offer a similarly dubious story. Having amassed an impressive $1.2 billion in cumulative investments by 2007, the SEZ regime has been described relatively successful in the African context. However, only one of the four SEZ locations specifically designated by the authorities has been developed. That zone hosted only 11 companies in 2009 and represented only around 5.5 percent of investments and 7.5 percent of employment of the whole SEZ scheme. All the rest of the impressive investment and employment numbers were generated by single-factory zones.[34]

Government officials can also use SEZs as an excuse to seize land. Land disputes driven by SEZ development are pervasive in some countries that lack the institutions to align the incentives to develop SEZs with making them beneficial. In India, SEZs have repeatedly been blamed for providing opportunities for officials to seize land from farmers without adequate compensation. Officials can allegedly obtain both money and political favors by leasing the designated zone space on the market.[35]

Similarly, in Vietnam, around 100,000 people are said to have been displaced when their villages turned into SEZs. Many of them claim to have been inadequately compensated.[36]

Since SEZs create spaces available for office buildings and factories rather than farms, the value of the land can increase significantly when converted into zones.[37] There are thus economically sound reasons for the pursuit of what is deemed a "conversion of the fertile land into cement structures."[38] The process is distorted, however, when driven by political, rather than business, concerns. If officials can use public resources and even pay below market price to farmers for their land, they have a strong incentive to introduce SEZs by land conversion. Because they are unlikely to account for the real cost of the land, they may do it regardless of whether SEZ industries are a better use of the land.

Policy makers can also use SEZs to gain popularity with voters. If they want to target a particular constituency, they may enrich it by locating an SEZ there and spending enough to make it "successful." They may also waste resources on promoting a popular industry in which the country does not have a comparative advantage. It does not matter whether the SEZ planners understand that the zone will on net be wasteful. They still have incentives to promote SEZs and claim to be promoting job creation.

Cutting the ribbon in front of a grandiose infrastructure project generates fame and supportive comments even if the project is a complete failure in the sense of benefiting the population as a whole. Policy makers thus have a proclivity for developing visible infrastructure projects, including SEZs with grand gates, as these signal leadership and active development policy. This bias is particularly problematic where resources are scarce. In that case especially, SEZ planners should focus instead on providing less costly, but often more important, regulatory incentives in the zones. Better regulations are however often lacking in SEZ schemes in poorer countries, even though a solid legal framework for SEZs is presumably much cheaper than massive infrastructure investments.

The lack of a solid legal framework can certainly be an obstacle to the success of SEZs. One example of this is the SEZ scheme in Senegal, which was introduced in the 1970s and had problems for decades due to its opaque and unpredictable rules. As a result, despite the government's investments in infrastructure, the zones in Senegal attracted disappointingly few investors and developers.[39]

South Africa seems to have neglected the importance of rules in the SEZs too. The country has better infrastructure than most other African countries, and its SEZ scheme offers duty-free imports and tax exemptions. However, it is still hard to invest in the zones because of South African social regulations, such as burdensome labor laws, from which no exemptions apply in the zones. As a result, the zones are not seen as attractive enough to many foreign investors.[40]

Cuba made a similar mistake with its SEZs, which were introduced as late as 1997. Its zones offer foreign investors substantial tariff and tax exemptions. Combined with the low wages of the country and an opening up of the American consumers market, Cuba looks well placed to compete with other SEZ schemes in Latin America. However, the SEZs do not offer exemptions from the country's labor laws. This means that they require companies to hire workers through a state-run labor company. Cuba has a dual currency system, and because this public company pays workers in the near worthless Cuban peso, the workers receive far less than the companies pay in wages. Thus, while wages are low, the cost of labor for companies is slightly higher than in the Dominican Republic, for instance.

Cuban labor laws combined with restricted access to the US market made the Cuban SEZs unattractive to investors. As a result, the project was more or less abandoned in 2004, as businesses closed or moved out, and SEZ permits were revoked. In 2013, the Cuban government issued a decree for renewed development of one of the country's old SEZ site, at the port of Mariel. It offers generous tax breaks, including labor and profit taxes, to investors. Yet the problem with the dual currency, which keeps labor artificially expensive, remains. It may therefore come as no surprise that as previously, initial investments in the zone are mainly in warehousing and shipping, not in labor-intensive manufacturing.[41]

SEZs can serve other kinds of political goals. Ghana's government opened its flagship SEZ at the port of Tema in 1995. It has been seen as a way to strengthen its ties with the Malaysian government, as part of a broader objective to turn the country's policy orientation toward an East Asian model of state-led development.[42] The contract to develop the zone, as well as the privilege to run the country's port authority, was given to Business Focus, a

Malaysian company with close ties to the Malaysian government. When disputes erupted between the company and the Ghanaian government, the project halted. The SEZ was then essentially deserted until 2005, when the World Bank pledged money for the project.[43]

Besides extracting rents from businesses, landowners, voters, and other governments, central-government policy makers can also use SEZs to extract rents from local officials. If an SEZ is expected to generate employment, local officials should benefit from hosting it. More economic activity means a better economic legacy, which increases the chances for the current local administration to remain in office after the next election. This may induce a local official to lobby or bribe people in the central government to place the SEZ in his or her jurisdiction. To boost its rents as much as possible, the central government can make clear that the local leader who makes the highest contribution also gets the SEZ.

Local rent-seeking

Local officials can use SEZs to rent-seek too. If they are responsible for the procurement process for SEZ infrastructure, they can extract bribes from firms willing to supply it, as well as from potential SEZ investors. The incentive problem might therefore not be solved simply by electing benevolent people to the central government. Unless the system is completely robust also at local levels of governance, SEZ policies will avoid the plague of rent-seeking only if all government officials at all levels are completely benevolent. Alas, this is unlikely to be the case.

If rent-seeking is more prevalent at the local level than the central level, then the incentive problem might increase when local policy makers have more discretion in setting and executing SEZ policies. Decentralization of decision-making is therefore not as safe a solution to the incentive problem as it is to the knowledge problem.

By the unofficial nature of corruption schemes involving SEZs, people will never hear about most of them. Once in a while, though, scandals break out and a corrupt deal is exposed. While the SEZs in China were successful in the long run, the scheme was tainted with corruption during its first few years. In 1985, a smuggling scandal was revealed in Hainan, one of the country's first zones. Local officials apparently turned a blind eye to a massive illegal scheme of shipping cars from the SEZ to China proper. Thanks to tariff exemptions, the vehicles could be supplied to the country more cheaply than through the legal route. The revelation tarnished the reputation of China's SEZs, but the corruption was fortunately limited enough to not sink the project as a whole.[44]

In the case of Russia, the corruption related to SEZs seems to have been more widespread. After the break-up of the Soviet Union in the 1990s, Russia opened up several SEZs. These zones, however, have been described as centers for oligarchs engaged in corruption and crime rather than as business-friendly zones. Because the legal environment was more secure outside the SEZs, the zones did not become a source of economic progress in the country.[45] It was only in 2005, when the government poured infrastructure and administrative resources into the zones, that they started to grow.[46] Nevertheless, recent analyses of SEZ performance find that the zones can show little in the form of innovative success. In addition, tourism and recreational zones, port SEZs, and the program as a whole have all been described as inefficient.[47]

Rent-seeking by the bureaucracy

Low-level officials can contribute to the deterioration of an SEZ scheme too. Government bureaucrats involved in executing SEZ policies are certainly in a position to abuse their power. Their tasks may include issuing licenses to companies who wish to operate in SEZs, and inspecting whether SEZ firms and developers live up to factory standards or other regulations. Such tasks give them the opportunity to delay the admissions process or prevent investors from operating by referring to various regulations and criteria. To resolve the situation, SEZ investors may need to give the bureaucrats some form of under-the-table inducement.

Low-level corruption can make companies into common-pool resources for corrupt officials. Such local graft puts pressure on small firms, forced to pay corrupt officials performing numerous inspections and regulatory requirement to this end.[48] When low-level corruption is pervasive, the system can become so unpredictable and costly for companies that they cannot profit from any investments.[49]

The more layers of government bureaucracy SEZ investors must pass through to obtain their permits and other documents, the higher the risk that the officials they encounter will demand more in bribes than the extra profits the investors might make.[50] If so, companies will exit the scheme, and even an SEZ with the potential to succeed and benefit the country will be left empty.

One of the inducements for businesses to locate in an SEZ is access to so-called single-window or one-stop shops. These are meant to lower the administrative costs of doing business and hence attract more investors. In many cases, though, companies need to go through a daunting bureaucratic process to register and operate in SEZs. This indicates the lack of incentives for bureaucracies to make the process easy.

Navigating the bureaucracy has for long been the bane of SEZ firms in India, a country rife with low-level corruption. SEZ applicants have for long needed approval from numerous bureaucracies. By 2005, 15 different authorities were involved in this process, and a majority of SEZ acknowledged to frequently making non-official payments.[51]

Some SEZ bureaucracies are so opaque and complicated that they seem to exist only for bureaucrats to enrich themselves. It is hard to know whether such flaws arise as officials set up obstacles that SEZ firms have to pay to overcome, or are simply due to bureaucrats shirking on the job.

In Lesotho, SEZ firms can take care of all the necessary permits, migration and labor issues, and utility connections in one business-facilitation center. While this sounds great, just getting all the necessary permits still took on average 90 days only a few years ago. To what extent such sluggishness is due to corruption is naturally hard to tell but it may be no better if it is simply caused by a lack of incentive to make the bureaucracy more efficient. As officers in Lesotho's SEZ center still report to their respective ministers, no level of the bureaucracy really has the incentive to coordinate the administration and introduce better oversight of service provisions.[52]

When low-level rent-seeking is so sever it scares all investors away, the central government cannot avoid seeing that there is a problem. However, an even greater inefficiency persists if investors stay and perpetuate a costly regime. This can happen when the country devotes so many resources to an SEZ that businesses find it worthwhile to invest despite the rent-seeking. This means that the more resources the government devotes to SEZs, the higher is the risk that they will be used for rent-seeking purposes. As more government resources are invested in them, previously corruption-free projects can attract rent-seeking officials.[53]

In addition to such blatantly corrupt ways to extract rents, government bureaucrats also have some subtler options. For one, they may use their responsibility to execute SEZ policies as an excuse to increase their staff and thus expand their agencies. By claiming that executing the job is more expensive and demanding than it really is, they can demand more resources from the government, thus becoming both wealthier and more important. Another incentive to expand their agencies is the extra time for coffee breaks and afternoon golf rounds that additional staff allows.

Such bureaucracy shirking is possible because it is difficult for the government to know the actual cost of an efficient agency.[54] Bureaucrats are therefore unlikely to get caught defrauding the central government by consuming more resources than they need. As a result, the SEZ scheme can become more expensive than warranted, which increases the likelihood of SEZs resulting in a net cost to the economy.

While bureaucrats usually manage to hide this conflict of interest, the clash between the motives of policy makers and bureaucrats sometimes becomes evident. In Nigeria, a conflict over the SEZ program with the customs authorities went on for a couple of decades. The SEZ incentives included tariff exemptions, and the customs officials refused to give up an important source of revenues by implementing the policy. They therefore allowed only a small part of the customs exemptions promised to SEZ investors.[55]

Solving the incentive problem: limited corruption

Solving the incentive problem means aligning the interest of selfish officials with beneficial policies. We cannot count on electing benevolent people to the central government, let alone all the local governments and bureaucracies in a country. The best thing to do is therefore to look for a system where self-interested people will not harm the economy.

As with the knowledge problem, dealing with the incentive problem does not require making the system perfect. For the knowledge problem, it may suffice to delegate decisions to local officials with knowledge that is better than that of central-government officials though still worse than that of market actors. Similarly, for the incentive problem, a solution need not rid the system of rent-seeking completely. Some rent-seeking, even in the form of illicit corruption, may not doom an SEZ scheme. The zones might even have corruption to thank for their existence, if that was the motivation for policy makers introducing them.

Scholars have previously shown how corruption can be beneficial to an economy. Leff argued in the 1960s that corruption allows the most efficient producers to obtain production quotas since they can afford to pay the highest bribes to decision-makers.[56] Lui, as well as Beck and Maher, subsequently showed how bribes might help bring about socially optimal outcomes.[57] Others have argued that rent-seeking can be the very reason some policy makers introduce beneficial policies.[58]

We might imagine a simple scheme where policy makers swap SEZ licenses for rents in the form of favors and money. Let us also assume they care only about rents and not at all about their reputations as SEZ promoters. If the policy makers want to keep the scheme running, they will have to limit their level of graft. They cannot demand all of a company's revenues, for instance, as that would bankrupt it. Just like a tyrant plundering his poor subjects, they do not want to steal so much from producers that they perish.[59] Once SEZ businesses start disappearing under the pressure of graft, moreover, the officials cannot count on any new victims being willing to replace the old.

Because most SEZ investors are mobile, they will move to preferable regimes long before going bankrupt under the pressure of rent-seeking. Corrupt officials therefore face limits on what they can demand in rents. The officials might need to strike a bargain with the investors. The officials introduce an SEZ scheme where the investors enjoy fiscal incentives and a plethora of free infrastructure and services. In return, the investors give a share of their benefits from the scheme in brown envelopes to government officials. In this way, policy makers can design the SEZs as a convenient tool for transforming public funds in the form of tax expenditures into cash in their own pockets.

While blatantly corrupt, this kind of setup may cause officials, driven by their incentives to extract rents, to benefit the economy as a whole. There is waste of public resources on the one hand, but an opportunity for businesses to increase investments and employment on the other.

The problem with such an arrangement, however, is that neither the SEZ officials nor the businesses have an incentive to keep the level of rents low enough to generate net benefits for the economy. The businesses have an incentive to ask for more fiscal benefits and more government spending in the SEZs, requests that give officials an opportunity to raise their demands for bribes. The higher the sums involved, the less likely it is that the economy as a whole might actually benefit from the scheme.

Whether the corruption scheme is beneficial depends to a large extent on whether the SEZ firms are already in the country. Take the example of a foreign company that receives tax benefits worth $8 million while the government spends $2 million to provide infrastructure worth $1 million to the company. The company may then be willing to pay almost $9 million under the table to move to the SEZ. The public loses only $2 million since it would otherwise not have received any taxes from the company. If the company's contribution to the economy is higher than that, the scheme should be beneficial. If, by contrast, the company is merely shifting location within the country to the SEZ, the government loses out on $10 million. The chances of the scheme being beneficial to the economy are then miniscule. With the officials taking most of the extra profits generated from operating in an SEZ, a domestic company will hardly be able to expand much and will instead just shift its activities from one place to the other.

It is unlikely, though, that this scheme would work with international firms. If they get the above fiscal benefits and infrastructure provision in exchange for $9 million in kickbacks, they will likely seek a better offer from another government. Foreign companies are also more likely constrained by laws in their home country that deter them from engaging in bribery. In addition, their cost of moving to an SEZ in another country is lower than that of domestic companies, which are therefore more willing to accept having to pay the bribes.

The SEZ planners, not caring about inviting companies that will benefit the country the most, therefore have little incentive to pursue international inves-tors. This means a bribery deal is more likely struck between the government and its domestic firms, making it unlikely to benefit the economy. The result is a scheme reliant on corruption that for incautious observers nevertheless looks successful because it attracts investors.

Even if a corruption scheme like this does turn out to be marginally bene-ficial for the economy as a whole, it is unlikely to remain so. Many of the costs for a company relocating to an SEZ are fixed costs, such as setting up new production facilities, hiring new staff, and establishing new supply chains. The benefit from locating in an SEZ, by contrast, is the value of all the future tax exemptions and infrastructure support. A company may assess the yearly net benefit of their SEZ status, and offer bribes to officials accordingly.

However, once the SEZ bribery scheme is agreed on and the fixed costs incurred, the company will be reluctant to move again and face the same fixed costs if the yearly bribery costs start rising. The government officials therefore have the incentive to renege on their promises and raise the illicit fee for the SEZ investor. Even if people in the current administration shake the CEO's hand and promise not to raise the illicit rents, the officials cannot guarantee that their successors will not do the same. With time, the agreement is thus likely to deteriorate, as subsequent administrations can enrich themselves by breaking any graft limiting promises. This dynamic means that governments cannot commit to limited interventions through corrupt agreements.[60] Similar agreements in the SEZ context are therefore unlikely to be sustainable, and will thus hardly be beneficial.

Solving the incentive problem: democracy

Political actors often have little to gain by investing in projects that add the highest social value.[61] One way to give them the incentive to promote general welfare is to connect their payoffs to people's perceptions of their economic policy making. A democratic system is one that makes officials responsible for the economic outcomes of their actions to at least half of their constituency. With popular voting and checks and balances, policy makers can take credit for people getting jobs and for favorable production, investment, and export statistics. They thus have the incentive to introduce and execute beneficial policies.

Needless to say, democratic leaders also have incentives that do not align with decisions that promote economic welfare. Populist leaders appeal to people's sentiments rather than rationality. Nationalist and racist agendas appeal to people with talk of patriotism and preserving an ethnically homogeneous national state. Democratic leaders can also trade policies for campaign contributions, just like autocrats trade favors for rents.

Nevertheless, the political bias in a democratic system is toward the benefit of the people rather than repression. Leaders in a democracy are also more reluctant to engage in rent-seeking due to the risk of being caught. If they are exposed as corrupt, voters can punish them in the next election if they have not already been disqualified from serving in office.

Democracy is more likely to discipline the behavior of policy makers in a decentralized system, where there is a clearer connection between their actions and economic outcomes. SEZ planners seated in the country's capital may have little to fear politically if a couple of SEZs fail to generate economic growth or increase aggregate employment. There are, after all, many factors besides the SEZs that they can blame for the adverse statistics.

At the local level, by contrast, an SEZ can play an important and clear role in the economy. Therefore, while decentralization alone is not a solution to the incentive problem, it strengthens the disciplinary power of democratic institutions.

Democracy cannot completely prevent an SEZ scheme to serve rent-seeking purposes. Democratic policy makers have the incentive to locate SEZs in jurisdictions where they hope to boost support, which are likely to be in suboptimal locations from an economic standpoint. If the society is sufficiently open, though, investigative journalists have a chance to expose such devious tactics.

As we have seen, bureaucrats, not being elected by voters, might have incentives to engage in corruption. However, policy makers with a stake in the outcome of an SEZ have the incentive to put effort into making their agencies act in accordance with the spirit of the policy. This may be through positive inducements such as paying higher salaries, which was a key tool for Singapore to get rid of corruption in its bureaucracy.[62] Policy makers might also try to tie the bureaucrats' compensation to their performance. A tougher approach is to monitor agencies better or punish bureaucrats more harshly when caught shirking or rent-seeking. With their political career on the line, the policy makers will want to find the system that best aligns the bureaucrats' behavior with their own intentions.

Solving the incentive problem: private zones

We have already examined the potential of privately developed SEZs to solve the knowledge problem, thanks to their private provision of SEZ infrastructure and services. For the very same reason, private zones can also solve the incentive problem. Private developers have the incentive to make their SEZs as attractive as possible, at the lowest possible cost. This includes both finding the best SEZ locations and creating attractive business environments.

The profits of private developers are aligned with the societal benefits of the zone. Unlike policy makers, private developers can only provide infrastructure or other benefits at their own expense. They will only do so if the SEZ firms are prepared to pay for it because it enhances their profit prospects. Therefore, the developer cannot charge more in fees and land rent than the additional profits a company enjoys by locating in the SEZ.

There is also no point in a private developer extracting bribes from an investor, unless it is illegally plotting with the investor to avoid paying some tax. Between private parties, a bribe is just another fee, and there is generally no point in making it illicit.

A private developer does of course not provide all benefits that an SEZ company enjoys. The company also benefits from the government's tax breaks and regulatory exemptions. The private developer should want to exploit this when setting the rental price. If it sets land rents high enough that there is no room for the government to extract bribes from the firms in exchange for SEZ status, all of the surplus of SEZ firms goes into the pockets of the developer. If the officials demand that the private developer share some of its margin with them, the developer may simply lower the land rents and host more companies, thus lowering the profit margin the officials are trying to claim. Private zones are therefore difficult for corrupt officials to kidnap.

Fiscal benefits are not merely transfers from the government to private developers. If entry into the SEZ development market is open and fair, there is competition among developers for investors. Their incentive is then to offer the best services and business climate, which benefits the SEZ investors. The only way a government can earn rents is to constrain the number of SEZ developers. If they start functioning as an oligopoly, they can earn excess profits that allow the government to extract rents from them in exchange for keeping them as part of the scheme. However, such a setup could probably be pursued only by the central government, which would be better off simply abolishing the private SEZ model if it is eager to maximize its rents.

There is an additional risk of inefficiency for the private SEZ model. Because of the risk that officials will start extracting rents from SEZ companies if zone developers lower their land rents, the developers might provide more services and infrastructure than optimal. However, there are good reasons to believe that the private SEZs provide a level of services closer to optimal than public ones. Private investors generally have the incentive to find the optimal level of services to offer to SEZ companies. The better the services, the more the companies will pay in land rent. There is a limit to companies' willingness to pay for more services though, and private developers can find this level by trial and error.

Besides providing utilities such as electricity and water, private zones in several countries offer mail service, garbage collection, and even fire squads. Honduras has SEZs that offer administrative services, such as payroll and human resources. Some even offer manufacturers labor for lease.[63]

In contrast to privately developed SEZs, public zones tend to offer fewer and more basic services to their investors. This could be because governments are underestimating the benefits of providing services or know they lack the proficiency to do it right. More plausibly, this is because policy makers find it easier to use fiscal incentives to attract investors. Private developers do not have that option and can attract more investors only by offering a better business climate.

The private developer thus tends to pursue a strategy of quality, and the public one a strategy of price. This can give them very different clients, just as the producer of a good will attract poorer consumers by competing on price rather than quality.[64] Publicly developed zones that compete on lower costs tend to cater to investors with tight margins. Such companies have most of the features governments allegedly want to avoid in SEZ investors. They tend to offer low wages and be more "foot-loose", as they constantly look for the cheapest investment climate. This short-termism also means that they invest little in training for their employees. The sought-after technology and knowledge transfers are thus less likely to materialize.

Private developers, by contrast, compete on quality and service differentiation, and often obtain SEZ firms to match this approach. On most social and environmental indicators, private zones perform better than public ones. Although there are also many high-quality public zones, it seems as though a country should introduce private zones if it wants to leave the sweatshop model of SEZs.[65]

Single-factory zones are generally private SEZs in the sense that their infrastructure, which may just be a part of a building downtown, is supplied privately. However, this feature does not make single-factory zones robust. Instead, single-factory zones should be efficient vehicles for rent-seeking. For a government that wants to extract bribes from investors, single-factory zones are more targeted. As part of a private SEZ scheme, they stand out in having removed the private developer from the picture. The government can thus allow the single-factory firm to operate as normal and simply extract kickbacks from the single-factory zones in exchange for their fiscal benefits. If these companies are domestic, such a scheme would be merely a transfer from the public purse to the pockets of government officials.

Single-factory zones were shown earlier to be a possible solution to the knowledge problem. While this is true, it should be clear by now that they create obvious incentive problems. This is because their structure makes them function as targeted benefits to companies, with little resemblance to other SEZs.

Good outcomes promote good institutions

This chapter has dealt with how good institutions promote economic progress in the SEZ context. It is also worth noting a reciprocal effect. Institutions that have good economic results are more likely to be maintained, strengthened, and replicated. Successful privately developed zones make other countries see the benefits to be had in privatizing their schemes. Prospective private developers can also use examples of previous private zones to lobby the government to introduce such a scheme, arguing that it will make the policy makers look good.

Similarly, a democratic system with a successful SEZ is more likely to introduce more of them while also strengthening its democratic elements. Seeing the benefits of an SEZ, voters will demand more of them and policy makers will have the incentive to oblige. With greater interest in the scheme, the people will also be more interested in knowing how it works and performs. This encourages transparency via news coverage and other forms of scrutiny of SEZs, which strengthen the disciplining effect of the democratic system.

Solutions to the knowledge problem also encourage stronger institutions. When policy makers realize that local leaders make better decisions about SEZs, they are less likely to recentralize decision-making and administration. Also, when they observe the superior performance of private actors in developing SEZs, they will increasingly adopt this model. Such a process of learning has made private development into something of a "best practice" for SEZs.[66]

Conclusion

A robust political economy is a system plagued neither by the knowledge problem nor by the incentive problem. As we have seen, SEZ planners may need to seek different measures for attenuating the two problems, not all of which are consistent with each other. A politically decentralized system has a better chance of solving the knowledge problem. Decentralization should also help solve the incentive problem in the context of a democratic system because it strengthens the connection between economic performance and a policy maker's success in office. On the other hand, decentralization also risks exacerbating the incentive problem by encouraging more low-level corruption.

Private SEZs tend to solve both the knowledge problem and the incentive problem. Private developers know their markets and thus the prospects of SEZs. In pursuit of profits, they also have the incentive to develop zones in a manner that benefits the economy as a whole. In several countries, private SEZ developers start with a parcel of land and must then supply all of the zone's buildings, roads, utilities, garbage collection, fire squads, and much more. The only possible infrastructure cost for the government lies in connecting the SEZ with nearby cities, ports, and highways.

Private investors are no more benevolent than corrupt policy makers or bureaucrats, but their profit motive drives them to invest in locations and production facilities that create the highest value. The growing popularity of private SEZs may be due to both their ability to efficiently attract many investors and their ability to genuinely benefit an economy.

The robust political economy framework provides some rough guidelines to estimate whether an SEZ scheme is beneficial. Because the net benefit of an SEZ depends on factors we cannot measure, we can still never know for sure. We do not know, for instance, how much corruption is actually taking place, what the optimal level of infrastructure and services is, or whether international SEZ firms would invest in a country in the absence of SEZs. What we can do is to look at the institutional setup of a scheme to assess the opportunities, risks, and biases toward errors and misconduct.

The robust political economy framework is a more powerful framework to weigh benefits and costs than the cost-benefit analyses, which only rely on macroeconomic data and alternative cost approximations. Yet the two frameworks share an emphasis on the economic net benefit. They both weigh the costs for the tax payers against the benefits SEZ investors can be expected to bring, and focus on static metrics like investments and employment.

The next chapter, by contrast, will discuss a more dynamic benefit that SEZs might bring: the promotion of countrywide economic reform. While the current chapter analyzed how SEZs may avoid underperforming the status quo, the next chapter raises the bar and looks at SEZs at their very best.

Notes

1 Lavoie 1985; Boettke 1998; Horwitz 1996.
2 Ikeda 2005; Kirzner [1979] 1985; Mises 1929: 25.
3 Lavoie 1985: 52–54.
4 Warr 1987; Moran 2011: 16.
5 Norman 2014; Charles 2015.
6 All Africa 2011; Liquid Africa 2004.
7 Xue-qiang and Si-ming 1990; Pak 1997: 76; Yeung et al. 2009: 225.
8 Studwell 2013.
9 See, e.g., Harrison and Rodríguez-Clare 2009: 4.

10 Keck 1988.
11 Farole and Akinci 2011: 41.
12 CNZFE 2004; CNZFE 2009.
13 National Congress 2007.
14 Engman 2011: 61.
15 Nadvi 1998.
16 Miller and Côté 1985: 120.
17 Seshadri and Storr 2010: 362.
18 Desrochers and Sautet 2004.
19 Martin and Sunley 2003.
20 Xuan 2015.
21 Kathuria 2016.
22 Aggarwal 2005: 16, 42–44.
23 Auty 2011: 213.
24 Costachie 2008; FIAS 2008; Farole 2010: 3; 145; Engman 2011: 49; Iwulska et al. 2015: 67
25 Vijayabaskar and Babu 2016.
26 FIAS 2008: 4, 46, 26–28.
27 Makabenta 2002: 61; Malapad 2016
28 Engman 2011: 49, 59.
29 Bell 2016.
30 Gwosdz et al. 2008.
31 Bowen et al. 2002: 461.
32 Wallis 2006.
33 Baissac 2011: 5. As an additional twist, as much as $150 million of the single-factory-zone investments originated from a single phosphate manufacturer.
34 Farole 2010: 8–9; 2011: 61.
35 Levien 2011.
36 Action Aid Vietnam 2005.
37 Farole and Moberg 2014: 8.
38 Khan 2008: 14.
39 Baissac 2011: 15–16.
40 Moran 2011; McCallum 2011.
41 Willmore 2000; Feinberg 2012; Frank 2013; Whelan 2015.
42 Ansah 2006.
43 Farole 2010: 4.
44 Crane 1990.
45 Tuominen and Lamminen 2008.
46 Rybakov 2009.
47 Yankov et al. 2016.
48 Frye and Shleifer 1997.
49 Easterly 2002: 247.
50 Shleifer and Vishny 1993.
51 Aggarwal 2005.
52 Farole 2011: 216.
53 Beaulier and Subrick 2006.
54 Niskanen 1971.
55 Farole and Moberg 2014: 10.
56 Leff 1964.
57 Lui 1985; Beck and Maher 1986.
58 Cowen et al. 1994; Bhagwati 1980; Bhagwati and Srinivasan 1980.
59 McGuire and Olson 1996.
60 Haber 2002: xv.
61 Moberg and Wagner 2014.

62 Quah 1995: 398.
63 Engman 2011: 60.
64 Hirschman 1970: 47.
65 FIAS 2008: 21, 46.
66 Farole 2010: 15.

References

Action Aid Vietnam. 2005. "Migrant Workers in Vietnam: A Summary Research Report." *Action Aid Vietnam*Hanoi: Action Aid International Vietnam.

Aggarwal, Aradhna. 2005. "Performance of Export Processing Zones: A Comparative Analysis of India, Sri Lanka, and Bangladesh." *Indian Council for Research on International Economic Relations (ICRIER) Working Paper* No. 155. Available at: http://icrier.org/pdf/wp155.pdf (accessed 29 October 2016).

All Africa. 2011. "Ten Years After, Is the Calabar Free Trade Zone Working?" *All Africa Global Media*, Dec. 19, 2011. Available at: http://allafrica.com/stories/201112190775.html (accessed 29 October 2016).

Ansah, Eric S. 2006. "Close Encounters Between Africa and Asia Ghana's Look East Policy and the Making of Malaysia's Overseas Investors." *PhD Dissertation* University of Amsterdam Faculty of Social and Behavioral Sciences. Available at: http://dare.uva.nl/document/39579 (accessed 29 October 2016).

Auty, Richard. 2011. "Early Reform Zones: Catalysts for Dynamic Market Economies in Africa." In: *Special Economic Zones: Progress, Emerging Challenges, and Future Directions* (Thomas Farole and Gokhan Akinci eds.). The World Bank, Washington, D.C., 207–226.

Baissac, Claude. 2011. "Senegal's Special Economic Zones program: Historical performance, contribution to reform, and prospects." *World Bank memo*, Oct. 11, 2011.

Beaulier, Scott A., and J. Robert Subrick. 2006. "Poverty Traps and the Robust Political Economy of Development Assistance." *Review of Austrian Economics* 19(2–3): 217–226.

Beck, Paul J., and Michael W. Maher. 1986. "A Comparison of Bribery and Bidding in Thin Markets." *Economics Letters* 20: 1–5.

Bell, Tom W. 2016. "Special Economic Zones in the United States: From Colonial Charters, to Foreign-Trade Zones, Toward USSEZs." *Chapman University, Fowler Law Research Paper* No. 16–02. Available at: http://ssrn.com/abstract=2743774 (accessed 29 October 2016).

Bhagwati, Jagdish N. 1980. "Lobbying and Welfare." *Journal of Public Economics* 14: 355–363.

Bhagwati, Jagdish N., and Thirukodikaval N. Srinivasan. 1980. "Revenue Seeking: A Generalization of the Theory of Tariffs." *Journal of Political Economy* 88(6): 1069–1087.

Boettke, Peter J. 1998. "Economic Calculation: The Austrian Contribution to Political Economy." In: *Advances in Austrian economics*, Vol. 5 (Peter J. Boettke, Israel M. Kirzner, and Mario J. Rizzo). JAI Press Inc., Greenwich, CT, pp. 131–158.

Bowen, John T. Jr, Thomas R. Leinbach, and Daniel Mabazza. 2002. "Air Cargo Services, the State and Industrialization Strategies in the Philippines: The Redevelopment of Subic Bay." *Regional Studies* 36(5): 451–467.

Charles, Eyo. 2015. "Non-Functionality of Calabar Seaport, EPZ Worry APC Elders." *Daily Trust*, Nov. 17, 2015. Available at: http://allafrica.com/stories/201511181006.html (accessed 29 October 2016).

CNZFE (National Free Zones Council). 2004; 2009. Yearly statistical publications. Available at: http://www.cnzfe.gob.do/transparencia/index.php/estadisticas/inform e-estadisticos-anuales (accessed 29 October 2016).

Costachie, Silviu. 2008. "Free Zones, Some Theoretical Aspects." *Annals of the University of Craivora: Series Geography* 11: 138–146.

Cowen, Tyler, Amihai Glazer, and Henry McMillan. 1994. "Rent Seeking Can Promote the Provision of Public Goods." *Economics and Politics* 6(2): 131–145.

Crane, George T., 1990. *The Political Economy of China's Special Economic Zones.* M. E. Sharpe Inc., Armonk, New York and London, England.

Desrochers, Pierre, and Frédéric Sautet. 2004. "Cluster-Based Economic Strategy, Facilitation Policy and the Market Process." *The Review of Austrian Economics* 17(2/3): 233–245.

Easterly, William. 2002. *The Elusive Quest for Growth: Economists' Adventures and Misadventures in the Tropics.* The MIT Press, Cambridge, MA and London, England.

Engman, Michael. 2011. "Success and Stasis in Honduras' Free Zones." In: *Special Economic Zones: Progress, Emerging Challenges, and Future Directions* (Thomas Farole and Gokhan Akinci eds.). The World Bank, Washington D.C., pp. 47–68.

Farole, Thomas. 2010. "Case Studies of Special Economic Zones: Ghana." *World Bank memo*, Washington D.C.

Farole, Thomas. 2011. *Special Economic Zones in Africa: Comparing Performance and Learning from Global Experience.* The World Bank, Washington, D.C.

Farole, Thomas, and Gokhan Akinci (Eds.). 2011. *Special Economic Zones: Progress, Emerging Challenges, and Future Directions.* The World Bank, Washington, D.C.

Farole, Thomas, and Lotta Moberg. 2014. "It Worked in China, so Why not in Africa? The Political Economy Challenge of Special Economic Zones." UNU-WIDER Working Paper 152/2014. Available at: https://www.wider.unu.edu/publica tion/it-worked-china-so-why-not-africa (accessed 29 October 2016).

Feinberg, Richard E. 2012. "The New Cuban Economy: What Roles for Foreign Investment?" *Brookings.* Latin America Initiative at Brookings. Available at: https://www.brookings.edu/research/the-new-cuban-economy-what-roles-for-for eign-investment/ (accessed November 5, 2016).

FIAS (The World Bank's Facility for Investment Climate Advisory Services). 2008. *Special Economic Zones: Performance, Lessons Learned, and Implications for Zone Development.* World Bank Group, Washington, D.C.

Frank, Mark. 2013. "Cuba Bids to Lure Foreign Investment with New Port and Trade Zone." *Reuters*, Sep. 22, 2013. Available at: http://www.reuters.com/article/us-cuba -investment-idUSBRE98M12H20130923 (accessed 29 October 2016).

Frye, Timothy, and Andrei Shleifer. 1997. "The Invisible Hand and the Grabbing Hand." *American Economic Review* 87(2): 354–358.

Gwosdz, Krzysztof, Woyciech Jarczewski, Maciej Huculak, and Krzysztof Wieder-man. 2008. "Polish special economic zones: Idea versus practice." *Environment and Planning C: Government and Policy* 26: 824–840.

Haber, Stephen (Ed.). 2002. *Crony Capitalism and Economic Growth in Latin America: Theory and Evidence.* Hoover Institution Press, Stanford, CA.

Harrison, Ann and Andrés Rodríguez-Clare. 2009. "Trade, Foreign Investment, and Industrial Policy for Developing Countries." NBER Working Paper No. 15261.

Hirschman, Albert O. 1970. *Exit, Voice, and Loyalty: Responses to Decline in Firms, Organizations, and States.* Harvard University Press, Cambridge, MA.

Horwitz, Steven. 1996. "Money, Money Prices, and the Socialist Calculation Debate." In: *Advances in Austrian Economics*, Vol. 3 (Roger Koppl and Steven Horwitz eds.), pp. 59–77.

Ikeda, Sanford. 2005. "The Dynamics of Interventionism." In: *Advances in Austrian Economics*, Vol. 8 (P. Kurrild-Klitgaard ed.). Emerald Group Publishing Ltd., Bingley, UK, pp. 21–58.

Iwulska, Aleksandra, Jouanjean, MarieAgnes, Lotta Malin JohannaMoberg, Jose DanielReyes, Miguel Eduardo SanchezMartin, Cristian UgarteRomero, RafaelVan Der Borght, SwarnimWaglé. 2015. *How to Sustain Export Dynamism by Reducing Duality in the Dominican Republic: A World Bank Trade Competitiveness Diagnostic.* World Bank Group, Washington, D.C. Available at: http://documents.worldbank.org/curated/en/2015/03/24383476/sustain-export-dynamism-reducing-duality-dominican-republic (accessed 29 October 2016).

Kathuria, Vinish. 2016. "What Causes Agglomeration – Policy or Infrastructure? A Study of Indian Organised Manufacturing." *Economic & Political Weekly* 51(21): 33–44.

Keck, Otto. 1988. "A Theory of White Elephants: Asymmetric Information in Government Support for Technology." *Research Policy* 17(4): 187–201.

Khan, Saeed. 2008. "India's SEZ – Business Zones Development: Economic Performance, Social/Environmental Impacts." *SSRN*The Jamnalal Bajaj Institute of Management Studies, Mumbai. Available at: http://ssrn.com/abstract=1292195 (accessed 29 October 2016).

Kirzner, Israel M. [1979] 1985. *Discovery and the Capitalist Process.* University of Chicago Press, Chicago.

Lavoie, Don. 1985. *National Economic Planning: What is Left?*Ballinger Publishing Company, Cambridge, MA.

Leff, Nathaniel H. 1964. "Economic Development through Bureaucratic Corruption." *American Behavioral Scientist* 8(3): 8–14.

Levien, Michael. 2011. "Special Economic Zones and Accumulation by Dispossession in India." *Journal of Agrarian Change* 11(4): 454–483.

Liquid Africa. 2004. *"Federal Government's Export have Started Yielding Fruits."* Liquid Africa Holdings Limited, Jul. 25, 2004.

Lui, Francis T. 1985. "An Equilibrium Queuing Model of Bribery." *Journal of Political Economy* 93(4): 760–781.

Makabenta, Maria Peregrina. 2002. "FDI Location and Special Economic Zones in the Phillipines." *Review of Urban and Regional Development Studies* 14(1): 59–77.

Malapad, Anna Rose R. 2016. Personal correspondence with Anna Rose R. Malapad, Philippine Economic Zone Authority, Aug. 23, 2016.

Martin, Ron, and Peter Sunley. 2003. "Deconstructing Clusters: Chaotic Concept or Policy Panacea?" *Journal of Economic Geography* 3(1): 5–35.

McGuire, Martin C. and Mancur L. Olson. 1996. "The Economics of Autocracy and Majority Rule: The Invisible Hand and the Use of Force." *Journal of Economic Literature* 34(1): 72–96.

Miller, Roger, and Marcel Côté. 1985. "Growing the Next Silicon Valley." *Harvard Business Review* 63(4): 114–123.

Mises, Ludwig von. [1929] 1977. *A Critique of Interventionism.* Translation copyright by Margit von Mises. Available at: https://mises.org/library/critique-interventionism (accessed November 6, 2016).

Moberg, Lotta, and Richard E. Wagner. 2014. "Default Without Capital Account: The Economics of Municipal Bankruptcy." *Public Finance and Management* 14(1): 30–47.

Moran, Theodore H. 2011. "International Experience with Special Economic Zones (SEZs): Using SEZs to Drive Development in Countries around the World." *Report Commissioned by Center for Development and Enterprise.* Available at: http://cata log.ihsn.org/index.php/citations/52296 (accessed 29 October 2016).

Nadvi, Khalid. 1998. "Knowing Me, Knowing You: Social Networks in the Surgical Instrument Cluster of Sialkot, Pakistan." *Institute of Development Studies*Institute of Development Studies, University of Sussex. Available at: https://www.ids.ac.uk/ idspublication/knowing-me-knowing-you-social-networks-in-the-surgical-instrum ent-cluster-of-sialkot-pakistan (accessed November 6, 2016).

National Congress (Congreso Nacional). 2007. Law 56–07 (Ley No. PI-56–07). Available at: https://www.dgii.gov.do/legislacion/leyesTributarias/Documents/56-07. pdf (accessed 29 October 2016).

Niskanen, William A. 1971. *Bureaucracy and Representative Government.* Aldine-Atherton, Chicago.

Norman, Martin. 2014. "Have 'Special Economic Zones' Entered the 21st Century Yet? A Tale of Two Cities." *Private Sector Development Blog*, The World Bank. Available at: http://blogs.worldbank.org/psd/have-special-economic-zones-entered-21st-century-yet-tale-two-cities (accessed 29 October 2016).

Pak, Chŏng-dong. 1997. *The Special Economic Zones of China and Their Impact on Its Economic Development.* Greenwood Publishing Group, USA.

Quah, Jon S. T. 1995. "Controlling Corruption in City-States: A Comparative Study of Hong Kong and Singapore." *Crime, Law & Social Change* 22(4): 391–414.

Rybakov, Leonid. 2009. "Special Economic Zones: Foreign direct investment boosts Russian economy." *Telegraph*, Apr. 24, 2009.

Seshadri, Triyakshana and Virgil Henry Storr. 2010. "Knowledge problems associated with creating export zones." *The Review of Austrian Economics* 23(4): 347–366.

Shleifer, Andrei, and Robert W. Vishny. 1993. "Corruption." *The Quarterly Journal of Economics* 108(3): 599–617.

Studwell, Joe. 2013. *How Asia Works: Success and Failure in the World's Most Dynamic Region.* Grove Press, New York.

Tuominen, Karita, and Eero Lamminen. 2008. "Russian Special Economic Zones." Electronic Publications of Pan-European Institute 18/2008. Available at: http://www. utu.fi/fi/yksikot/tse/yksikot/PEI/raportit-ja-tietopaketit/Documents/Tuominen%20and %20Lamminen%201808%20web.pdf (accessed 29 October 2016).

Vijayabaskar, M., and M. Suresh Babu. 2016. "The Politics of Urban Mega-projects in India." *Economic & Political Weekly* 51(17): 85.

Wallis, John Joseph. 2006. "The Concept of Systematic Corruption in American History." In: *Corruption and Reform: Lessons from America's Economic History* (Edward L. Glaeser and Claudia Goldin eds.). University of Chicago Press, Chicago, pp. 23–62.

Warr, Peter G. 1987. "Export Promotion via Industrial Enclaves: The Philippines' Bataan Export Processing Zone." *The Journal of Development Studies* 23(2): 220–241.

Whelan, Robbie. 2015. "Shipping Line CMA CGM Signs Deal for Cuba Logistics Hub." *Wall Street Journal*, May 11, 2015. Available at: http://www.wsj.com/articles/ shipping-line-cma-cgm-signs-deal-for-cuba-logistics-hub-1431373531 (accessed 29 October 2016).

Willmore, Larry. 2000. "Export Processing Zones in Cuba." DESA Discussion Paper No. 12. Available at: http://www.un.org/esa/desa/papers/2000/esa00dp12.pdf (accessed 29 October 2016).

Xuan, Minh. 2015. "Ho Chi Minh City: Many Districts Propose to Remove Industrial Cluster Planning." *Sai Gon Giai Phong*, Jan. 07, 2015. Available at: http://www.saigon-gpdaily.com.vn/Hochiminhcity/2015/1/112205/ (accessed 29 October 2016).

Xue-qiang, Xu, and Li Si-ming. 1990. "China's Open Door Policy and Urbanization in the Pearl River Delta Region." *International Journal of Urban and Regional Research* 14(1): 49–69.

Yankov, Kirill V., Anton K. Moiseev, and D. A. Efgrafov. 2016. "Yankov Problems and Prospects of Special Economic Zones in Russia." *Studies on Russian Economic Development* 27(3): 311–317.

Yeung, Yue-man, Joanna Lee, and Gordon Kee. 2009. "China's Special Economic Zones at 30." *Eurasian Geography and Economics* 50(2): 222–240.

3 SEZs as drivers of reform

By solving the knowledge and incentive problems associated with SEZs, a government can create zones that benefit the country economically. However, SEZs can bring benefits other than economic ones. Increases in such performance aggregates as production, exports, and employment are, after all, inevitably limited and therefore easily outweighed by the costs of resource misallocation and rent-seeking.

This chapter will discuss the more dynamic benefits of SEZs. Because these are usually ignored in an SEZ analysis, such benefits of SEZs can in fact be easily underestimated. The aim is to show that the largest benefits of SEZs are political, not economic, and that SEZs are at their very best when they help solve political problems. Political economy benefits are more dynamic and more transformative, and can scale in a way that marginal improvements in macroeconomic aggregates cannot.

When only the economic side of SEZs is considered, one cannot refute the most powerful criticism of the policy: If a government wants to promote economic development, it should not introduce such patchy and limited reforms as SEZs. Whatever business activity SEZs encourage would also come about by lowering taxes, tariffs, and regulatory burdens more widely. Non-discriminatory fiscal measures also avoid the SEZ-related inefficiency costs.

This line of argument can be refuted, however, by taking into account some potential political benefits. In contrast to the mainstream scholarship on SEZs, the political economy approach thus reveals both the most damaging sides of SEZs, such as corruption and resource misallocation, and their largest benefits. While the previous chapter focused on the hidden costs, this one deals with the less obvious benefits.

Can SEZ dynamics solve economic problems?

At this stage in this book, the case for SEZs is weak at best. While people often praise them for increasing investments, employment, and exports in a country, such benefits are higher than the costs only under the right institutional and political circumstances. Even if SEZs are better than the status quo, they may be inferior to broader economic reforms, which can bring about the same economic benefits without misallocating resources, favoring certain industries, or encouraging wasteful rent-seeking.

Even ignoring the insight about the knowledge and incentive problems, it is not strange that theoretical models of SEZs might reveal them as wasteful.[1] Any employment of a person or investment of a dollar in an SEZ would come about to an even greater extent if the government introduced more general and smaller reductions in taxes and tariffs in the country as a whole. However, in a less technical strand of SEZ research, scholars have also put forth some theories about plausible dynamic economic benefits of SEZs. These have in common the suggestion that, accounting for less immediate or obvious effects, SEZs can be superior to broader reforms.

This chapter presents the most credible dynamic benefits, starting with the economic effects in this section and continuing with the political benefits in the next. The chapter will then describe a different political mechanism that others have not suggested but which has the potential of generating the most radical change in an SEZ country.

Fostering backward linkages

A well-cited benefit of SEZs is so-called backward linkages. These are the connections formed as SEZ investors purchase inputs and services from domestic non-SEZ firms. The theory is that as SEZs attract investors, domestic firms experience higher demand for the primary material and services that these new companies need. This encourages both more domestic investment in already-existing sectors and the development of new ones.[2]

The backward-linkages reasoning rests on Albert O. Hirschman's theory of the benefits of unbalanced growth for economic development.[3] If one sector of the economy enjoys more investment than others, it induces investments in the lagging sectors that form parts of the growing sector's supply chain. The rest of the economy is thus pulled into a higher growth territory thanks to the progress of the sector enjoying the initial added investments.

The benefits of unbalanced growth can certainly be questioned. For a start, it is not clear what sectors should be selected to lead and pull the rest of the economy along. There is therefore a risk that policy makers choose a sector that lacks the potential to play this role. Furthermore, if resources are devoted to one sector, other sectors risk forming bottlenecks holding the economy back as a whole.[4] Finally, more-even growth should make it easier for linkages to form between businesses, as more sophisticated companies will more likely purchase inputs from suppliers with similar standards.

Regardless of the merits of unbalanced growth, the theory is particularly non-applicable in the SEZ context. This is because, due to the nature of zones, SEZs are more likely to discourage already-existing backward linkages than to form new ones. Most SEZ models offer some form of tariff exemption to encourage imports. This is an important incentive for exporting manufacturers who need access to the cheapest raw material to compete internationally.

However, by encouraging imports of raw material, the tariff exemptions also discourage companies from forming backward linkages because they make it cheaper to import goods than to buy them domestically.[5] If this were not the case, the SEZ companies would not need the tariff exemptions in the first place. It is particularly important to offer tariff exemptions if the raw material does not exist in the host country. In that case, though, it becomes even less likely that domestic companies will try to produce it.

It is quite easy to see why tariff exemptions would discourage backward linkages. When a tariff is added to the international price of a good, the domestic producers can charge as much as the world price and the tariff added together. Domestic companies may therefore be indifferent between buying locally and importing. When companies become SEZ firms and can buy inputs more cheaply from abroad, their domestic suppliers lose some of their customers. As such, a clothes manufacturer may buy cotton domestically while the tariff is in place, but start importing cotton when it becomes tariff exempt.

If domestic firms lose many of their customers as the customers move into SEZs and become tariff exempt, the domestic firms probably need to lower their prices in response. If they cannot, however, they may disappear as a result of the SEZs. Domestic firms will be less affected, though, if the SEZ producers formed only a small part of their customer base. If so, an SEZ scheme means the domestic firms still enjoy the protection of tariffs and are not incentivized to meet their international competitors' prices.

The weak connection between the SEZ firms and domestic import-substituting firms tends to diminish even further over time. Trade protection guarantees import-substitution firms an artificially high price for their goods and thus encourages them to stagnate by not increasing quality or lowering costs. Meanwhile, international competition encourages SEZ firms to become increasingly sophisticated, which leads to increasingly stringent quality requirements for the material they use. Any international investor that is technologically sophisticated will likely turn to already established suppliers in other countries.[6] Increasing sophistication thus further widens the gap between what import-substitution firms produce and what SEZ firms demand.

As SEZ firms no longer depend on domestic suppliers, they have no need to stay in a particular industry to secure domestic supplies. The SEZ sector can therefore diversify into new industries, further weakening its ties to the domestic protected industries. The divide between SEZ firms and domestic import-substitution firms thus widens further with time. This development path runs in exactly the opposite direction predicted by the theory about SEZs igniting a country's industrialization as SEZ investors pull domestic firms into higher forms of production via backward linkages.

Some industries are more likely to generate backward linkages than others, of course. The sector most likely to do so is probably agriculture because it cannot import the land it uses. However, agricultural SEZs are often formed out of already-existing domestic firms, so that no new linkages are actually formed. Only international agricultural companies that invest in a country's SEZs and cultivate new land areas can form new linkages, in this case between the landowners and the agribusiness. Ironically, the very goal of SEZs is often to diversify a country away from agriculture and into more-sophisticated industries. Therefore, governments tend not to promote agriculture to be the main land use of new SEZs. Governments try instead to lure in high-tech manufacturers, often with the rationale of beneficial linkages.

Thus, the great paradox of SEZs: Countries use them to promote sectors in which they do not have a comparative advantage, such as manufacturing or high technology, rather than agriculture. As a result, SEZ investors are unlikely to find domestically produced inputs for their production. Meanwhile, sectors such as agriculture, where backward linkages can more easily be formed, are the least popular sectors to expand.

Not only theory fails to support the idea that SEZs promotes backward linkages, but empirical findings suggest a similar conclusion. Evidence of such linkages is largely absent, even in countries with large markets and plenty of established local industries where linkages would be most expected.[7] A country may have a successful SEZ scheme by conventional measures of zone production and employment but still fail to develop backward linkages. Bangladesh, for instance, which is a prominent garment exporter, has few linkages even though SEZ firms are "not actively prohibited and, in theory, are encouraged" to purchase inputs domestically.[8]

Governments that actively encourage backward linkages tend to do so through tax breaks and tariff exemptions to domestic companies that sell to SEZ companies. They may even designate selling to SEZ firms as exports, and thus allow these companies also to become SEZ firms with all the benefits that entails. The problem is that if domestic firms must receive the same incentives as SEZ firms to sell to them, it is questionable whether this really constitutes backward linkages. The power of the argument on backward linkages is, after all, that SEZs can spur activities in sectors that do not receive the SEZ benefits themselves. If the chain of linkages is broken when a sector does not receive SEZ benefits, it is a stretch to call it backward linkages.

Several Asian SEZ schemes, while prominent employers, have become isolated enclaves, with only limited backward linkages with the domestic economy.[9] Another case of weak backward linkages is the Dominican Republic, which has its own chapter in the case-study part of this book. Its SEZs stand for an estimated 58 percent of the country's exports and 3.6 percent of total employment.[10] Still, the zones have largely failed to form backward linkages. Instead, they have developed what is likened to islands of high performance in a sea of slow development.[11] Backward linkages were primarily observed in the Dominican Republic before the 1980s. This was before textiles took off and the scheme was still dependent on agriculture.[12]

Countries that have managed to promote backward linkages have often done so at a high cost. Firms in the Masan Zone in South Korea are credited for buying an unusually large share of their inputs domestically. However, in this case, local companies that supplied SEZ investors were also given special benefits. The government also devoted resources to technical training for the SEZ suppliers.[13] Honduras has applied similar tactics to create backward linkages, by extending tax and tariff exemptions to non-SEZ companies.[14] In this way, domestic suppliers in practice become single-factory zones – firms receiving SEZ benefits without having to relocate to a zone.

A government can also move potential domestic suppliers into SEZs and promote their competitiveness by giving them SEZ benefits. This gives domestic companies better access to SEZ firms, but blurs the definition of backward linkages even further.

SEZs thus lack natural tendencies to create backward linkages. These form primarily when the government introduces additional incentives or resources targeted at creating particular business connections. There seems to be little support for the notion that SEZs spur development in a country by pulling the rest of the economy along via backward linkages.

Concentration of government resources on infrastructure

Another line of argument for why SEZs can have greater economic benefits than broader reforms is that they allow for pooling of government resources. Infrastructure is one example. By supplying one location with superior infrastructure, the government can allegedly attract foreign investors that would not find any one location in the country attractive if the infrastructure was distributed evenly.

Companies that shun investing in developing countries often cite the lack of infrastructure as a major reason. For a place to be remotely of interest, a reliable and constant supply of electricity and water, along with accessible infrastructure such as roads and ports, is a necessary, although not sufficient, condition. The country's average infrastructure quality is irrelevant for an investor as long as its area has access to good facilities and a decent port. It does not matter if the rest of the economy relies on mud roads and lacks reliable electricity supply.

SEZs are seen as a useful tool to concentrate government spending on infrastructure and utilities in a particular location when the government cannot provide it in the country as a whole. To meet the demands of foreign investors, the reasoning goes, the government should concentrate its resources in limited areas.

The main problem with this way of thinking is that, by concentrating resources in a few zones, the government runs a great risk of falling prey to the knowledge problem. Whatever location and whatever type of zone it chooses to invest in, the investment may cause a great misallocation of resources. Large government infrastructure spending also risks falling into the trap of numerous incentive problems, due to the rent-seeking opportunities it provides. Therefore, even if resource concentration is warranted, it comes with serious risks of waste if the government pursues it.

Because private SEZ development is the best way to avoid the knowledge and incentive problems related to infrastructure, the government should leave those investments to the private sector. If it is true that resource concentration yields high benefits, private developers will try to capitalize on that fact by developing infrastructure hubs. The benefit of infrastructure concentration can thus be an explanation for private investments in clusters, but not a rationale for the concentration of government-financed infrastructure.

In addition to its practical problems, resource concentration may not even be warranted, as it targets the wrong metric. The level of foreign investments is not a proxy for development. It is important to remember that the goal of SEZs should be economic development in general, not growth in the investments that often go along with it. Investors bring capital and employment opportunities, but if these benefits come at the expense of basic infrastructure for people in the country as a whole, the policy may not be a net benefit.

Concentrating resources for policing of corruption and crime

Another form of government resource concentration is that of policing against crime. If the government cannot afford to police the country as a whole, it can instead concentrate its limited resources in a particular area. Multinationals are highly sensitive to a country's reputation for crime. To attract them, the authorities need to provide secluded environments where they can safely invest.

This argument has merit to the extent that crime prevention is a more justifiable government obligation than SEZ infrastructure investment. In contrast to infrastructure provision, policing is not as easily privatized. The government therefore has to decide on where to direct its policing resources. In countries where a thinly stretched police force cannot possibly control a lawless country, it may need to concentrate its resources out of necessity.

However, this is quite a weak argument for SEZs per se. Concentrating policing is a way to benefit not only foreign investors but also the people given an opportunity to find a safe area in the country. In fact, the most important benefit such resource concentration provides may be the protection of domestic businesses. This does not imply that such a policy should necessarily be combined with an SEZ with tariff and tax exemptions.

The argument about concentrating resources for policing corruption and crime can thus not be dismissed out of hand. However, when considering that resource concentration in this field may be a necessity for many different reasons, it is a weak argument in favor of SEZs, as opposed to other ways of concentrating police resources.[15]

SEZs as a way to overcome the knowledge problem of reforms

The examples above regarding linkages or concentration of resources are all economic arguments for why SEZs are better than broader reforms. There are also a couple of ways in which governments could use SEZs to find and implement the right policies. These arguments are more political than economic, as they rely on improving the knowledge of policy makers about what the best policies are. The SEZs then become tools to identify the best policies and spread them more widely throughout the country.

Arguments about SEZs as solutions to the knowledge problem are more convincing than the economic arguments for SEZs about backward linkages and resource concentration. However, as I will argue in the next section, SEZs can do the most good for a country by solving incentive problems stifling reform.

The knowledge arguments about SEZs guiding a government toward broader reforms have some empirical support. Several countries that previously relied on SEZs have subsequently introduced SEZ-like policies in the country as a whole. Some Asian countries with low-tariff SEZ schemes have subsequently abandoned them and instead opened up to trade more broadly.[16] In Central America, Honduras has hosted SEZs since the 1970s. Throughout the years, it expanded the scheme several times. Finally, in 1998, it declared that the whole country was a "free zone area."[17] Taiwan has similarly seen its SEZ investments virtually disappear after growing 61 percent annually for more than a decade. By the early 1980s, the country itself had improved so much, with less trade protection and better infrastructure, that the SEZs had lost their previous appeal.[18]

The persistently low export share of South Korea's manufacturing zones might seem alarming to the casual observer. After introducing its first zone in 1970, SEZ exports rose to $175 million in a couple of years. Between 1975 and the mid-1980s, SEZ exports grew at an annual rate of 41 percent. Nevertheless, by 1985, the share of SEZ exports was only 2.9 percent of the country's total. This was because, parallel to the rise of Korean SEZs, the country as a whole was becoming a bigger exporter. If anything, this would point to the success of the SEZ scheme, which may nevertheless be perceived as irrelevant and even a failure for the country based on the SEZs' export share.[19]

Rather than being indications of SEZ failure, the diminishing role of zones may thus point to a positive national development. The most useful SEZs may actually be those whose importance as exporters and job creators diminish the most. If SEZ policies spread through the introduction of more zones, they become less "special." Rather than a sign of failure, this indicates that the SEZs have helped spread zone policies by setting examples for the rest of the country.

In what follows, I will discuss the two main ways in which SEZs may be spreading reforms by helping policy makers overcome their ignorance of their effects. One is through the usage of SEZs as test-beds and the other as show-cases for reform. I will argue that these theories about SEZs overcoming knowledge problems, while not inaccurate, hardly suggest that SEZs can play a pivotal role in a country's transformation. The latter part of this chapter therefore focuses on the most powerful way in which SEZs can change a country as a whole, namely by changing the incentives of the ruling elite.

SEZs as policy test beds

The test-bed argument for SEZ reform says that a government that seeks to improve an economy can introduce SEZs to become more knowledgeable about the effect of SEZ policies. This scenario implies a benevolent government seeking to improve its knowledge about how to achieve economic improvements. It can use SEZs as Petri dishes for economic policies, places where it can observe policies' effects before introducing them in the country as a whole.

Using SEZs for policy experiments has several advantages. Because of their limited space, it is relatively easy to accomplish the required changes in administration and to change the expectation of market participants accordingly. Their smallness also means that, if a policy turns out to be ill suited for the country, there is less damage done than would have been the case if the policy was applied simultaneously throughout the country.

The opportunity to try out different policies in different areas in the same country also gives a better sense of a policy's general effects. Often, different policies are adopted only in different countries. This makes it tough to discern their effects because of the multitude of other factors influencing economic and social performance. Comparing two countries with different policies can lead to misinterpretations due to cultural and historical differences that influence economic development. There are fewer such differences among SEZs within a country. Using SEZs as test beds can thus make the government more confident in introducing beneficial policies in the country as a whole. As such, SEZs as test beds are not ends in themselves but tools for broader economic reform.

There are some cases in which countries seem to have been using SEZs to try out new policies. Before liberalizing its telecommunication services, Jamaica introduced SEZs free from the state monopoly. In Kuwait and other countries in the Middle East, SEZs have been used to experiment with the effect of foreign ownership.[20] Labor laws can also become more flexible, first in an SEZ and later in the country as a whole. One recent example is Japan, where the prime minister is pursuing SEZs with more flexible labor laws to test how they may work in the country as a whole.[21]

The first SEZs in China have been described as a way to test capitalism before implementing it nationwide. The government may have been cautious about implementing a new economic regime in the country because of the unknown effects of such a shift. It therefore introduced SEZs as test beds for capitalism, where businesses could make their own decisions about investments, production, and marketing, and where even foreign ownership of companies was allowed.[22]

Although the theory of governments using SEZs as test beds for policy reform holds some truth, it is hardly the main reason governments introduce them. Nor is it what helps a country ultimately reform. First of all, it is implausible that governments would simply not know the effects of most SEZ policies, as the most common changes that SEZs bring are quite universal. Lower taxes do, on average, mean more business activity, as do all other ways SEZs can lower the cost of doing business, such as more streamlined administrative procedures and lighter regulations. Lighter labor-market regulations make companies more willing to hire, which boosts employment. The government may not know the precise magnitude of the effect of such policies. But while SEZs can demonstrate the general effect of a policy, they cannot show precisely how big the effect will be in the country as a whole.

It is quite possible that the perception of SEZs as test beds for policy reform spread as governments gave the impression of being wise and calculating in proposing change. Using SEZs for experiments looks like a scientific and pragmatic approach to policy making, in contrast to regular partisan politicking. Many leaders surely cherish a legacy like that of the benevolent statesman in the spirit of the late Lee Kuan Yew of Singapore.

However, the test-bed theory relies on a unified government, with officials joining up behind a leader ready to perform the policy experiments that will alleviate their ignorance. As we know from the real world, governments consist of people with different goals and interests who possess different knowledge. These individuals form complex networks of interactions among different personalities with varying agendas, values, and knowledge, the aggregate of which we call a government.[23] Because of this internal heterogeneity, the impasse policy makers need to solve is to convince others in power about the benefits of the policy they are proposing.

SEZs as showcases

Policy makers claiming to be using SEZs as policy test beds may just want to show others something they already know. If they were to implement a policy that others strongly oppose, this might create a backlash that stifles reform. It is then more tactical to initially limit the policies to SEZs. Reform opponents can then change their minds when they see the potential benefits of new policies. Therefore, rather than being useful as test beds for reform, SEZs are more handy for policy makers trying to prove to others in government the benefits of a policy, perhaps to establish their credibility as leaders. This is the case for why SEZs are in fact more useful as showcases for policy reforms.

The argument for SEZs as showcases is different from that about test beds because it assumes that only some people in charge already know what the best policies are. By creating examples out of small areas, they can then gain sufficient support for the new policies from current reform opponents.

One version of the showcase argument is that a unified government can use SEZs to demonstrate policy effects to the general public. If the people do not understand the benefits of a policy the administration introduces, they may vote their leaders out of office before the benefits become evident. SEZs can then be a tool for showing the people the results of a policy the government wants to implement in full.

While this reasoning is plausible, it relies on the misleading view of government as a unified, monolithic entity, when the reality is far more complex. It also relies on the government possessing superior knowledge even though officials themselves often make incorrect assessments about a policy's effects.

If we look at the government as a heterogeneous network of people, it becomes clear that while some officials might understand the benefits of a policy, others will not. For those recognizing the need for a policy, it is likely that those standing in the way of its implementation are other government officials, not ordinary people. The pro-reform officials therefore need to find ways to convince their peers in power rather than their voters.

An SEZ-led reform has two main benefits compared to immediate countrywide reforms. For one, a broader reform might not be doable because too many interests stand in its way ready to block it. Also, even if pro-reformers can pursue the change they seek countrywide, this may cause clashes within the government that will threaten their position of power.

SEZs are useful as showcases only for certain kinds of policy changes. People in government are unlikely to need to demonstrate the effects of fiscal benefits, such as tax breaks and tariff exemptions. Most people do not need convincing that businesses prefer to pay less tax. There is also little point in using low-tax SEZs to make a case for low taxes nationwide, even if they attract plenty of investments. Extending tax exemptions to all firms in a country would put too much strain on most government budgets for policy makers to go down that path.

Zones that attract businesses based on fiscal incentives are therefore not useful as showcases for reforms. Small and simple zones, like export processing zones, fall into this category. They are generally industrial parks where governments try to boost exports and other business activities primarily by exempting companies from tariffs, taxes, and some administrative costs. Being so different from the economy as a whole, export processing zones can hardly function as showcases for other liberal policies.

SEZs are more useful to demonstrate the result of regulatory liberalization. They can, for instance, allow more foreign ownership or abolish local monopolies. Because such regulations do not necessarily imply an outlay for the government, they can be extended nationwide if proven beneficial in the zones.[24] The larger and more diverse an SEZ is, the more useful it should be to show the effect of any regulatory change in the country, by serving as a smaller model for the economy as a whole.

Deregulation in the labor market is one important area of regulatory reform where SEZs can work as showcases for reform. Both the people and powerful government officials may fear the effects of uncertain working conditions and therefore oppose change. If the government introduces it nevertheless, political infighting might erupt among the elites, or voters might turn against the administration at the next election. Reform opponents may, however, accept an SEZ with looser regulations as an exception to the rule. As companies invest in the zone and start hiring people, unemployment drops in the area and social conditions improve. When witnessing the improved quality of life of SEZ workers, voters and government officials alike should start supporting wider changes in the same direction.

Japan's prime minister is introducing SEZs meant to alleviate the burden on investors of some of the country's famously rigorous labor laws, by making it easier for companies to fire their employees. The zones are also meant to introduce various reforms in areas such as business creation, agriculture, education, and medical care.[25] These SEZs could give the government the opportunity to gradually introduce policies in an area where any countrywide reform would meet too much political resistance to be realized.[26] The Japanese government is also discussing SEZ reforms that will open up the market for foreigners to work in several professions, including those in fashion, animation, and cooking, for which it is currently difficult for foreigners to obtain visas.[27]

The role of SEZs as showcases for reform has also been attributed to the case of China. Communist party leaders seemingly needed to repudiate the perception that, as some claimed, capitalism would cause spiritual pollution for the socialist people. Shenzhen and other capitalistic pockets in the country could then show that economic progress was possible without spiritual decay. This allowed the policy makers to make the case for further liberalization.[28]

The distinction between SEZs as test beds and as showcases may not always be clear. The government may, for instance, believe that more foreign ownership will have beneficial economic effects. They may not know, however, how much political resistance such a change would provoke, so they launch an SEZ where foreign ownership is permitted. As such, they are using the SEZ as a test bed for political resistance rather than for possible economic effects. If the SEZ itself does not cause rebellion, it may also work as a showcase for reform and thus increase the likelihood that the policy can spread. As reform opponents see that foreigners do not cause economic imbalances and insecurity, they are less likely to resist broader reforms in this direction.

In a similar vein, a government might use SEZs both as test beds and as showcases to abolish state monopolies. For businesspeople enjoying the monopoly privileges, any reform in this area is anathema. If the government abolishes monopolies completely, the privileged companies can arrange power cuts, water shortages, and transportation havoc. However, they may choose not to protest if free competition is allowed only within particular zones. The minimal risk the zone imposes to their market share is not worth incurring a fight with the government to avoid. SEZs are thus a way for the government to test the eagerness of monopoly holders to protest against change. Meanwhile, the zones demonstrate the benefits of competition to both the public and potential competitors. When the government later expands the concept to more areas, it will enjoy more public support and new businesses will be ready to compete with the former monopolies.

Because SEZs are good as test beds and showcases only for changing regulations, they clearly have limited use. They will bring meaningful changes only to countries whose development constraints are regulatory rather than fiscal. Also, if the main attraction of an SEZ is its fiscal benefits, one cannot point to the zone to make the case for any special regulatory policies it may also contain.

The main flaw of both the test-bed and showcase theories is that they only apply if people in government are benevolent and are therefore willing to implement a policy when they see its beneficial effects. Where leaders are benevolent, SEZs can contribute to their development pursuits in their role as test beds and showcases for policies. However, relying on benevolent leaders assumes away the main problem of many underdeveloped countries. The reason many places are poorly governed is that officials lack the incentives to see first to the people's welfare and will only promote it if it is consistent with their self-interest. Luckily, the best case for SEZs as tools for reform is that they can change the incentive structure of self-interested leaders. I will argue this case in the next section.

SEZs at their very best: overcoming the incentives against reform

At their very best, SEZs can change the incentives of people in power. Rather than tools of benevolent leaders, SEZs can do most good when they help a country escape economic stagnation caused by a system of rent-seeking. The SEZs' most important role in a country's development is thus not as test beds or showcases for reforms. In these roles, SEZs may serve only to alleviate the knowledge problem of policy makers who do not know what policies may benefit their country. This does not address the incentive problem that leads officials to use SEZs for unproductive rent-seeking. As test beds or showcases, they are also not of much use in the face of the incentives policy makers have to avoid broader economic liberalization.

At their very best, SEZs can change the incentives of powerful elites by providing them with a higher payoff from economic liberalization than from the rent-seeking opportunities protectionist policies provide. By dismembering a political system of rent-seeking, SEZs can have a powerful impact on a country's development trajectory.

The big development problem

A pervasive and fundamental problem in economic development is that governing elites often do not have an incentive to promote economic progress.[29] Market-distorting and anticompetitive policies benefit government officials, who can offer privileges to businesses and demand favors in return.[30] These anticompetitive policies include trade barriers, monopolies, and business regulations that allow companies to benefit from trade quotas, monopoly rights, and regulatory exemptions.

There are limits to the extent to which the governing elite can extract rents. Even as oppressive authoritarians, they need to maintain some level of economic growth by refraining from taking everything the people have. If their rent-seeking is too oppressive, businesses will have nothing left for further production that can provide extractable rents in the future.[31]

Despite these limits to rent-seeking, people in power can derive a large share of their revenue from illicit rents, which they can use to buy votes, give out political favors, or simply enhance their own lifestyle. They therefore want to find the optimum level of rent-seeking, where their total gains are the greatest.

In making this calculation, the elite must consider the effect a rent-seeking system has on the economy as a whole and its impact on their personal gains. Because a system of rent-seeking relies on anticompetitive policies, promoting the rent-seeking system suppresses economic growth which deprives government officials of tax revenues.

The rent-seeking system still persists as long as the tax-revenue losses that affect individual policy makers are smaller than their rent-seeking gains. This does not seem an unrealistic scenario. Rents are, after all, usually the keep of the official who can extract them. Tax revenues, by contrast, are shared in a common pool among the elite. This easily makes the gains from rent-seeking larger for the individual decision-maker than the gains from promoting a more competitive and prosperous economy that yields higher tax revenues. Self-interested government officials are therefore rational in trying to preserve an anticompetitive system.[32]

Because officials benefit from a corrupt system, an economy can be stuck in an uncompetitive and economically repressive state without enough powerful people advocating change. It is therefore curious that some countries have in fact managed to enact reforms. The Western world was once mired in the kind of rent-seeking and corruption that keep many developing countries impoverished today. European rulers acted on motives that discouraged them from promoting growth, finding ways to intervene in the economy through feudalism, state ownership, or regulations.[33] Such systems would change only when the elites found that they could benefit from liberalization or when rent-seeking became too costly.[34] Only as the elites had the proper incentives would they switch from trying to maximize rent-seeking to maximizing tax revenues.

A central question in development economics is how such a shift in favor of reform can come about.[35] Some suggestions rely on some kind of external shock that pushes the political system out of its equilibrium. Sudden technological progress, for instance, may take rulers by surprise, change the balance of power, and allow for a more inclusive system to be introduced.[36] The governing elite may also be surprised by social movements that surface after having festered for a while. The people's uprising may form new revolutionary powers that destroy the old power structures.[37] Game changing revolutions may also erupt if the state suddenly puts too much pressure on citizens, or is weakened in the face of competitors for power.[38]

A country may hope one day to get the right people in power at the right time, who can reform a repressive and illiberal regime. The story of the benevolent new authoritarian leader who stands up to the conservative establishment is well cited in accounting for some famous growth miracles.[39]

However, while countries occasionally end up lucky, suggestions of revolutionary technological, social, or leadership shifts do not provide much understanding of how currently illiberal states can be made to reform. Authoritarian regimes can certainly be induced to lower their repression in the face of new economic circumstances.[40] However, in the absence of such fortunate developments, illiberal countries will most likely remain so. Even though efficiency enhancing reforms would generate sufficient surpluses to compensate those who lose their rent-seeking privileges, such arrangements are not politically feasible.[41] Therefore, as long as rent-seeking benefits those in power, the people may wait for decades and generations to get lucky.

To understand the role SEZs can play in generating change, we need to understand just how difficult it is to solve this development problem. In many countries, a majority of members of the governing elite prefer to live off rent-seeking rather than taxation because the former is more lucrative. They could increase tax revenues by promoting competition and openness, but would then need to give up much of their illicit rents. Even if some minority of the elite sees greater profit opportunities in liberalization and higher tax revenues, they will have nowhere near the political power needed to change policies in their favor.

This is where SEZs enter the picture. The minority in favor of liberalizing reforms can come together and form a coalition to promote the introduction of a zone. Such a proposal has a greater chance of passing in a protectionist-leaning government than broader, countrywide reforms. The pro-reform minority may thus be able to reach a majority agreement on an SEZ to liberalize a small part of the country.

The central government must agree on the SEZ policy, of course, and many powerful people will be against it. However, like other modest reforms, an SEZ looks less threatening to reform-averse officials. The new SEZ can be located in an area with the best potential to attract investments. This gives the officials who benefit from the SEZs the ability to compensate, with money or favors, enough anti-reformers for the SEZ proposal to pass. Not all elites who prefer the rent-seeking system need to be compensated, of course – only enough of them to form a majority. Presumably, this will be those with the least to lose from reform and those least threatened by the zone.

Elites with different areas of opportunity

Let us take a closer look at the necessary conditions for an SEZ to appear in a political climate hostile to liberalizing reforms. One assumption is that the members of a country's ruling elite face different trade-offs between rent-seeking and taxation. This may be because some policy makers care more about their reputation and legacy than others, and may want to be associated more with a country's reforms. However, differences in preferences among the elites should also depend on the jurisdiction in which they have their interests.

There are many reasons why the interests of people in government are geographically connected. In a federal system, they may be locally elected or appointed, and thus formally represent different parts of the country. A similar, more informal, system of representation prevails in countries with tribal and ethnically fractional traditions, as powerful people seek primarily to benefit their home regions. In other contexts, the elite may create crony ties with businessmen by promoting local monopolies or other local businesses.

Different locations generate different levels of rents versus tax revenues. A remote region may be better territory for a local monopoly, as it is better shielded from competition. This provides more opportunities for rent-seeking. An abundance of natural resources is also an opportunity to establish a monopoly that will rent-seek to keep its privileged position.

A coastal region, by contrast, is better equipped to attract competitive businesses with the promise of higher levels of tax revenues. Another important revenue source is property rents. A region that can increase property values through development and industrialization allows the local elite to benefit from a more open economic system.

The heterogeneity of jurisdictions thus creates some elites for and others against reform. Yet, even within the reform and anti-reform coalitions, people are not homogenous. Some are marginally for or marginally against, while others have very strong pro- or anti-reform preferences. We can imagine lining up all the members of the elite, with the person most strongly against reform on one end and the one most strongly in favor on the other. They thus form a continuum of preferences, where nobody makes the same cost-benefit evaluation as another. A few people in the middle will be almost indifferent to change, because their gains from it would roughly be equivalent to their losses. Elite members who are marginally in favor of keeping the rent-seeking system will take a stand against reform. However, they are still the ones pro-reformers could persuade with only modest compensation.

An SEZ should be located where it can promote the highest boost in tax revenue, which is presumably near the coast or similarly commercially attractive areas. This places the official benefiting from the zone in a good position to compensate anti-reformers. An SEZ may also benefit from a location that is a good distance from the areas of the officials that they need to persuade to support the zone. If the zone is so close to their turf that it severely disrupts their rent-seeking opportunities, they may demand too high a compensation for accepting the SEZ's introduction.

The role of political and fiscal decentralization

Decentralization plays a crucial role in SEZ-driven reform. The first thing to note is that locally connected policy makers need some degree of political decentralization, as this allows them to influence their level of economic liberalization. Some officials prefer to pursue rents and will want to introduce local monopolies, repressive regulations, and other policies that induce businesspeople to bribe them. Others, who are pursuing tax revenues instead, want to liberalize the economy to the extent that they can, and want to invest in a good local business climate. Which approach they prefer depends primarily on the opportunities their geographical areas offer.

We must also recognize the importance of fiscal decentralization. Fiscal decentralization allows locally connected leaders to keep a substantial amount of the tax revenues they generate. This is a vital condition for their incentive to pursue liberalization. In a fiscally centralized system, rent-seeking may always be superior. If all tax revenue is distributed evenly by the central government to all jurisdictions in a country, a powerful person with interests in a region would see little reason to boost the tax intake. To make a trade-off between rent-seeking and tax revenues possible, rules must also paint a sufficiently clear picture of the share of the tax proceeds that stays with the local government.

While fiscal decentralization gives local elites the incentive to pursue reform, political decentralization is what makes it happen. Even in the absence of SEZs, in a politically decentralized system, different areas will have different local policies and hence different degrees of liberalization. SEZs can then provide an area with even higher growth potential than what is possible by local policy making alone. Tariffs, business taxes, and regulations are, after all, often decided at the national level. The only way for a local leader to relieve companies of them is therefore to introduce a policy that provides the exemptions SEZs offer.

If all policies are determined by the central government, reform-minded officials will hardly see value in pursuing SEZs. The central government may then impose policies in the zone that are against the interest of the officials, such as granting local monopoly rights that make the area unfriendly to businesses and keep investors away. If local leaders cannot change such destructive policies, they have little prospect of raising tax revenues much and are better off resorting to rent-seeking. Both political and fiscal decentralization thus play important roles in the trade-off elites face between raising tax revenue and rent-seeking.

The role of liberalizing externalities

It may seem obvious that an official with an interest in higher tax revenues in an area will want an SEZ. But why would others who favor liberalization join a coalition to support an SEZ in another region? If they are affected at all by another region's SEZ, this might be because businesses from their area relocate to the SEZ. Yet this assumption overlooks some important points.

First of all, pro-reformers want to support SEZs in other areas as a way to increase their own chance of getting SEZs in the future. Local leaders who vote against an SEZ in another region cannot count on support from other pro-reformers if they want to host SEZs themselves.

Second, pro-reformers have the incentive to support liberalization elsewhere because of its beneficial external effects. A country with SEZs is perceived as more open overall, even if the scheme is geographically limited. SEZs signal that the government is pursuing pro-trade policies and has a welcoming attitude toward foreign investors. This is beneficial for officials trying to attract foreign capital, even if they do not have an SEZ in their jurisdiction. A foreign investor may rather invest in an SEZ if the neighboring region is not rotten with rent-seeking. Local leaders who already have SEZs will also support other zones, both because they create a generally business-friendly country and because they might want to host more SEZs in the future.

Another important external effect of an SEZ is to help leaders in other areas become more market friendly. An SEZ sets an example for them of how to transition from a rent-seeking system to one based on taxation. When local policy makers know how the transition is best made and can be more certain of its costs, they are more likely to change to the tax-based system.

These external effects serve two purposes. Not only do they promote the formation of pro-SEZ coalitions, but they also help to expand them. By creating better opportunities for raising tax revenues in a jurisdiction, they make rent-seeking relatively less attractive to pursue. Some local elites who only marginally favor rent-seeking over liberalization and taxation can start to marginally favor liberalization when their prospects for tax collection improve. To boost their tax-revenue opportunities further, they have an incentive to support new SEZ initiatives. This means they no longer need any compensation for this support. The fewer the people in power who oppose reform, the easier it will be for the next official pursuing a new SEZ to persuade a majority of the governing elite to support it.

One SEZ thus increases the probability for the next one, which makes the introduction of a third zone even easier, and so on. This process should take a while since the external effects might only materialize after the SEZ has been operational for some time. Therefore, this kind of process will likely be gradual and slow. As the number of SEZs in the country increases, they also increase the revenue opportunities for other, more liberalized regions. Eventually, a majority of government officials will have the incentive to promote openness and liberalization, at which point suggestions of broader nationwide reforms can win majority support.

Because this development can take a long time, anti-reformers may not demand full compensation for all the costs in lost rents the SEZs may impose on them in the future. They may anticipate that zones will weaken their rent-seeking prospects and one day lead to reform. However, if this scenario is far away in the future, they are more likely to discount such costs heavily and accept a smaller payment today. They may also correctly anticipate that they will leave their current position of power before the country adopts broader reforms. Their successors will assume the future costs while they can enjoy the immediate rewards.

The necessary conditions for this SEZ-driven reform process are different interests among the elites, fiscal, and political decentralization. If the elites all share an interest in preserving the rent-seeking system, nobody will take the initiative of local reform, and the reform process will never take hold. If a majority of the elites instead share an interest in reform, change can come without SEZs, and introducing them would only be an unnecessary detour. Fiscal decentralization gives local leaders a reason to try to increase their tax revenues. If they must share the tax revenues with all the other localities, they will not want to give up any of their rent-seeking revenues to increase their tax take. Finally, political decentralization is what allows policies to vary in different areas according to the preferences of the local elites.

There are a few other necessary assumptions in this narrative. If the external effects of an SEZ are not great enough, for instance, one SEZ may not provoke the creation of another. Another potential obstacle to this dynamic is a very polarized elite. If there are no elites in the middle of the preference spectrum who are almost indifferent between rent-seeking and taxation, it will be hard for pro-reformers to build their coalition by persuading powerful people to switch sides. Luring powerful people with a large stake in rent-seeking over to their side may simply not be feasible. There are thus several contexts in which SEZs cannot set in motion a process toward countrywide reforms.

Nevertheless, SEZs at least offer the possibility of a reform process when all other routes are blocked. For a country stuck in the rent-seeking equilibrium, SEZs are a tool for reform that does not rely on technological or social change. SEZs can lead to countrywide reform in a situation where a majority of the ruling elite is initially against change. In the absence of any other way for a political minority to induce the central government to pass its proposals for reforms, SEZs are therefore a tool for liberalization worth pursuing.

Reform stability

For a country moving out of a system of rent-seeking, a crucial question is whether it can avoid falling back in. Some paths to reform are miserably unstable because they fail to change the incentives of the people in power. If rulers are removed from office by force or threats, or are cajoled to step down, this may do little to change the nature of the prevailing regime. New people entering office will face the same incentive structure as their predecessors, and may engage in as much rent-seeking. Even if all new rulers happen to be absolutely benevolent, the government may remain reformed only as long as these people are in power. With institutions unchanged, the rent-seeking system can easily be revoked when the next ruler takes over.

The process of SEZ-driven reform proposed here is different. Government officials do not change their way of governing because they are forced to or bribed. They do not become different persons who value the welfare of the people more than previously. Rather, in their pursuit to maximize personal gains, they eventually choose rationally to promote a liberalized system. As the country liberalizes gradually, their interest in favor of reform is increasingly entrenched. Marginal pro-reformers become stauncher supporters as the rest of the country reforms. As SEZs spread and eventually lead to broader liberalizing reforms, there is no force pulling the economy back to the rent-seeking status quo.

The pursuit of liberalization thus spreads like an epidemic throughout the economy. Once an area gets the bug, it will tend to never rid itself of it. While some will decry the loss of the stable rent-seeking equilibrium that once prevailed in the country, most will prefer to switch to the side of the pro-reformers, simply because this is in their interest.

Conclusion

This chapter began by introducing a few plausible theories of how SEZs can be preferable for a country to broader reforms. As we saw, backward linkages do not give much support for SEZs. It is actually quite implausible that new backward linkages would form under the incentive structure of an SEZ. The arguments for using SEZs to concentrate infrastructure and policing resources are also quite weak.

SEZs are more credible as tools for solving political problems on the path toward broader economic liberalization. For a government wanting to pursue reform, they could help solve some knowledge problems, by serving as policy test beds or showcases for new policies. However, whether as showcases or test beds, SEZs are likely only to play a smaller role in a country's reform process by speeding up regulatory reforms or avoiding some mishaps on the way.

SEZs can play a far superior role as a tool for a pro-reform political minority. They can allow an economy to break free from a situation in which government officials seek to maintain a rent-seeking system that they have an interest to preserve. SEZs may thus do the greatest good when they are not part of a government's development agenda but are pursued despite the reluctance of most people in power.

Because several conditions are necessary for this to happen, there may be few countries that will ever be candidates for this kind of SEZ-driven reform. First of all, the situation probably needs to be bad enough to begin with. In a system that is already sufficiently liberalized, SEZs may be useful as test beds and showcases by demonstrating the effects of marginal policy improvements. However, a relatively liberalized country would have little chance of experiencing the powerful dynamic of a liberalization avalanche that the minority-led SEZ reform process can produce.

The United States, for instance, has its foreign trade zones, some of which may have been launched despite a resistance against liberalization at the federal level. However, these zones are hardly promoting liberalization in the country in the radical way suggested in this chapter. This is because in an already-competitive system, with relatively low, predictable, and non-discriminatory taxes and tariffs, rent-seeking should already be quite low.[42] In such a case,

SEZs are more likely to do harm by creating new opportunities for rents. SEZs introduced in a liberalized economy are also more likely to be a way for policy makers to create opportunities for rent-seeking than a result of minority-driven demand for further liberalization.

For the reform dynamic to take off, there also needs to be sufficient decentralization, and jurisdictions need to be different enough to create a spectrum of interests among local government officials. Thus, while SEZs have much potential to promote economic development, we should expect such SEZ-driven reform to be a rare event. As I will show in the case study section, China is the most likely case to fit this narrative. Hopefully, we will see more developments of this kind.

Notes

1 See e.g., Hamada 1974.
2 Wong and Chu 1984: 2, 9; FIAS 2008: 37; Farole 2011: 225; White 2011: 193. Backward linkages can be measured in the value of domestic purchases of SEZ firms. The concept does not include so-called technology transfers, which is another often-cited linkage effect between SEZs and their neighboring economy. Technology transfers may occur as foreign SEZ investors integrate and collaborate with domestic companies. However, this concept is inherently hard to measure and can therefore only be suggested through anecdotes on SEZ schemes. The evidence is also mixed regarding the connection between foreign investments and such intangible spillovers as technology transfers (Basile and Germidis 1984; Rhee et al. 1990: 3; Aggarwal 2007: 13; Schrank 2008: 1381; Farole and Winkler 2014: 7).
3 Hirschman 1958.
4 Myint 1973: 107.
5 Wong and Chu 1985: 15.
6 Farole et al. 2014: 34.
7 Farole 2011: 226.
8 Shakir and Farole 2011: 32.
9 Amirahmadi and Wu 1995: 836, 841–2.
10 CNZFE 2015: 26.50; Central Bank 2016: Labour Market.
11 Kaplinsky 1993; Burgaud and Farole 2011: 178; Sánchez-Ancochea 2012. The export figures are based on the first quarter of 2016.
12 White 2011: 194.
13 Jenkins et al. 1998: 6.
14 Engman 2011: 55.
15 Rather than a way to concentrate spending, SEZs could help to root out corruption and crime if they introduce institutional and governance reforms instead of expending resources that are needed elsewhere (Wei 1999). However, if such reforms would come for free, they should be applied to the country as a whole.
16 Cling and Letilly 2001: 24.
17 Engman 2011: 49.
18 Burman 2006: 10.
19 World Bank 1992: 27.
20 FIAS 2008: 43.
21 *Economist* 2014.
22 Sit 1985: 75, 84; Wong and Chu 1985: 34–35; Ge 1999: 1281; Chen 1996: 175; Yeung et al. 2009: 223; Leong 2013: 550, 552.
23 Wagner 2007: 7; Eusepi and Wagner 2011.

24 FIAS 2008: 43.
25 Office of the Prime Minister 2016.
26 *Economist* 2014; HSBC 2014.
27 Nikkei 2016.
28 Crane 1990: 94; Wijnbergen and Willems 2014: 16.
29 For analysis and derivations on this theme, see, e.g., Acemoglu and Robinson 2000; 2012: ch. 8; Haber 2002; Kang 2002; Rose-Ackerman 2006; Nye 2009; Brollo et al. 2013.
30 Buchanan et al. 1980; Tullock 1967; Tullock 2005; Mitchell 2012.
31 McGuire and Olson 1996.
32 Nye 2009: 54. Even if the government officials calculate that, in a competitive economic system, their revenues might be larger, they may still be unable to accomplish the change. This is because even if they rewrite the constitution to incorporate the reforms, government officials may be incentivized to reverse the progress under the wrong circumstances (Leeson 2011). Market actors can thus suspect that the old system will return, and choose not to make the investments needed for the new system to take root.
33 Ekelund and Tollison 1981: 24–25, 80–81, 93; Boettke 2001: ch 8: 140–153; Nye 2007: ch. 7: 89–109; Braithwaite 2008: ch. 1.
34 Ekelund and Tollison 1981: 27; Nye 2009: 59.
35 See e.g. Frye and Shleifer 1997; Blanchard and Shleifer 2001; Acemoglu and Robinson 2012: ch. 3 and 11.
36 See, e.g. North and Weingast 1989; Acemoglu et al. 2005.
37 See, e.g. Tilly 1993: 15, 216; Tilly 2004: ch 1: 1–41, 177; McAdam et al. 2001: Part I, II; Tilly and Wood 2009; Åslund 1999.
38 Tilly 1993: 237.
39 Haggard et al. 1990: 26; Gilson and Milhaupt 2010; Sachs 2012.
40 Wintrobe 1990.
41 Buchanan 1980.
42 Buchanan and Congleton [1998] 2006.

References

Acemoglu, Daron, and James Robinson. 2000. "Political Losers as a Barrier to Economic Development." *American Economic Review* 90(2): 126–130.

Acemoglu, Daron, and James Robinson. 2012. *Why Nations Fail: The Origins of Power, Prosperity, and Poverty.* Crown Publishing Group, New York.

Acemoglu, Daron, Simon Johnson, and James Robinson. 2005. "The Rise of Europe: Atlantic Trade, Institutional Change, and Economic Growth." *American Economic Review* 95(3): 546–579.

Aggarwal, Aradhna. 2007. "Impact of Special Economic Zones on Employment, Poverty, and Human Development." *Indian Council for Research on International Economic Relations (ICRIER) Working Paper* No. 194. Available at: http://www.democraciaycooperacion.net/IMG/pdf/1-working_paper_194.pdf (accessed 29 October 2016).

Amirahmadi, Hooshang, and Weiping Wu. 1995. "Export Processing Zones in Asia." *Asian Survey* 35(9): 828–849.

Åslund, Anders, 1999. "Why Has Russia's Economic Transformation Been So Arduous?" Conference Paper, *Annual Bank Conference on Development Economics*, Washington, D.C. Available at: http://ssrn.com/abstract=187548 (accessed 29 October 2016).

Basile, Antoine, and Dimitrios A. Germidis. 1984. *Investing in Free Export Processing Zones*. OECD Publishing, Paris.

Blanchard, Olivier, and Andrei Shleifer. 2001. "Federalism With and Without Political Centralization: China versus Russia." In: *International Monetary Fund: IMF Staff Papers, Vol. 48: Transition Economies: How Much Progress?* pp. 171–179. Available at: https://www.imf.org/External/Pubs/FT/staffp/2001/04/ (accessed 29 October 2016).

Boettke, Peter J., 2001. *Calculation and Coordination: Essays on socialism and transitional political economy*. Routledge, London and New York.

Braithwaite, John. 2008. *Regulatory Capitalism: How it Works, Ideas for Making it Work Better*. Edward Elgar, Cheltenham.

Brollo, Fernanda, Tommaso Nannicini, Roberto Perotti, and Guido Tabellini. 2013. "The Political Resource Curse." *American Economic Review* 103(5): 1759–1796.

Buchanan, James M. 1980. "Reform in the Rent-Seeking Society." In: 1980. *Toward a Theory of the Rent-Seeking Society* (Buchanan, James M., Robert D. Tollison, and Gordon Tullock eds.). Texas A&M University Press, Texas, pp. 359–367.

Buchanan, James M., and Roger D. Congleton. [1998] 2006. *Politics by Principle, Not Interest: Towards Nondiscriminatory Democracy*. Cambridge University Press, Cambridge, UK.

Buchanan, James M., Robert D. Tollison, and Gordon Tullock (Eds.). 1980. *Toward a Theory of the Rent-Seeking Society*. Texas A&M University Press, Texas.

Burgaud, Jean-Marie, and Thomas Farole. 2011. "When Trade Preferences and Tax Breaks are No Longer Enough: The Challenge of Adjustment in the Dominican Republic's Free Zones." In: *Special Economic Zones: Progress, Emerging Challenges, and Future Directions* (Thomas Farole and Gokhan Akinci eds.). The World Bank, Washington, D.C., pp. 159–181.

Burman, Anirudh. 2006. "Special Economic Zones: Issues in Corporate Governance." *SSRN Working Paper*. Available at: http://ssrn.com/abstract=954934 (accessed 29 October 2016).

Central Bank. 2016. "Labour Market." Statistics available at: http://www.bancentral.gov.do/statistics/labour_market/ (accessed 29 October 2016).

Chen, Jean Jinghan. 1996. "The Impact of Public Construction Investment upon Special Economic Zones – the Chinese experience." *Construction Management & Economics* 14(2): 175–182.

Cling, Jean-Pierre, and Gaëlle Letilly. 2001. "Export Processing Zones: A Threatened Instrument for Global Economy Insertion?" *DIAL Working paper* DT/2001/17. Available at: http://ideas.repec.org/p/dia/wpaper/dt200117.html (accessed 29 October 2016).

CNZFE (National Free Zones Council). 2015. Yearly statistical publication. Available at: http://www.cnzfe.gob.do/transparencia/index.php/estadisticas/informe-estadisticos-anuales (accessed 29 October 2016).

Crane, George T., 1990. *The Political Economy of China's Special Economic Zones*. M. E. Sharpe Inc., Armonk, New York and London, England.

Economist, The. 2014. "Economic Zones for Japan: Some More Special than Others." *The Economist*, Mar. 31, 2014. Available at: http://www.economist.com/blogs/banyan/2014/03/economic-zones-japan (accessed 29 October 2016).

Ekelund, Robert B., and Robert D. Tollison. 1981. *Mercantilism as a Rent-Seeking Society: Economic Regulation in Historical Perspective*. Texas A&M University Press, Texas.

Engman, Michael. 2011. "Success and Stasis in Honduras' Free Zones." In: *Special Economic Zones: Progress, Emerging Challenges, and Future Directions* (Thomas Farole and Gokhan Akinci eds.). The World Bank, Washington D.C., pp. 47–68.

Eusepi, Giuseppe, and Richard E. Wagner. 2011. "States as Ecologies of Political Enterprises." *Review of Political Economy* 23(4): 573–585.

Farole, Thomas. 2011. *Special Economic Zones in Africa: Comparing Performance and Learning from Global Experience.* The World Bank, Washington, D.C.

Farole, Thomas, and Deborah Winkler. 2014. "Context, Objectives, and Methodology." In: *Making Foreign Direct Investment Work for Sub-Saharan Africa: Local Spillovers and Competitiveness in Global Value Chains* (Thomas Farole and Deborah Winkler eds.). The World Bank, Washington, D.C., pp. 7–22.

Farole, Thomas, Cornelia Staritz, and Deborah Winkler. 2014. "Conceptual Framework." In: *Making Foreign Direct Investment Work for Sub-Saharan Africa: Local Spillovers and Competitiveness in Global Value Chains.* (Thomas Farole and Deborah Winkler eds.). The World Bank, Washington, D.C., pp. 23–55.

FIAS (The World Bank's Facility for Investment Climate Advisory Services). 2008. *Special Economic Zones: Performance, Lessons Learned, and Implications for Zone Development.* World Bank Group, Washington, D.C.

Frye, Timothy, and Andrei Shleifer. 1997. "The Invisible Hand and the Grabbing Hand." *American Economic Review* 87(2): 354–358.

Ge, Wei, 1999. "Special Economic Zones and the Opening of the Chinese Economy: Some Lessons for Economic Liberalization." *World Development* 27(7): 1267–1285.

Gilson, Ronald J., and Curtis J. Milhaupt. 2010. "Economically Benevolent Dictators: Lessons for Developing Democracies." *The American Journal of Comparative Law* 2010: 227–288.

Haber, Stephen (Ed.). 2002. *Crony Capitalism and Economic Growth in Latin America: Theory and Evidence.* Hoover Institution Press, Stanford, CA.

Haggard, Stephan, Byung-Kook Kim, and Chung-in Moon. 1990. "The Transition to Export-Led Growth in South Korea, 1954–1966." The World Bank, Country Economics Department, *Working Paper Series* 546.

Hamada, Koichi. 1974. "An Economic Analysis of the Duty-Free Zone." *Journal of International Economics* 4(3): 225–241.

Hirschman, Albert O. 1958. *The Strategy of Economic Development.* Yale University Press, New Haven, CT.

HSBC. 2014. "Japan Economics Comment: Abe's Trojan horse takes another step." *HSBC: Global Research – Economics*, Mar. 31, 2014.

Jenkins, Mauricio, Felipe Larrain, and Gerardo Esquivel. 1998. "Export Processing Zones in Central America." *Harvard Institute for International Development Working Paper* 646.

Kang, David C. 2002. *Crony Capitalism: Corruption and Development in South Korea and the Philippines.* Cambridge University Press, Cambridge, UK.

Kaplinsky, Raphael. 1993. "Export Processing Zones in the Dominican Republic: Transforming Manufactures into Commodities." *World Development* 21(11): 1851–1865.

Leeson, Peter T. 2011. "Government, Clubs, and Constitutions." *Journal of Economic Behavior and Organization* 80(2) 301–308.

Leong, Chee Kian. 2013. "Special Economic Zones and Growth in China and India: An Empirical Investigation." *International Economics and Economic Policy* 10(4): 549–567.

McAdam, Doug, Sydney Tarrow, and Charles Tilly. 2001. *Dynamics of Contention.* Cambridge University Press, New York.

McGuire, Martin C. and Mancur L. Olson. 1996. "The Economics of Autocracy and Majority Rule: The Invisible Hand and the Use of Force." *Journal of Economic Literature* 34(1): 72–96.

Mitchell, Matthew. 2012. *The Pathology of Privilege: The Economic Consequences of Government Favoritism.* Mercatus Center, George Mason University, Arlington, VA.

Myint, Hla. 1973. *The Economics of the Developing Countries, 4th Ed.* Praeger Publishers, New York.

Nikkei. 2016. "Japan to Ease Visa Rules on Foreign Animators, Designers." *Nikkei Asian Review,* Mar. 2, 2016. Available at: http://asia.nikkei.com/Politics-Economy/Policy-Politics/Japan-to-ease-visa-rules-on-foreign-animators-designers (accessed 29 October 2016).

North, Douglass C., and Barry R. Weingast. 1989. "Constitutions and Commitment: The Evolution of Institutional Governing Public Choice in Seventeenth-Century England." *The Journal of Economic History* 49(4): 803–832.

Nye, John V.C. 2007. *War, Wine, and Taxes: The Political Economy of Anglo-French Trade, 1689–1900.* Princeton University Press, Princeton, NJ.

Nye, John V.C., 2009. "Why Do Elites Permit Reform?" In: *The Annual Proceedings of the Wealth and Well-Being of Nations 2008–2009,* Vol. 1 (Emily Chamlee-Wright ed.). Beloit College Press, Beloit, WI.

Office of the Prime Minister. 2016. "Regulatory Reform Menu." *Office of the Prime Minister* Available at: https://www.kantei.go.jp/jp/singi/tiiki/kokusentoc/menu.html (accessed 29 October 2016).

Rhee, Yung Whee., Katharina Katterbach, and Janette White. 1990. "Free Trade Zones in Export Strategies." World Bank Industry and Energy Department, PRE, *Industry Series Edward Elgar Publishing Paper* No. 36.

Rose-Ackerman, Susan. 2006. "Introduction and Overview." In: *International Handbook of the Economics of Corruption* (Susan Rose-Ackerman ed.). Edward Elgar Publishing, Cheltenham, UK and Edward Elgar Publishing Inc., Northampton, MA, pp. xiv–xxxiv.

Sachs, Jeffrey. 2012. "Reply to Acemoglu and Robinson's Response to My Book Review." *jeffsachs.org* Available at: http://jeffsachs.org/2012/12/reply-to-acemoglu-and-robinsons-response-to-my-book-review/ (accessed 29 October 2016).

Sánchez-Ancochea, Diego. 2012. "A Fast Herd and a Slow Tortoise?" *Studies in Comparative International Development* 47(2): 208–230.

Schrank, Andrew. 2008. "Export Processing Zones in the Dominican Republic: Schools or Stopgaps?" *World Development* 36(8): 1381–1397.

Shakir, Hye Mustafizul, and Thomas Farole. 2011. "The Thin End of the Wedge: Unlocking Comparative Advantage through EPZs in Bangladesh." In: *Special Economic Zones: Progress, Emerging Challenges, and Future Directions* (Thomas Farole and Gokhan Akinci eds.). The World Bank, Washington, D.C. pp. 25–45.

Sit, Victor F.S. 1985. "Special Economic Zones in China: A New Type of Export Processing Zone?" *The Developing Economies* 23(2): 69–87.

Tilly, Charles. 1993. *European Revolutions: 1492–1992.* Blackwell Publishers, Oxford.

Tilly, Charles. 2004. *Contention and Democracy in Europe 1650–2000.* Cambridge University Press, Cambridge, UK.

Tilly, Charles and Lesley J. Wood. 2009. *Social Movements, 1768–2008.* 2nd ed. Paradigm Publishers, Boulder, CO.

Tullock, Gordon. 1967. "The Welfare Costs of Tariffs, Monopolies, and Theft." *Western Economic Journal* 5(3): 224.

Tullock, Gordon. 2005. *The Selected Works of Gordon Tullock, Vol. 5: The Rent-Seeking Society* (Charles K. Rowley ed.). Liberty Fund, Indianapolis.

Wagner, Richard E. 2007. *Fiscal Sociology and the Theory of Public Finance: An Exploratory Essay.* Edward Elgar Publishing Ltd.

Wei, Shang-Jin. 1999. "Special Governance Zone: A Practical Entry-Point for a Winnable Anti-Corruption Program." *9th International Anti-Corruption Conference*, Durban, South Africa, 10–15 December, 1999. Available at: http://9iacc.org/papers/day2/ws1/dnld/d2ws1_sjwei.pdf (accessed 29 October 2016).

White, Justine. 2011. "Fostering Innovation in Developing Economies through SEZs." In: *Special Economic Zones: Progress, Emerging Challenges, and Future Directions* (Thomas Farole and Gokhan Akinci eds.). The World Bank, Washington, D.C., pp. 183–205.

Wijnbergen, Sweder J. G. van, and Tim Willems. 2014. "The Learning Dynamics and Support for Economic Reforms: Why Good News Can Be Bad." *World Bank Policy Research Working Paper* 6973.

Wintrobe, Ronald. 1990. "The Tinpot and the Totalitarian: An Economic Theory of Dictatorship." *American Political Science Review* 84(03): 849–872.

Wong, Kwan-Yiu and David K. Y. Chu. 1984. "Export Processing Zones and Special Economic Zones as Generators of Economic Development: The Asian Experience." *Geografiska Annaler. Series B, Human Geography* 66(1): 1–16.

Wong, Kwan-Yiu, and David K.Y. Chu. 1985. *Modernization in China: the case of the Shenzhen special economic zone.* Oxford University Press, Hong Kong.

World Bank. 1992. *Export Processing Zones.* The World Bank, Washington, D.C.

Yeung, Yue-man, Joanna Lee, and Gordon Kee. 2009. "China's Special Economic Zones at 30." *Eurasian Geography and Economics* 50(2): 222–240.

4 SEZs as promoters of liberalization or protectionism

We have come quite a way in understanding the disparate effects SEZs can have on an economy. At their worst, they cause resource misallocations or serve as vehicles for corruption that bring more harm than good to an economy. At their best, SEZs are vital tools for minority elites to implement economic reforms countrywide. SEZs can also play a variety of less extreme roles. Even if they fail to bring countrywide reforms, they can still have a net benefit on the economy. The aim of this chapter is to understand the political economy of this middle ground scenario.

If the government solves the knowledge and incentive problems associated with SEZs, they should be better than the status quo. But what if the alternative to SEZs is not the status quo? If policy makers choose to introduce SEZs instead of broader reforms, the SEZs can actually be seen as a negative for the country. This insight is a central criticism of SEZs. Albeit better than the status quo, they are only a second-best solution to broader reforms, which the government should pursue in the name of economic development. SEZs can therefore be good for a country only if their political alternative is reform stagnation.

This chapter will look at how a government may choose SEZs to avoid broader economic reforms and what the implications are for their economic benefits. As in the previous chapter, I will assume policy makers to be self-interested. Here, though, the focus is not on the internal struggle for policy influence but the actions of a government that tries to maximize rents in every instance. Rather than making a trade-off between taxes and rents, the government as a whole tries to maximize rents only.

We can think of the government as one of consensus among the elite about the preeminence of rent-seeking over taxation. Alternatively, we can allow for the possibility of a pro-reformist minority elite, but assume that it never manages to influence the political agenda and even less to set any liberalization avalanche in motion. As a result, government acts as if it were unified in favor of rent-seeking.

That a government chooses SEZs on the basis of rent-seeking does not mean the zones cannot be successful. But the scheme will not be created in a way that leads to the kind of dynamic process toward reform that we saw in the previous chapter. The current chapter will therefore show why we see so many moderately successful SEZs.

The paradox of moderately successful SEZ schemes

In a 1992 report, the World Bank argued that, rather than tariff-free zones, a country should look to "economywide duty-free import systems."[1] One can show the logic of this statement with a simple theoretical model of duty-free zones. In a version by Miyagiwa, SEZs increase national welfare under certain assumption, but is still a second-best solution to the inefficiencies that trade protection causes.[2] We know by now that SEZs may actually be the best option if they help overcome obstacles to broader economic reforms. However, such a political dynamic can happen only under circumstances that might not prevail often enough.

The reality is that many SEZ schemes, while not absolute failures, do not lead to economy-wide reforms. They may boost investments and employment, along with increasing and diversifying a country's exports, yet fall short of changing the economy outside the zone boundaries.

According to the mainstream view, such schemes present success stories because they generate favorable macroeconomic data. However, favoring one geographical area over another or granting special benefits to companies in industrial parks is clearly not the quickest way to economic prosperity. SEZs risk reallocating capital to suboptimal places while the government loses out on revenues. Companies that enjoy SEZ benefits will presumably invest more in the economy. However, a more general lowering of taxes and tariffs should accomplish the same in the aggregate, without the distortionary side effects. If the government wants to promote economic growth, it should therefore pursue broader reforms, which are more likely to benefit a larger share of the population.

Economic development can therefore hardly be the motivation of a unified government introducing SEZs. As we have seen, corruption can be one motivation. Superficially successful SEZ regimes could just be fronts for cronyism and corrupt dealings. However, such schemes are unlikely to function as well and attract as much foreign investment as they often do. As we have seen, it is hard for a government to maintain an agreement to exchange SEZ benefits for rents. There is also little empirical support for the suggestion that all or most SEZ schemes are corrupt. In many cases, investors can attest to the absence of corruption, swearing by a transparent and honest process for gaining SEZ status. Many countries also have professional and independent SEZ authorities that seem transparent and non-corrupt.

The question then becomes, what is the motivation behind the introduction of moderately successful SEZ schemes, if people in government are using them neither as tools for reform nor as vehicles for corruption? There is in fact another important role that SEZs can fulfill. Officials can use SEZs to preserve a system of rent-seeking from which they benefit. Because SEZs are a middle way between liberalization and protectionism, they are handy tools for policy makers who are torn between those two policy directions. Protectionism provides opportunities for rent-seeking. However, if people in government are pressed to provide some liberalization, they can use SEZs to accomplish this in only a limited way. To understand this reasoning, we must first examine why protectionism persists in the first place.

Why pursue protectionism?

For decades after WWII, protectionism was the trade regime of choice for many developing countries. The rationale for protectionism was often the pursuit of import-substituting industrialization, which relies primarily on the infant-industry argument. By discouraging imports through import tariffs and quotas, this argument goes, domestic demand increases for goods that would otherwise be imported. This allows for more domestic production and hence investments and employment. Domestic industries develop and grow and after some time they become ready to compete internationally. By then, protectionism is no longer necessary and the government can safely remove all tariffs. If, by contrast, the domestic industries never enjoy protectionism, they cannot develop because they will always lack demand for their products in the face of competition from imported goods.

There are several problems with this reasoning. The higher domestic prices protectionism provides discourage domestic firms from working to meet the standards of their competitors in other countries. They have no reason to incur the costs of reaching greater sophistication if that only means they will lose their government support. Higher prices for their goods also deprive domestic consumers of purchasing power. Low demand overall discourages production in all domestic sectors. Protectionism can thus increase the relative share of particular industries in the economy but without increasing its overall development.

After decades of protectionism worldwide, it became evident that countries pursuing import-substituting policies performed worse than more liberalized economies. By the 1980s, the infant-industry argument had largely fallen out of favor. Still, protectionism did not disappear. Although tariff rates steadily declined, governments continued to proclaim the necessity of protecting one industry or another with tariffs and quotas. It has become increasingly clear that protectionism persists less due to the belief in the infant-industry argument and more because of political interests.

A growing scholarship in political economy has shone light on the political incentives behind various trade policies. Trade restrictions are ways for governments to favor particular businesses. Import quotas become valuable assets for firms wanting to import, which are therefore inclined to bribe the government to obtain them. Tariffs serve to raise prices on particular goods, which benefits domestic producers. Domestic producers thus have a reason to bribe the government for the right tariffs.

Various protectionist policies allow governments to extract rents from the businesses to which they extend special treatment. Whether in the form of money or favors, such rents can either enrich the individual policy maker or help keep a governing coalition together.[3] There are thus several ways in which both individual policy makers and governments can benefit from trade protection.

The clearest way to illustrate the role of SEZs in protectionism is to consider how a government as a whole benefits from import tariffs. The rents they gain come about as businesses try either to raise or lower tariff rates. To influence tariffs, businesses have the incentive to lobby the government through campaign contributions, public support for government policies, and various kickbacks. People in government can then respond to the most generous among rent-seekers by providing what they ask for. To encourage more lobbying, the government should respond with higher tariffs the more that companies offer to pay for trade protection. In this way, tariffs can offer a rich source of income for government officials.

Not all businesses lobby to raise the tariffs on particular goods. Some firms rely on imports for much of their production, and therefore have an incentive to counter-lobby for lower tariffs instead. To maximize its rents, the government can encourage a bidding war between the trade antagonists trying to buy the government's allegiance.[4]

Take a shoemaker and a leather maker as an example. The shoemaker needs leather to make the shoes, and this can be either imported from abroad or bought domestically. In the absence of tariffs, with international trade in leather, the price at home and abroad for leather at a particular quality will be roughly the same. To stay in business, domestic leather producers cannot charge more for their wares than a price just above the international level, so that importing the leather is not worth the cost of transportation. This competition between leather makers benefits the shoemaker, who can buy the leather cheaply at home. If something happens with the domestic supply, the shoemaker can always turn to the international market and get leather at roughly the same price.

Domestic leather makers, by contrast, will not be happy with the free trade regime. If the government can impose a 50 percent tariff on leather, the domestic producers can both enjoy a higher price and make sure to keep the shoemakers as customers. With the tariff, the price of imported leather increases to 150 percent of the international price, plus transportation costs. This means leather makers can raise domestic leather prices to just above 150 percent of international prices before the shoemaker will turn abroad for supplies. This arrangement is clearly beneficial for the leather maker but damaging for the importing shoemakers.

The government can exploit the conflicting interests of the leather makers and shoemakers by setting a leather tariff that reflects their contributions to the rent-seeking tariff bidding game. The tariff they set cannot be so high that the shoemaker finds it pointless to lobby or leaves the country. Yet it must be high enough that the domestic leather makers feel it is worth lobbying for.

The government's rents under protectionism, liberalization, and an SEZ regime

The prospects of rents are a powerful rationale for policy makers to maintain their protectionist regime. For each good in the economy, they can set a tariff rate that reflects the lobbying efforts of different sides with a stake in the domestic price. If an exporting firm sees that a tariff can be decreased through lobbying, it has the incentive to lobby. Import-substituting firms are similarly incentivized to lobby if the tariff increases as a result. To maximize the lobbying efforts of both sides, the government needs to be sufficiently responsive in its tariff adjustments and sufficiently reliable in its response that the companies know the lobbying is worthwhile.

As a rationale for keeping the protectionist system in place, the government may use the rhetoric of the infant-industry argument even though the real reason to protect domestic industries is self-interest. As long as a government can, it should want to keep the tariff-rate competition in place among industries and businesses.

Trade liberalization would cause the government to lose these rents. If it were to either remove the tariffs or fix them at a low rate, import-substituting industries would no longer see a point in lobbying to raise them. Companies that import the goods would be better off thanks to lower prices but would no longer need to lobby the government to keep tariffs low. Government officials would thus lose the rents from both sides of the tariff lobbying game.

SEZs offer an alternative that helps the government keep some of its rents while promoting partial trade liberalization. SEZs can address the wishes of the importers by offering them tariff-free imports. At the same time, the zones leave protectionist tariffs in place for the rest of the economy, preserving the protection of import-substituting firms. SEZs thus allow industries on both sides of the tariff game to get the policies they want.[5]

Mauritius' SEZ scheme exemplifies this set-up. While they opened up the economy on some fronts, the government maintained high barriers to trade. As such, it provided incentives to both exporters and import-competing companies.[6]

This setup comes at a cost for the people of the country, who both pay high domestic prices due to the tariffs and subsidize exporters through the tax system. The setup also does not increase the government's rent streams, even though it may win the loyalty and gratitude of the lobbying factions. Because firms within SEZs already enjoy low tariffs, they do not have a reason to lobby for them. The only lobbying they may want to pursue is for the government to keep the regime in place, but this they can do collectively and presumably at a lower cost than when each business or industry group lobbies to lower particular tariffs.

Import-substitution firms offer a more stable source of rents for the government. Even though they can keep their tariffs, they still need to lobby for them to some extent. Policy makers may be aware that tariffs hurt the economy and therefore risk causing economic problems that may punish the people in power politically. Also, tariffs are generally unpopular among members of the public, who seek to keep prices down. If word gets around that the cost of living is rising due to the government's ineffectual policies, the people may revolt or at least express discontent at the voting booth. Government officials should thus see a risk in keeping prices high against the wishes of the general public.

How much this public pressure affects how governments set import tariffs is unclear, and presumably varies among different systems. Scholarly studies on the matter are not conclusive, although several point to at least some popular influence on trade protectionism in democratic systems, besides that of lobbying business interests.[7] However, governments that adhere to public pressure could also end up increasing protectionism to shield jobs from foreign competition, as opposed to preserving people's purchasing power through trade liberalization.[8]

Government officials likely want some kind of reward from import-substituting industries for keeping tariffs up outside the SEZs. Still, the rents they can extract are much higher when all business interests must lobby and counter-lobby in the struggle to set tariffs. SEZs therefore seem like a less attractive option for policy makers who are intent on maximizing their rents. Before looking into why the government would introduce SEZs, let us look more closely at the effect the scheme has on the importing exporters and domestic import-substitution industries.

Winners and losers from SEZs

With the introduction of SEZs, an exporting shoe manufacturer can become an SEZ firm, which allows it to import cheaper leather from abroad. The shoe manufacturer is clearly better off compared to when it was in the protectionist system. Its new opportunity to import leather allows it to expand, hire more people, and generate higher profits.

The outcome for the domestic leather producer is less clear. Import-substitution firms still need to put some effort into lobbying, but they now face less resistance to high tariffs, as the importing exporters are no longer lobbying to keep tariffs down. Only the pressure from the general public stands in the way of very high tariffs. Because people are often either poorly informed or poorly organized, their influence will be quite small. The domestic leather producer thus obtains higher tariffs on leather at a lower lobbying cost. An SEZ regime is also a way to cement the protectionist policies of a country, as the risk of general liberalization diminishes with the lower pressure from exporting interests.

However, SEZs also have their downsides for domestic leather producers. For one, they lower the demand for protected goods. Some of the leather company's customers are SEZ companies, which will be lost as they turn abroad for inputs. Therefore, the more future SEZ firms a domestic industry has as customers, the less likely it is to gain from the zone regime. Another downside for import-substituting firms is that SEZs might ultimately result in higher taxes for non-SEZ firms. If domestic firms that previously paid taxes in full get tax exemptions for entering SEZs, the government will lose out on revenue. To compensate for the loss, it may choose to raise taxes on other firms in the economy.

It is thus unclear whether import-substituting firms come out as winners or losers from the SEZ introduction. In the long run, however, most import-substituting firms should neither lose nor benefit much from the presence of SEZs. If they gain from SEZs through lower costs on lobbying, this windfall should encourage more people from other sectors of the economy to invest in import-substituting industries. Any benefit these companies see from protectionism dissipates as new companies seek to compete for the same profits.[9] If the sector comes out as a loser from SEZs, some import-substituting firms will leave for other areas of the economy. With fewer companies in the import-substituting business, competition for inputs is lower while prices of the goods are higher, thus leaving the level of profits for the remaining companies about the same as previously.

Why a government would liberalize

Because governments are better off with a protectionist system, it seems they should always stick to a rent-seeking system without even partial liberalization. While an SEZ regime preserves some of the government's rents, it is still inferior to standard protectionism from the government's perspective. However, there are a couple of ways in which the government can be either induced or pressured to promote such partial trade liberalization.

First, government officials may see that they can gain a large one-off rent contribution that outweighs the long-run rent losses. The importers who will invest in SEZs are the big winners from the zone regime, and may therefore offer to reward the current administration for introducing it. Various economic and technological developments can drive the emergence of a manufacturing export sector that can exert such political powers. When the sector becomes large enough, policy makers can expect an SEZ regime to yield lots of rents thanks to its great value to the exporters. SEZs can thus drive liberalization through the same mechanism as technological and economic change, by increasing the size and power of pro-trade interests.[10]

SEZ exporters likely invest with a time horizon that is longer than the time policy makers expect to stay in office. Their compensation to the government for introducing SEZs can therefore be larger than the present value of the policy makers' loss. When the officials are no longer in power, they will not care that they cannot receive much rent through protectionism. As long as they do not worry about their successors in office being in a worse situation, they are better off obtaining the reward today and leaving the costs for future administrations to bear. Businesses, by contrast, who invest for decades ahead, can better take account of the value of future benefits.

The other case where a government may pursue partial liberalization is when they are subjected to external pressure for economic reform. One source of external pressure may come from abroad. In trade negotiations or other international diplomatic contexts, policy makers may be forced to please their more powerful counterparts in foreign governments. External pressure can also come from domestic opinion leaders. People in academia or vocal media outlets can start raising arguments about the cost of protectionism and making people more aware of the burden it imposes on them.

If the government is bound to pursue liberalization, either as a way to earn more rents or because of external pressure to do so, SEZs offer a way to avoid liberalizing the economy as a whole. The government officials can earn their one-off rents from grateful exporters. At the same time, it keeps the some lobbying revenues that import-substitution industries supply in their pursuit of higher tariffs. If foreign governments, international organizations, or domestic opinion makers are pushing for liberalization, the government can use SEZs to appease them while keeping at least some of the rents in its revenue stream.

SEZs are perceived as a way to promote openness through export and trade. With them, governments can make a credible claim that they are actively doing something to promote trade. A government may even come across as a more credible liberalizer with SEZs than with more general tariff cuts, as the zones are a more active and visible policy measure. And while outsiders pushing for reform may hope for more, they may settle for the SEZ solution as a compromise. SEZs thus allow the government to placate the critics while avoiding general liberalization.

Why SEZs persist

Once introduced, SEZs are rarely abolished as long as they are not empty. This may seem curious since subsequent government administrations would be better off with a system that encourages more lobbying over protectionism. However, the political imperative for keeping the SEZs is similar to that for introducing them. If a government abolishes the SEZs, the SEZ firms might turn against it and deprive it of political support. If the previous government introduced them to earn a large one-off rent, then the loss of support from the sector should be as discouraging as its gain was alluring. This will be particularly true if, as is often the case, the SEZ regime has grown since its inception.

If outside pressure led to SEZs' introduction, it is unlikely to dissipate so as to allow the government to easily dismantle the regime. It is rather more likely that a step away from an allegedly pro-trade approach toward more protectionism would cost it more in political support than it previously gained by introducing SEZs. At a time when pro-trade arguments carry the most weight, steps back toward protectionism get more attention than further steps toward liberalization. For these reasons, governments have far more to lose by abolishing SEZs than they could gain from boosting the future stream of rents. Once established, SEZs are therefore unlikely to be abolished, regardless of their economic effects.

Why SEZs succeed without leading to reform

Many SEZ schemes turn out to be somewhere between clearly beneficial and clearly damaging to a country. At their worst, SEZs serve as vehicles for corruption or cause massive resource misallocations. These might attract little investment or clearly exhibit unnecessarily lavish and costly infrastructure. At their very best, SEZs bring countrywide reforms that eventually make the zones redundant.

When SEZs are used to preserve rents through partial liberalization, they can be placed somewhere in-between highly beneficial and severely damaging. They look successful compared to a protectionist status quo in the sense of attracting investors and bringing economic improvements, yet they fail to do more than that.

This middle-ground performance is easily explained by considering that governments can use SEZs to avoid economic liberalization. To please the people pushing for reform, they want to promote an SEZ scheme that is attractive to investors and an important source of exports. At the same time, the SEZs serve to maximize a government's rents by helping it circumvent countrywide liberalization.

An example of this system in action is Mauritius, which looks on the surface like a successful SEZ scheme. In place since 1971, the zones have since helped Mauritius become a manufacturing hub and boosted their tourism industry.[11] However, while the country opened up on one margin, it remained protectionist within import-substituting sectors. Policy-makers effectively divided the economy as to provide exporters with an open trade regime while shielding other firms from foreign competition.[12]

There is no reason to believe that any central government would use SEZs as a way to reform the country. If most people in government agree that rent-seeking should be preserved to the greatest extent possible, their only reason to introduce SEZs is to enhance their rent-seeking opportunities. They will thus not allow SEZs to function in a way that promotes broader reforms, like that described in the previous chapter.

The insight that SEZs can help governments avoid liberalization provides a novel way to view the dynamics of apparent SEZ success. A government may maintain a completely protectionist system as long as the import-substitution sector dominates the manufacturing export sector in size and power. With the growth of manufacturing exporters comes the pressure to liberalize, both from the companies themselves and politically influential outsiders. Governments may even act preemptively. Seeing the inevitable growth of a manufacturing and exporting sector in the country, a government might introduce SEZs to avoid the power clashes this may cause with the import-substituting industries.

SEZs can thus come about as the industrialization takes hold, but as a consequence of this development, rather than its catalyst. While the SEZs are praised for spurring the development, the reason for this is in fact the opposite – that SEZs emerge as a result of the imminent growth in manufacturing.

One reason SEZs are popular is the correlation between them and manufacturing growth. Several countries in East Asia saw both industrialization and the emergence of SEZs in the 1960s and 1970s. Most African countries saw a similar development take hold only in the 1990s, which was the time when SEZs became a popular policy. While this leads people to praise the SEZs as tools for promotion and development of manufacturing, the causation may in both cases go the other way around.

Once established, a unified government using SEZs for rent-seeking purposes will have the incentive to spur the growth of the SEZ sector by connecting it to the global economy. It must also prevent the zones from generating any external effects that may push the system as a whole toward liberalization and deprive the import-substituting firms of their protection. The government therefore has good reasons to keep the SEZs separated from the rest of the economy by, for instance, limiting their size and put fences around them. This may explain why so many seemingly successful SEZ schemes rely on industrial-park-style export processing zones.

In summary, there is an explanation for why this second-best solution comes about when it does not lead to reform. Rather than as a step toward general liberalization, SEZs are a way to avoid it. Without the bottom-up demand for SEZs whose liberalizing policies have external effects, the government can control the SEZ scheme and make sure it does not generate any dynamic for broader reforms. By keeping the scheme centralized, furthermore, it can see to it that no incentive emerges at the local level to pursue more efficient tax-revenue generation.

Finally, we should consider whether SEZs used to preserve rent-seeking are likely to be a net cost or benefit for the economy. It all depends on what the government would decide to do if it did not have SEZs as an alternative. The regime may have been forced to liberalize more broadly, in which case the SEZs would be a negative to the economy. In their absence, the outcome would be better for the country as a whole.

However, SEZs may benefit the economy if the political alternative is inferior. In this alternative scenario, the government officials may, for instance, find ways to pay the pro-reform interests off to stop their criticism. They may spend the same amount of money they would lose in tax revenue from the SEZs on bribes to think tanks and other advocates without getting any of the economic benefits of SEZs. If exporting businesses are among the liberalization advocates, these may be paid off by targeted fiscal benefits. Such a policy is inferior to SEZs in the same way that single-factory zones are, as they worsen the incentive problem and lack all the possible dynamic or agglomeration benefits of SEZs. Furthermore, because the pro-liberalization interest groups are likely to be domestic, any fiscal benefits to them are likely to be a loss to the government. SEZs, by contrast, can attract foreign investors, who do not impose the same losses.

If the government can pay off the pro-liberalization interests in this way, the economy would arguably be better off with SEZs instead. In such a case, we can say that the SEZs benefit the economy, even as tools to avoid broader reforms.

An overview of the political economy frameworks

The political economy frameworks presented in this book combine to give a fuller picture of when an SEZ scheme is beneficial. Chapter 2 explained that to understand whether SEZs are better than the status quo, we must take into account costs that most macroeconomic frameworks ignore. As Chapter 4 suggests, though, the status quo might not prevail in the absence of SEZs, and may therefore not be the proper benchmark for comparison. To fully take the political economy of SEZs into account, we must therefore ask whether SEZs are better than their political alternative.

As we have seen, SEZs tend to come about when the status quo of protectionism is under threat. Many SEZ schemes are therefore better than the status quo but are truly beneficial only if developments would have been worse in their absence. While this political-counterfactual reasoning will never amount to proof, it may be the best we can do when judging an SEZ scheme.

A short summary of the role SEZs can play under different political conditions helps summarize the theory part of the book. It is also helpful for our SEZ case studies. At their very best, SEZs are used by elite minorities to push for general reforms. As a middle case, SEZs are used to avoid broader reforms, in which case they can either be a marginal improvement on the status quo or inferior to the policy that would have prevailed in their absence. As a worst case, knowledge and incentive problems prevail, rendering SEZs even worse than the status quo. The case studies in the next section will serve as illustrative examples of these three possibilities.

Conditions	Effect and role of SEZs
Initiatives by a pro-reform political minority to push the country toward liberalization when the governing majority wants to preserve rents	At their best, as promoters of reform
Knowledge and incentive problems solved, but a tool to preserve rents for a government that would otherwise have avoided liberalization	Marginal improvement as a rent-seeking tool
Knowledge and incentive problems solved, but a tool to preserve rents for a government that would otherwise have liberalized further	Better than the status quo, but a way to avoid broader reforms
Knowledge and incentive problems unsolved	Worse than the status quo, due to waste and corruption

Notes

1 World Bank 1992: 1.
2 Miyagiwa 1986. The model builds on Young and Miyagiwa (1987) and is an extension of Hamada (1974).
3 Acemoglu and Robinson 2013.
4 For analyses of the interplay between interest groups over trade protection, see e.g. Alejandro 1967; Krueger 1974; Pincus 1975; Baldwin 1982; Baldwin 1989; Hillman 1982; Gallarotti 1985; Cassing and Hillman 1986; Eichengreen 1989; Dixit and Londregan 1995; Rodrik 1995; Grossman and Helpman 1996; Lee and Swagel 1997. Magee et al. (1989) call the free competition for tariff rates an "invisible foot economy." Economic actors driven by their self-interest under free competition to compete for rents will, to modify Adam Smith (1776: Book 5, Ch. 2, §9.), act as if led by an invisible foot in a way that imposes costs on the economic system as a whole. The rent-seeking dynamic does not apply only to tariffs, of course. Non-tariff barriers such as safety regulations can also be a potent protection for domestic firms and a deterrent to imports. However, since tariffs are an important fiscal benefit that is common for SEZs, they are the most relevant to discuss and the simplest example to use.
5 Rodrik 1999: 46.
6 Subramanian and Roy 2001: 19.
7 See, e.g., Caves 1976: 282; Marvel and Ray 1983: 192; Mayer 1984: 974; Grossman and Helpman 1994. Gawande and Bandyopadhyay (2000: 147) found that the US government seems to weigh the interest of business and the voting public fairly equally.
8 See, e.g., Riedel 1977.
9 Tullock 1975.
10 Rodrik 1994: 29; Tornell 1995; Acemoglu et al. 2005.
11 Baissac 2011.
12 Subramanian and Roy 2001: 15.

References

Acemoglu, Daron, and James A. Robinson, 2013. "Economics Versus Politics: Pitfalls of Policy Advice." *Journal of Economic Perspectives* 27(2): 173–192.

Acemoglu, Daron, Simon Johnson, and James Robinson. 2005. "The Rise of Europe: Atlantic Trade, Institutional Change, and Economic Growth." *American Economic Review* 95(3): 546–579.

Alejandro, Carlos F.Diaz. 1967. "The Argentine Tariff, 1906–1940." *Oxford Economic Papers, New Series* 19(1): 75–98.

Baissac, Claude. 2011. "Planned Obsolescence? Export Processing Zones and Structural Reform in Mauritius." In: *Special Economic Zones: Progress, Emerging Challenges, and Future Directions* (Thomas Farole and Gokhan Akinci eds.). The World Bank, Washington, D.C., pp. 227–244.

Baldwin, Robert E. 1982. "The Political Economy of Protectionism." In: *Import Competition and Response* (Jagdish N. Bhagwati ed.). University of Chicago Press, Chicago, pp. 263–292.

Baldwin, Robert E. 1989. "The Political Economy of Trade Policy." *Journal of Economic Perspectives* 3(4): 119–135.

Cassing, James H., and Arye L. Hillman. 1986. "Shifting Comparative Advantage and Senescent Industry Collapse." *American Economic Review* 76(3): 516–523.

Caves, Richard E. 1976. "Economic Models of Political Choice: Canada's Tariff Structure." *Canadian Journal of Economics* 9(2): 278–300.

Dixit, Avinash, and John Londregan. 1995. "Redistributive Politics and Economic Efficiency." *American Political Science Review* 89(4): 856–866.

Eichengreen, Barry. 1989. "The Political Economy of the Smoot-Hawley Tariff." In: *International Political Economy: Perspectives on Global Power and Wealth*. (Jeffry A. Frieden and David A. Lake eds.). Routledge, London and New York, pp. 37–46.

Gallarotti, Giulio M. 1985. "Toward a Business-Cycle Model of Tariffs." *International Organization* 39(1): 155–187.

Gawande, Kishore, and Usree Bandyopadhyay. 2000. "Is Protection for Sale? Evidence on the Grossman-Helpman Theory of Endogenous Protection." *Review of Economics and Statistics* 82(1): 139–152.

Grossman, Gene M., and Elhanan Helpman. 1994. "Protection for Sale." *American Economic Review* 84(4): 833–850.

Grossman, Gene M., and Elhanan Helpman. 1996. "Electoral Competition and Special Interest Politics." *Review of Economic Studies* 63(2): 265–286.

Hamada, Koichi. 1974. "An Economic Analysis of the Duty-Free Zone." *Journal of International Economics* 4(3): 225–241.

Hillman, Arye L. 1982. "The Declining Industries and Political-Support Protectionist Motives." *American Economic Review* 72(5): 1180–1187.

Krueger, Anne O. 1974. "The Political Economy of the Rent-Seeking Society." *American Economic Review* 64(3): 291–303.

Lee, Jong-Wha, and Phillip Swagel. 1997. "Trade Barriers and Trade Flows across Countries and Industries." *Review of Economics and Statistics* 79(3): 372–382.

Magee, Stephen P., William A. Brock, and Leslie Young (Eds.). 1989. *Black Hole Tariffs and Endogenous Policy Theory: Political Economy in General Equilibrium*. Cambridge University Press, Cambridge, UK, New York, USA and Victoria, Australia.

MarvelHoward P., and Edward J. Ray. 1983. "The Kennedy Round: Evidence on the Regulation of International Trade in the United States." *American Economic Review* 73(1): 190–197.

Mayer, Wolfgang. 1984. "Endogenous Tariff Formation." *American Economic Review* 74(5): 970–985.

McCallum, Jamie K. 2011. "Export Processing Zones: Comparative Data from China, Honduras, Nicaragua and South Africa." International Labour Organization, Working Paper No. 21, March 2011.

Miyagiwa, Kaz F. 1986. "A Reconsideration of the Welfare Economics of a Free-trade zone." *Journal of International Economics* 21(3): 337–350.

Pincus, Jonathan J. 1975. "Pressure Groups and the Pattern of Tariffs." *Journal of Political Economy* 83(4): 757–778.

Riedel, James. 1977. "Tariff Concessions in the Kennedy Round and the Structure of Protection in West Germany: An econometric assessment." *Journal of International Economics* 7: 133–143.

Rodrik, Dani. 1995. "Political Economy of Trade Policy." In: *Handbook of International Economics, Vol. 3*. (Gene M. Grossman and Kenneth Rogoff eds.). Elsevier Science B.V, Amsterdam.

Rodrik, Dani. 1999. *The New Global Economy and Developing Countries: Making Openness Work*. Johns Hopkins University Press, Baltimore, MD.

Rodrik, Dani. 1994. "The Rush to Free Trade in the Developing World: Why So Late? Why Now? Will It Last?" *National Bureau of Economic Research Working Paper* No. 3947.

Smith, Adam. 1776. *An Inquiry into the Nature and Causes of the Wealth of Nations.* W. Strahan and T. Cadell, London.

Subramanian, Arvind, and Devesh Roy. 2001. "Who Can Explain the Mauritian Miracle: Meade, Romer, Sachs, or Rodrik?" *International Monetary Fund Working Paper* No. 01.

Tornell, Aaron. 1995. "Are Economic Crises Necessary for Trade Liberalization and Fiscal Reform? The Mexican Experience." In: *Reform, Recovery, and Growth: Latin America and the Middle East* (Rudiger Dornbusch and Sebastian Edwards eds.). University of Chicago Press, Chicago, pp. 53–76.

Tullock, Gordon. 1975. "The Transitional Gains Trap." *The Bell Journal of Economics* 6(2): 671–678.

World Bank. 1992. *Export Processing Zones.* The World Bank, Washington, D.C.

Young, Leslie, and Kaz F. Miyagiwa. 1987. "Unemployment and the Formation of Duty-Free Zones." *Journal of Development Economics* 26(2): 397–405.

Part II

Case studies

The political economy frameworks in this book can help us interpret the apparent success or failure of an SEZ scheme, and help us predict whether SEZs will be beneficial. If it seems the SEZs are magnifying a country's problems, it probably has some unsolved knowledge and incentive problems. If a seemingly successful SEZ scheme does not lead to countrywide change, it may just be a way for the government to avoid reform and maximize its rents. If a country is turning into a larger version of its SEZ scheme, reform-minded elites may be using the SEZs as tools for change.

In this part of the book, I will use three case studies to illustrate three different levels of success – that of failure, middle ground, and success. The case studies are all indicative and relative. No case is perfect in the sense of being completely free from corruption throughout its history. At the same time, no case is so bad as to produce only unsuccessful zones. There are also always some unknown aspects of a country's inner politics, and we will never know the counterfactual political developments.

A political economy analysis nevertheless provides the most complete way to analyze SEZ regimes. With more than half the world's countries hosting SEZs, my selection of India, the Dominican Republic, and China is not in any way random. They are chosen because there is sufficient public information to study the cases in depth, as in the cases of China and India, or because I had the chance to conduct my own field studies there, as in the case of the Dominican Republic.

Looking at a particular country's SEZ scheme, the first question to ask is whether the country would have been better off without the SEZs. Using the framework from chapter 2, does it seem to be better off with SEZs than with the status quo? This depends on whether the country seems to have solved the knowledge and incentive problems associated with SEZs. If it has, the question is whether the SEZs seem to have led to countrywide reforms. In that case, the scheme has performed at its best.

If no reform process has come about, the level of SEZ success is somewhere in-between the best and worst cases. The SEZs can then be a successful way for policy makers to avoid liberalization as they try to maximize their rents. A better case in this middle-ground territory is one where SEZs bring marginal improvements, as policy makers would have stuck to more protectionism in their absence. Besides demonstrating how to analyze SEZs from a political economy perspective, the case studies will serve to make the theoretical discussions of the book clearer and more concrete.

5 The problems of India's SEZs

India introduced its first SEZ in 1965, and a decade passed before the second SEZ appeared. By 2002, the country had only seven SEZs.[1] These zones never attracted much investment or produced much of the country's exports, despite several improvements in SEZ incentives and much government attention to infrastructure and SEZ administration. They also have weak backward linkages to the rest of the economy. For these reasons, these SEZs are seen as not having made much of an impact on the economy.[2]

There have been some positive adjustments in Indian SEZ policy throughout the years. A main revision of India's SEZ regime came in 2005, with a new SEZ Act discussed later in this chapter. Because it is relatively new, it is still early to assess the full effects of the new SEZ law. The analysis of the role of SEZs in India's economic and political development will therefore mainly refer to the time before the new law. However, I shall note that while the number of SEZs has grown rapidly since the law's enactment, their actual performance is unclear. The zones have been described as quite unprofitable for the economy, and investments and employment have fallen short of expectations. Because of political resistance, the government has scaled back tax incentives, and it still seems uncertain what the rules for the SEZs will look like going forward.[3] Yet the SEZs have also been commended for the amount of investments, exports, and employment they have generated.[4]

The broader context

An overview of the economic history of India helps put the Indian SEZs in context. Between Indian independence in 1947 and the mid-1980s, the country was known for its sluggish rate of growth.[5] However, around 1985, things changed rapidly for India as GDP surged, a trend that continued throughout the 1990s and 2000s. While India's real GDP per capita grew at an average rate of just 1.7 percent per year between 1950 and 1985, its yearly average per capita growth rate increased to 4.6 percent between 1985 and 2010.[6]

Whether we are looking at macroeconomic data or the political context, it is hard to connect this breakthrough in economic progress with the SEZs, which at the time were small, few, and not particularly investor friendly. By

1976, when the scheme had been in place for over a decade, it was still restrictive toward foreign investments and had a business climate that seemed less attractive than the general business climate in most other countries.[7]

Until 1984, India still had only two SEZs, and by 1985, it had six zones employing 16,200 people in total. Before 1996, the share of Indian exports from the SEZs never exceeded 4 percent, and SEZ-related laws and procedures did not change until the 1990s.[8] Any significant changes in the broader economy during this time were therefore hardly results of the SEZ scheme.

While the SEZs produced little action, India's economy as a whole took off in the 1980s. There are various theories about why this shift came about, but none of them can connect it to the SEZs. One driver seems to have been an increase in domestic savings at the time, which channeled into investments in the country. The banking system was also developing. The amount of bank branches increased rapidly throughout the country, which created new economic opportunities. There were also some improvements in agriculture at the time, with high-yield fertilizers being widely implemented.[9] None of these trends point to SEZs playing any role.

Another observation is the big role services have played in India's economic growth since the 1980s. India is seen as having largely failed to promote a manufacturing base, which could provide employment to vast amounts of low-skilled workers. While some suggest services may be the new path to development for many countries, they have still not become the large-scale job creator that manufacturing has been in many developing countries. Because services generally require relatively skilled workers, they are unlikely

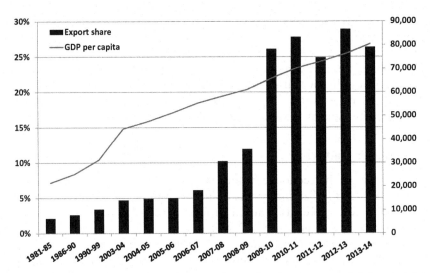

Figure 5.1 Exports from Indian SEZs as a share of national exports (left-hand scale), and real GDP per capita (right-hand scale, constant national currency).
Sources: Seshadri 2011b: 6; Department of Commerce 2016; Sivaramakrishnan 2016: 372; UN Trade Statistics 2016; IMF 2016.

to generate the kind of inclusive economic growth that can lift a whole population out of poverty.[10]

The lack of Indian manufacturing can be largely attributed to restrictive policies that prevented manufacturers from importing necessary inputs.[11] Perhaps even more severely, the government restricted the right to produce certain goods to small firms. Larger firms, which could have become international manufacturing champions in the production of items such as pencils, candles, shoes, garments, and toys, were banned from entering such markets.[12] The resulting lack of Indian manufacturing created a path dependency that lasts until this day, and there are still regulations in place hampering growth in the sector.[13]

Indian exports as a share of GDP have grown rapidly since 1986 but this has been in service industries rather than in manufacturing. The Indian population was relatively educated and could therefore take advantage of the new information technologies. Still, in contrast to the economy at large, the manufacturing sectors saw only limited adoption of information technologies.[14]

While SEZs could have played a role in filling the manufacturing vacuum, their modest growth made this impossible. The government also had a very different goal with the first SEZs, namely to earn foreign exchange to buy machinery for India's industrialization.[15] The latest push for SEZs, by contrast, has come out of recognition of the lack of a broad manufacturing base.[16]

It is also hard to see a connection between the Indian SEZs and any major policy changes. Ever since independence, India had a protectionist and centrally planned economic system. In the 1980s, the rhetoric of policy makers became more business friendly, and India saw some policy changes in the same vein. However, these were quite narrow and did not represent real economic liberalization.[17] The great political turnaround in India came in the 1990s, with substantial steps toward economic liberalization. These included fewer restrictions on FDI, more financial liberalization, and less protectionism in several areas of trade.[18]

During this time, the Indian SEZ scheme was still small, and showed no sign of generating a political dynamic toward reform. The SEZs never became sufficiently important to plausibly affect policy making. While Indian exports surged from the late 1980s, exports from the SEZs remained small in comparison. Only in 1998 did the share of SEZ exports of total Indian exports reach 5 percent. By then, zone employment was still only in the tens of thousands, in a country with more than a billion people.[19]

When looking at the first Indian SEZs in their political economy context, it seems even less likely that they benefited the country. An important feature of India's early SEZ scheme was its centralization. Zone policies were in the hands of an SEZ section within the ministry of commerce. The Board of Approval, which was placed just under this ministry, was responsible for allowing companies to enter the SEZs.[20] For a long time, only the central government could develop and operate SEZs. It was only in 1994 that state governments, agencies, and private developers could enter this domain.[21]

The dominance of the central government in SEZ decision-making suggests that the demand for the SEZs came from the very top. While the government was restricting trade and obstructing exports, some of the goals of the zones were to increase exports and enhance the country's trade balance aggregates.[22]

There is no indication, meanwhile, that the SEZs emerged through the kind of process driven by local interests that was described in Chapter 3, by which the SEZs could have been at their best. The dismal performance of the Indian SEZs and their small role in the economy at large support this notion. I will therefore start at the lowest possible level of SEZ performance, to understand whether the zones were at least better than the status quo.

A status quo comparison does not mean comparing India today with the country in 1965, when the zones were introduced. The status quo is rather today's India with all the policies it has introduced and changed throughout the years, but without the SEZs. This is also a different analysis from that of political alternatives, since such an analysis includes counterfactuals about what other policies might have been in place in the absence of SEZs. Only if the SEZs were better than the status quo is it worth asking whether they were better than their political alternative and if they might even have reformed the economy as a whole.

To understand whether the SEZs were likely a net contributor, we need to look at whether India had the institutional and policy environment that allowed it to solve the knowledge and incentive problems related to SEZs.

Did India solve the knowledge problem?

The context of the Indian SEZ scheme hints at its vulnerability to the knowledge problem. In the context of the government's economic planning, India's SEZs were part of a centralized system from the start. When the government considered the SEZ scheme, it had to take into account the distribution of resources in the country as a whole and assess how they would be used most productively. Many of the features of the country's SEZs, such as where the SEZs would be located, were often in the hands of the central government.[23]

Many of the flaws of Indian SEZs look like problems resulting from inadequate knowledge. Several SEZ locations turned out to be poor and unattractive to investors. The first SEZ was located in the port city of Kandla. Both Kandla and Falta, the location of another early SEZ seem unlikely to have been areas of naturally formed industrial clusters. Both locations allegedly lacked adequate social and economic infrastructure, as well as industrial culture.[24]

The location of the SEZ in Falta, established in 1985, seems more like an attempt at wealth redistribution than development policy. The area is situated in West Bengal, a state with one of the country's highest rates of unemployment at the time. The SEZ in Falta hardly changed that dismal state of affairs. Out of six SEZs in India in 2000, it stood for only 2 percent of SEZ employment, and only 1 percent of SEZ exports. The few early SEZs that were more productive were located in areas that already had high industrial performance. The Indian government frequently invested in backward areas. Perhaps it was doing its best to seize opportunities for industrialization that private investors failed to discover. Unfortunately, such centralized allocation of the country's recourses is highly vulnerable to the knowledge problem.[25]

The Indian SEZ planners got more things wrong than simply SEZ location. Infrastructure was inadequate in many of the zones, and communications, transport, and drainage were deficient. As with poor overall performance and bad location, this does not necessarily mean that the Indian SEZs were a failure. When zones are privately developed, bad locations or infrastructure should not result in any investment. If private developers mistakenly invest in an unprofitable location, only they incur the loss caused by the mistake.

Even if the government determines the location of private SEZs, it need not incur any losses. A lack of private investors and developers willing to invest in infrastructure simply signals that the government needs to find a better location. Alas, this was not the case in India, where the government for a long time initiated all zones and invested in much of the SEZ infrastructure.[26] In that context, the government may waste resources on infrastructure that, if not in demand, is a pure waste for the country's tax payers.

The legal framework for the SEZs had several flaws that made the zones particularly vulnerable to the knowledge problem. A central authority chose which firms could invest in SEZs, thus essentially picking winners and losers. There were criteria for SEZ investors, but because these were not binding, officials were applying more loosely defined criteria when picking the companies allowed to invest in SEZs.[27] Besides creating an obvious opportunity for rent-seeking, such a selection can easily lead to the choice of fragile companies that are unable to pay their land rent. A private developer, by contrast, has a strong incentive to develop an effective system for screening companies entering the zone.

The Indian legal framework also failed to account for the need of SEZ firms to subcontract some stages of production to firms outside the zones. Subcontracting rules were either costly to comply with or non-existent, which meant that only companies relying on imports instead of domestic sub-contracting preferred to locate in SEZs.[28]

The new SEZ Act of 2005 has potential to solve some of India's knowledge problems. Most importantly, the government now encourages privately developed SEZs. More of the burden of infrastructure supply is thus transferred from the public to the private sector.[29]

To get a zone approved, SEZ developers now turn primarily to the state governments, which in turn pass the proposal to the Board of Approval, an entity under the central government.[30] More state level involvement in the process implies more decentralization. Perhaps the most important aspect of increased authority for state entities is their ability to choose not to regulate how SEZ business should operate.[31] However, it is worth pointing out that India has a large population, with on average 45 million people per state, which is the size of the 30th largest country on earth. The knowledge problem of the central government may therefore be only slightly smaller for a state government.

Both the administration and regulatory powers over an SEZ now lie in the hands of a local authority, the zone's development commissioner. This concentration of roles in one body has been described as an "extreme centralization of governance institutions."[32] However, in contrast to a central government agency, a local SEZ authority should have a better understanding of local market conditions, and is therefore more suitable to exercise this role. Even though decision-making is centralized, it is at least taking place locally, and thus closer to the people with better market knowledge, which enhances the chance of alleviating the knowledge problem.

These are, however, only tenuous steps toward decentralization, and the new SEZ regime does not seem to address the knowledge problem with much vigor. The central government still has the opportunity to skew SEZ developments by having the final say in whether developers meet regulatory requirements. Entrepreneurs wanting to develop a private SEZ must present how much investment the zone is to attract and what kinds of facilities will emerge in it.[33] The SEZ program remains a top-down driven project, despite its decentralization of authority to the state level. The main authority for applications and approvals to establish SEZs still lies with a central government authority, the Board of Approvals.[34] State governments, having observed the disappointing performance of the new SEZs so far, have been largely reluctant to support zone projects. As a result, they have not passed the SEZ laws that would regulate state level SEZs. Such implicit discouragement from state governments will likely keep potential SEZ developers away from several Indian states.[35]

SEZ related land laws further contribute to the knowledge problem. A recent push to open new SEZs has raised much debate about the value of SEZ production versus farming. By May 2016, 417 zones had been approved under the new SEZ law.[36] This rapid expansion has been faulted for encouraging "land-grabbing" of farmland. At times, opponents of this dispossession have clashed with the police in violent uproars. SEZs have also been singled out as vehicles for unproductive real estate speculation.[37]

Such criticism would seem misplaced if farmers could choose to sell their land only when the price they received for it superseded the value of the revenue derived from farming the land. The problem in the India is that states regulate the sales price of land, which must be valued based on current land-use, thus preventing land from being sold for a higher price. Therefore, even if an SEZ developer sees the potential value of a piece of land as being twice that of its current use, they still cannot share this efficiency gain with the farmers that currently own the land. It is therefore not strange that farmers are reluctant to sell land, as they rarely benefit from it. To make SEZ possible on current farmland, the government steps in to help SEZ developers to accomplish land purchases.[38] The government enjoys eminent domain powers, which allow it to convert private land for "any public purpose or for a company."[39] This is made particularly defensible in the case of SEZs, as they are designated by law as public utility services.[40]

Land transactions at below-market price have aroused criticism about SEZ developers pricing farmers out from their land, causing "conversion of the fertile land into cement structures."[41] Some may think that suppressed prices and government mandated land conversions inevitably result in too much land being developed as SEZs at the expense of farming. Yet the real problem with government-mandated land pricing is that no cost-benefit analysis can be made of farming versus SEZ activities, which causes the wrong pieces of farm land to convert to SEZs. This is an obvious case of the knowledge problem. Without a market price as a signal of value, the government must make an assessment of what SEZ projects are warranted, and will inevitably sometimes make mistakes.

All this suggests that plenty of hit-and-miss policies have determined the fate of the Indian SEZs. The government made huge infrastructure investments in the early SEZs but SEZ companies still complained about its poor quality.[42] Much of this spending thus looks mistargeted, as it failed to meet the needs of businesses. While these policies made the knowledge problems particularly more severe in the first decades of Indian SEZs, the new rules are unlikely to overcome them to a large extent.

With luck, the SEZ scheme will see an increasing share of private developers, which will bring SEZ investments closer in line with market needs. There is, however, a risk that the government will step in to fill the infrastructure gaps in the meantime. Such efforts risk misdirecting resources and subsidizing private investments in inappropriate locations or industries. They thus prevent the SEZ scheme from developing into an efficient, market-based system.

Did India solve the incentive problem?

Much in the general political economy environment in India makes its SEZs susceptible to the incentive problem. Corruption is one of the banes of the Indian economy, and a great contributor to making the economy risky and unattractive to investors.[43] As with many developing countries, India has a nexus of crony relationships between businesses and the public sector.

Liberalizing policies in the 1980s and 1990s do not seem to have mitigated cronyism, and may even have increased it. The liberalization process allowed existing businesses with government contacts to benefit from privatizations. The Indian government only solidified the ties between businesses and the government as it rearranged property rights in favor of those with political connections. This was not a context in which the SEZs could promote a more competitive economy. Instead, they provided more opportunities for the government to grant favors to businesses.[44]

An indicator that political incentives, rather than social welfare, are driving an SEZ scheme is the inclusion of single-factory zones. As I discuss in the introduction of this book, single-factory zones resemble companies receiving targeted tax benefits, rather than zones. As such, they provide opportunities for officials to target fiscal benefits at particular businesses. In India, these are called export-oriented units and have been used widely since their introduction in 1980. By 1998, the government had approved 3,818 such units, 1,210 of which were operational, compared to 525 companies in export processing zones. In 2009, the number of operational single-factory zones had increased to 2,600.[45]

Lately, the increase in the number of new single-factory zones has been slowing down.[46] This development is part of a conscious effort to increase the share of larger SEZs, more reminiscent of the Chinese zone model.[47] The Indian 2005 SEZ Act aimed to create larger and more diversified zones, and set a minimum size for SEZs of 1,000 hectares. This is not impressive compared to the average size of 8,500 hectares of China's first SEZs, or the most prominent Chinese zone of Shenzhen, which covered 32,750 hectares already in 1980.[48] Still, the reorientation towards larger zones is promising from an incentive perspective, since smaller zones are more likely to serve as vehicles for benefits to particular companies.

The size requirements have however been significantly loosened. The minimum size was halved to 500 hectares, and this requirement applies only to zones with more than one form of production. Single-sector zones need only be 50 hectares and SEZs hosting "agro-based food processing" only 10 hectares. IT-zones are particularly privileged in this context, as they are exempt from any size requirements.[49]

These rules have generated small and IT dominated SEZs. Out of 513 SEZs approved by 2008, 40 percent were smaller than 20 hectares, 70 percent were smaller than 100 hectares, and 94 percent were smaller than 300 hectares. Only 3.7 percent seemed to live up to the promise of being large and diversified.[50] IT zones have flourished to constitute 63.5 percent of all SEZs. In the absence of minimum land requirement, it has been easier for them to establish production despite India's thorny land market.[51]

From the beginning of the new SEZ scheme, landowners protested against land acquisition for SEZs. Zones that were planned for thousands of hectares were forced to shrink significantly in the face of local resistance.[52] Responding to the disruptions, the government decided to limit the size of SEZs, the very opposite of encouraging larger zones, to 5,000 hectare. On top of this, states are free to impose even lower size limits.[53]

Because of India's regulated land market, private land owners have good reason to worry about SEZs making them landless. When compensated below market price, they cannot expect to find opportunities to buy the same amount of land elsewhere, as Indian officials have claimed. Not least because of the growing IT-industry, demand for land, and thus land prices, have been increasing.[54] At the same time, SEZ developers have good reasons to obtain land that they deem potentially profitable.

The system creates destructive incentives on all sides. SEZ developers have the incentive to lobby officials to acquire land. Land owners have the incentive to press the government for restrictions on SEZs, and decline price-suppressed land deals that normally would have made them and the country better off by being applied to more productive use. The government's incentive is to yield to political considerations in deciding whether to support exports and industrial investments through SEZs or respond to the demands of local land owners. When people cannot act on the basis of market prices for such an important asset as land, they will often fail to act in a socially constructive way.

Beyond these problems, corruption at the lower ranks of the government bureaucracy may be just as worrying as corruption connected to the central government. Corruption in the government bureaucracy is, unfortunately, a big problem in India.[55] Multiple levels of bureaucracy involved in business activity create several opportunities for graft, which is true also for the SEZ sector.

Before 1991, SEZ companies in India were required to obtain permission first from the Board of Approval, and then from the Secretariat of Industrial Approvals, the Ministry of Commerce, as well as state- and central-government departments. The procedures may have improved over time, but a 2004 survey found that a company still had to pass 15 different authorities to be approved as an SEZ company. In the same survey, 60 percent of companies said they frequently made "irregular payments," that is payments not on the books, both to customs-clearance and zone authorities.[56] If sufficiently widespread, such practices may prevent the SEZ regime from benefiting the country at large.

This situation might improve with the 2005 SEZ law's "single-window" facility, which is meant to be the Board of Approvals.[57] Making the registration process simpler can eliminate some opportunities for graft. In India generally, people wishing to start a business must go back and forth between agencies in a process that generally takes 270 days.[58] A one-stop-shop facility could therefore make a great difference.

So far though, the single window facility looks like a disappointment. The central government recognized this in 2010, as it directed state governments to set up the needed facilities for single window mechanisms at the state, instead of the central, government level.[59] Yet a survey published in 2015 found 64 percent of respondents reporting that no single-window clearance facility existed in the state.[60] Thus, while the planned single window facility of the SEZ scheme has been much touted, developers have had problems with getting clearances.[61] Many steps regarding registration in the new law are complicated and unclear.[62] As a result, notified zones have had problems attracting investors. In 2013, there were as many as 580 approved SEZs zones, not including single-factory zones. Two years later, 150 of them had been de-notified.[63] By December 2016, there were only 405 approved zones.[64]

There are clearly still many opportunities for such rent-seeking in the SEZ bureaucracy, even though the SEZ regime is moving in the right direction in protecting investors from low-level graft. Indicators of distorted incentives in the Indian case are evident both at the central and more local levels. And because of India's low-level corruption, there is an inevitable conflict between measures dealing with the knowledge problem versus the incentive problem. More centralization, such as federal-level single-window facilities, may alleviate rent-seeking while at the same time aggravating the knowledge problem.

Naturally, there are no precise data on the extent of rent-seeking associated with the SEZs. Furthermore, we can only guess how important rent-seeking prospects were for policy makers introducing the Indian SEZ regime. Despite official goals like earning foreign exchange and promoting manufacturing for exports, one cannot exclude the possibility that some of the rent-seeking opportunities they created were intentional. Despite recent attempts to reform the SEZ regime, it remains to be seen whether it can be organized to make India's SEZ scheme sufficiently attractive to honest investors.

Not better than the status quo

The discussion in this chapter suggests that India's SEZ planners have some way to go to solving some pressing knowledge and incentive problems. Centralized decision-making about Indian SEZs continues to cause knowledge problems. While this centralization could allow for more control over bureaucracies, in India, rent-seeking opportunities at the lower levels still create incentive problems.

Many reasons have been cited for the sluggish performance of Indian SEZs. Among them are a poor and complex bureaucracy, dysfunctional and unstable policies, and stringent labor laws.[65] However, these are most likely just symptoms of India's underlying political economy problems. As long as the knowledge problem persists, the risk is great that policy makers will introduce misguided policies. As long as incentive problems persist, the SEZ planners have little interest in correcting the flaws of the system.

India seems to have gained little from the SEZ scheme, when considering all the costs and more limited benefits it has brought since its inception. Therefore, the Indian SEZs do not seem to have been better than the status quo, and the country would likely have been better off in the absence of the SEZs.

Hopefully, Indian policy makers learn from the mistakes in the past and create an SEZ regime that will benefit the country going forward. Whether the SEZ Act of 2005 brought about sufficient changes may be too soon to tell. It seems in any case safe to say that so far, the countrywide liberalizations India embarked on decades ago, although not perfect, have been much more beneficial for the country as a whole.

Because the Indian SEZs seem not to have improved on the status quo, we need not ask whether the SEZs in India were an improvement compared to their political alternative. For this to have been the case, India would have initiated an even costlier industrial project in the absence of the SEZs, which is an implausible counterfactual story. As a central government project, it is also quite obvious that the zone regime was not part of a liberalization process driven by reform-minded elites.

Notes

1 Aggarwal 2004: 14.
2 Engman et al. 2007: 18; Palit and Bhattacharjee 2008: 19; Seshadri 2011a: 29.
3 Govardan and Srivastav 2012; Aggarwal 2016; Rahoof and Arul 2016: 51.
4 Bishesh and Banga 2016.
5 Rodrik and Subramanian 2005.
6 Penn World Table 2016, not PPP adjusted. IMF data suggests that the 1985–2010 figure is 5.3 percent (IMF 2016). As a comparison, China's per capita GDP grew between 1985 and 2010 at a rate of 8.9 percent.
7 Aggarwal 2004: 5.
8 Id.
9 Kotwal et al. 2011.
10 Ghani and O'Connell 2014; Cowen 2016; Rodrik 2016; Sharma 2016: 213.
11 Cowen 2016: 25.
12 Das 2006.
13 Cowen 2016: 25.
14 Kotwal et al. 2011: 1180.
15 Seshadri 2011a: 26.
16 Dohrmann 2008: 62.
17 Rodrik and Subramanian 2005; Kochhar et al. 2006.
18 Kochhar et al. 2006: 13.
19 Aggarwal 2004: 10, 13; Penn World Table 2016. Macroeconomic data also indicate that the Indian zones had no effect on the country's trade balance (Seshadri 2011a: 30–31).
20 Aggarwal 2005: 15–16.
21 Ranjan 2006: 8.
22 Seshadri 2011a: 29.
23 Seshadri and Storr 2010.
24 Kundra 2000: 66.
25 Seshadri and Storr 2010: 357.
26 Gopalakrishnan 2011: 143.
27 Seshadri and Storr 2010: 360.
28 Seshadri and Storr 2010: 358.
29 Gopalakrishnan 2011: 143; Palit and Bhattacharjee 2008: 174.
30 Dohrmann 2008: 66; Department of Commerce 2016.
31 Burman 2006: 5.
32 Dohrmann 2008: 69; Gopalakrishnan 2011: 148.
33 Palit and Bhattacharjee 2008: 114.
34 Dohrmann 2008: 66.
35 Govardan and Srivastav 2012.
36 Department of Commerce 2016.
37 Roy 2009: 79; Levien 2011; Levien 2012; Seshadri 2011b: 84.
38 Seshadri 2011b: 12.
39 Rajagopalan and Tabarrok 2014: 6.
40 Department of Commerce 2006: §5 (g).
41 Khan 2008: 14; Levien 2011; Mitra 2007: 13.
42 Aggarwal 2004: 1, 26.
43 See e.g. Keshava 2008: 18.
44 Mazumdar 2008: 13–15.
45 Seshadri 2011a 36; EOU India 2016.
46 East Asia Forum 2016.
47 Dohrmann 2008: 62; Seshadri 2011a: 28.
48 Herlevi 2016: 12.

49 SEZ Division 2013.
50 Mukhopadhyay and Pradhan 2009: 70–71
51 Id.: 70; Seshadri 2011b: 8.
52 Anwar and Carmody 2016: 125.
53 Dohrmann 2008: 76; Department of Commerce 2007.
54 Anwar and Carmody 2016: 126–27.
55 Transparency International 2011.
56 Aggarwal 2004.
57 Dohrmann 2008: 66; Department of Commerce 2016: About, Introduction.
58 Palit and Bhattacharjee 2008: 116.
59 Business Standard 2010.
60 PHD Research Bureau 2015: 43.
61 Id.: 178.
62 Harding 2011: 164.
63 ASSOCHAM 2015.
64 Department of Commerce 2016: About, Approved SEZs in India.
65 Ranjan 2006: 23; Keshava 2008: 11–12; Seshadri and Storr 2010.

References

Aggarwal, Aradhna. 2004. "Export Processing Zones in India: analysis of the Export Performance." Indian Council for Research on International Economic Relations (ICRIER) Working Paper 148.

Aggarwal, Aradhna. 2005. "Performance of Export Processing Zones: A Comparative Analysis of India, Sri Lanka, and Bangladesh." *Indian Council for Research on International Economic Relations (ICRIER) Working Paper* No. 155. Available at: http://icrier.org/pdf/wp155.pdf (accessed 29 October 2016).

Aggarwal, Aradhna. 2007. "Impact of Special Economic Zones on Employment, Poverty, and Human Development." *Indian Council for Research on International Economic Relations (ICRIER), Working Paper* No. 194. Available at: http://www.democracia ycooperacion.net/IMG/pdf/1-working_paper_194.pdf (accessed 29 October 2016).

Aggarwal, Aradhna. 2016. "Special Economic Zones in India: growth engines or missed opportunity?" *East Asia Forum*, Feb. 19, 2016. Available at: http://www. eastasiaforum.org/2016/02/19/special-economic-zones-in-india-growth-engines-or-missed-opportunity/ (accessed 29 October 2016).

Anwar, Mohammad Amir, and Pádraig Carmody. 2016. "Bringing Globalization to the Countryside: Special Economic Zones in India." *Singapore Journal of Tropical Geography* 37: 121–138.

ASSOCHAM (The Associated Chambers of Commerce & Industry of India). 2015. "Set up a single-window clearance system for speedy approvals of special economic zones: ASSOCHAM plea to govt." *ASSOCHAM* Nov. 30, 2015. Available at: http:// www.assocham.org/newsdetail.php?id=5357 (accessed 29 October 2016).

Bishesh, Bithikaa, and Shradha Banga. 2016. "Special Economic Zones in India as a Regional Development Stimulator." *Imperial Journal of Interdisciplinary Research* 2(6): 1318–1322.

Burman, Anirudh. 2006. "Special Economic Zones: Issues in Corporate Governance." *SSRN Working Paper*. Available at: http://ssrn.com/abstract=954934 (accessed 29 October 2016).

Business Standard. 2010. "Create Single-Window Clearance for SEZs: Govt Tells States." *Business Standard*, Feb. 12, 2010. Available at: http://www.business-standard.

com/article/economy-policy/create-single-window-clearance-for-sezs-govt-tells-states-110021200075_1.html (accessed 29 October 2016).

Cowen, Tyler. 2016. "Economic Development in an 'Average is Over' World." Working Paper. Available at: https://www.gmu.edu/centers/publicchoice/faculty%20pages/Tyler/ (accessed 28 October, 2016).

Das, Gurcharan. 2006. "The India Model." *Foreign Affairs* 85(4), Jul. 1, 2006.

Department of Commerce. 2006. "SEZ Rules Incorporating Amendments up to July, 2010." Published in Part II, Section 3, Subsection (i), of the *Gazette of India Extraordinary*, Feb. 10, 2006. Available at: http://www.sezindia.nic.in/goi-policies-sra.asp (accessed 29 October 2016).

Department of Commerce. 2007. "Notification." *The Gazette of India*, Extraordinary, Third Amendment, Part 2, Section 3, Sub-Section 2, Oct. 17, 2007. Available at: http://www.sezindia.nic.in/goi-policies-sra.asp (accessed 29 October 2016).

Department of Commerce. 2016. Ministry of Commerce and Industry Home-page, available at: http://www.sezindia.nic.in/index.asp (accessed 29 October 2016).

Dohrmann, Jona Aravind. 2008. "Special Economic Zones in India: An Introduction." *Asien* 106: 60–80.

East Asia Forum. 2016. "India's EOUs Flourished… So What Happened?" *Economy Watch*, Jun. 20, 2016. Available at: http://www.economywatch.com/features/Indias-EOUs-Flourished-So-What-Happened0620.html (accessed 10 October 2016).

Engman, Michael, Osamu Onodera, and Enrico Pinali. Pinali. 2007. "Export Processing Zones: Past And Future Role In Trade And Development." *OECD Trade Policy Working Paper*, No. 53, OECD Trade Directorate. Available at: http://search.oecd.org/officialdocuments/displaydocumentpdf/?cote=TD/TC/WP(2006)39/FINAL&docLanguage=En (accessed 29 October 2016).

EOU India. 2016. "Facts and Figures." Export Promotion Council for EOUs and SEZs, homepage. Available at: http://eouindia.gov.in/fact_figure.htm#111 (accessed 29 October 2016).

Ghani, Ejaz, and Stephen D. O'Connell. 2014. "Can Service Be a Growth Escalator in Low Income Countries?" *World Bank Policy Research Working Paper* 6971. Available at: http://documents.worldbank.org/curated/en/823731468002999348/pdf/WPS6971.pdf (accessed 29 October 2016).

Gopalakrishnan, Shankar. 2011. "SEZs in India: An economic policy or a political intervention?." In: *Special Economic Zones in Asian Market Economies* (Connie Carter and Andrew Harding eds.). Routledge, New York, pp. 139–155.

Govardan, D., and Vikas Srivastav. 2012. "What SEZ? With Problems Galore, There's Nothing so Special about Special Economic Zones." *The Financial Chronicle*23 November 23. Available at: http://wwa.mydigitalfc.com/news/what-sez-535 (accessed 29 October 2016).

Harding, Andrew. 2011. "The Indian Special Economic Zones Act 2005: Implications for modeling the law and governance of SEZs." In: *Special Economic Zones in Asian Market Economies* (Connie Carter and Andrew Harding eds.). Routledge, New York, pp. 156–171.

Herlevi, April A. 2016. "What's So Special about Special Economic Zones? China's National and Provincial-Level Development Zones." *Isanet* Available at: http://web.isanet.org/Web/Conferences/AP%20Hong%20Kong%202016/Archive/3a83092a-cbfa-4526-85d7-3ca39931b3b4.pdf (accessed 29 October 2016).

IMF (International Monetary Fund). 2016. "World Economic Outlook Database." Available at: http://www.imf.org/external/pubs/ft/weo/2016/01/weodata/index.aspx (accessed November 3, 2016).

Keshava, S.R. 2008. "The Effect of FDI on India and Chinese Economy: A Comparative Analysis." *Second Singapore International Conference on Finance*2008. Available at: http://ssrn.com/abstract=1089964 (accessed 29 October 2016).

Khan, Saeed. 2008. "India's SEZ – Business Zones Development: Economic Performance, Social/Environmental Impacts." *SSRN*The Jamnalal Bajaj Institute of Management Studies, Mumbai. Available at: http://ssrn.com/abstract=1292195 (accessed 29 October 2016).

Kochhar, Kalpana, Utsav Kumar, Raghuram Rajan, Arvind Subramanian, and Ioannis Tokatlidis. 2006. "India's pattern of development: What happened, what follows." NBER Working Paper No. 12023. Available at: http://www.nber.org/papers/w12023 (accessed 29 October 2016).

Kotwal, Ashok, Bharat Ramaswami, and Wilima Wadhwa. 2011. "Economic Liberalization and Indian Economic Growth: What's the Evidence?" *Journal of Economic Literature* 49(4): 1152–1199.

Kundra, Ashok. 2000. *The Performance of India's Export Zones: A Comparison with the Chinese Approach*. SAGE Publications.

Levien, Michael. 2011. "Special Economic Zones and Accumulation by Dispossession in India." *Journal of Agrarian Change* 11(4): 454–483.

Levien, Michael. 2012. "The Land Question: Special Economic Zones and the Political Economy of Dispossession in India." *Journal of Peasant Studies* 39(3–4): 933–969.

Mazumdar, Surajit. 2008. "Crony Capitalism and India. Before and After Liberalization." *Working Paper* 2008/04, Institute for Studies in Industrial Development, New Delhi.

Mitra, Siddhartha. 2007. "Special Economic Zones in India: White Elephants or Race Horses." *SSRN* Available at: http://ssrn.com/abstract=969274 (accessed 29 October 2016).

Mukhopadhyay, Partha, and Kanhu Charan Pradhan. 2009. "Location of SEZs and Policy Benefits What Does the Data Say?" *MPRA Paper* No. 24333, University Library of Munich, Munich, Germany.

Palit, Amitendu, and Subhomoy Bhattacharjee. 2008. *Special Economic Zones in India: Myths and Realities*. Anthem Press, London, New York andDelhi.

Penn WorldTable. 2016. Data available at: http://www.rug.nl/research/ggdc/data/pwt/?lang=en (accessed 29 October 2016). Methodology found in: Feenstra, Robert C., Robert Inklaar and Marcel P. Timmer. 2015. "The Next Generation of the Penn World Table" forthcoming in *American Economic Review*.

PHD Research Bureau. 2015. "SEZs in India: Criss-Cross Concerns." *PHD Chamber of Commerce*.

Rahoof, Abdul TK, and P. G. Arul. 2016. "An Evaluation of Special Economic Zones (SEZs) Performance Post SEZs Act 2005." *Universal Journal of Industrial and Business Management* 4(2): 44–52.

Rajagopalan, Shruti, and Alexander T. Tabarrok. 2014. "Lessons from Gurgaon, India's Private City." *GMU Working Paper in Economics* No. 14–32, Oct. 24, 2014. Available at: http://ssrn.com/abstract=2514652 (accessed 29 October 2016).

Ranjan, Ram Krishna. 2006. "Special Economic Zones: Are They Good for the Country?" Centre for Civil Society, New Delhi. *Working Paper Series* 15(2006): 2009–2010.

Rodrik, Dani. 2016. "Premature Deindustrialization." *Journal of Economic Growth* 21(1): 1–33.

Rodrik, Dani, and Arvind Subramanian. 2005. "From 'Hindu Growth' to Productivity Surge: The Mystery of the Indian Growth Transition." *IMF Staff Papers* 52(2): 193–228.

Roy, Ananya. 2009. "Why India Cannot Plan Its Cities: Informality, Insurgence and the Idiom of Urbanization." *Planning Theory* 8(1): 76–87.

Seshadri, Triyakshana. 2011a. "Is the Path to Higher Exports in India Paved with Export Zones?" *Journal of South Asian Development* 6(1): 25–41.

Seshadri, Triyakshana. 2011b. "Special Economic Zones in India: Landed Before Take-off." Dissertation Chapter 4 in dissertation, *George Mason University.* Available at: http://www.triya-seshadri.com/documents/Triya_Seshadri_Job_Paper.pdf (accessed 29 October 2016).

Seshadri, Triyakshana and Virgil Henry Storr. 2010. "Knowledge Problems Associated with Creating Export Zones." *The Review of Austrian Economics* 23(4): 347–366.

SEZ Division. 2013. No. D.12/45/2009-SEZ. Government of India, Ministry of Commerce and Industry, Department of Commerce (SEZ Division), New Delhi, Sep. 13, 2013. Available at: http://www.sezindia.nic.in/goi-policies-sra.asp (accessed 29 October 2016).

Sharma, Ruchir. 2016. *The Rise and Fall of Nations: Forces of Change in the Post-Crisis World.* W.W. Norton, New York.

Transparency International. 2011. *Daily Lives and Corruption: Public Opinion in South Asia.* Available at: www.transparency.org (accessed 29 October 2016).

UN Trade Statistics. 2016. "Table 36: Imports and exports and indices for countries in national currency." Available at: http://unstats.un.org/unsd/trade/data/tables.asp#monthlytotal (accessed 7 November 2016).

6 How SEZs reformed China

China is the country people most associate with SEZs. The Chinese zones were a prominent part of the country's reforms in the 1980s, and their success sparked a renewed interest in SEZs throughout the world. Modern SEZs had already existed for two decades in other countries when China introduced its zone regime in 1979, but with the rise of the Chinese SEZs, the number of zones began to surge around the world. An ingredient in the Chinese zone recipe was to allow for large zones that could host all kinds of activities. Such all-inclusive SEZs, sometimes covering whole cities, offer more dynamic benefits than the classical industrial parks. The Chinese model is therefore one that many countries have tried to emulate ever since.

China introduced one of its first SEZs in Shenzhen, a city adjacent to Hong Kong. This zone offers a remarkable story of a small fishing village of 20,000 people that grew on the back of its SEZ into a megacity of over 10 million people. However, the Chinese SEZ scheme as a whole had a sluggish start. The process of introducing the first Chinese SEZs was long and rough, and filled with disagreements. The scheme was deemed unprofitable in its first few years, as the proceeds from foreign investments in the zones barely covered the cost of infrastructure. It may have seemed at the time that the Chinese SEZ scheme was about to go a similar way to that of India. As in India, much Chinese SEZ investment went into real estate speculation, and the public sector was heavily involved in SEZ development. Large amounts of smuggled goods also passed from mainland China via Shenzhen to Hong Kong, while other goods were smuggled from abroad to mainland China via the SEZs.[1]

For a while, there was talk of cancelling the SEZ project, but the zones were spared and more of them were introduced instead. In 1984, the fifth SEZ opened along with 14 "coastal cities" with SEZ-like benefits, located along the Chinese coast. A major breakthrough for SEZ policies came in 1992, when all 22 provincial capitals were declared SEZs. Between 1990 and 1995, the proportion of Chinese municipalities hosting SEZs grew from 24 percent to 69 percent, compared to just 9 percent in 1985. By 2008, this share had increased to an impressive 92 percent.[2]

While not all Chinese SEZs have been successful, much points to the Chinese scheme as a whole having been beneficial, not least thanks to its dynamic

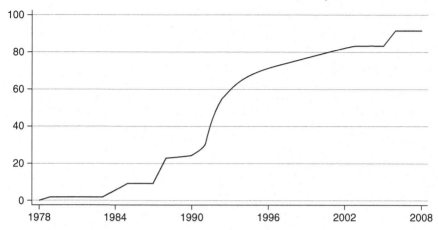

Figure 6.1 Percentage of Chinese municipalities with SEZs across time.
Source: Wang 2013: 134.

effects. Policies that initially showed up only in SEZs were subsequently implemented in other regions, and some even in the country as a whole. It thus seems that the SEZs played in important role in the opening of the Chinese economy.[3] However, scholars who reach such conclusions rely primarily on macroeconomic indicators. A discussion about the policy from a political economy angle will help us better understand the nature of the SEZs' contribution.

Did China solve the knowledge problem?

China has for a long time relied on political decentralization to solve knowledge problems in the country. Scholars have previously noted the benefits of the Chinese decentralized, albeit authoritarian, system.[4] The country is centralized in the sense that the central government can both appoint and dethrone local officials. But because most policy making is decentralized, economic performance of an area is a reflection of policy choices made at the local level. Local governments can thus change policies based on market conditions that the central government would fail to detect. The conduct of China's regional governments has been likened to "a conglomerate or ... a holding company," due to the system of decentralized policy making and clear property rights of subnational governments.[5]

Decentralization also allowed local officials to be innovative with SEZ policies.[6] The SEZ scheme itself was designed in a decentralized fashion, so that locally appointed committees could decide which foreign investors to approve, what infrastructure to supply, and how to regulate the use of land.[7] There are good reasons to believe that this decentralized system played an important role in the success of the SEZs. Local SEZ authorities had sufficient knowledge about market conditions and local businesses to adjust their policies and regulations accordingly. They, rather than the central government, supplied much of the initial infrastructure and oversaw access to utilities. By and large, local officials promoted a good business climate for SEZ investors, with functional administrations and efficient regulations.[8]

Initially, authority over the zones was only semi-decentralized, being divided between local, regional, and state levels. The SEZ scheme was then allowed more decentralization around the years 1981–82, and later in 1984, when factory managers in the zones obtained substantial responsibilities. This development coincided with SEZ industrial investments taking off and the SEZs becoming profitable.[9]

The importance of decentralization is also reflected in the superior performance of zones that enjoyed additional autonomy. The government granted Shenzhen, near Hong Kong, and Pudong, part of the city of Shanghai, special hub-provincial status, which meant their governments obtained more autonomy over local regulations. This was partly in recognition of their importance, but also a way to allow officials overseeing the SEZs to make the necessary policy changes.[10] The Shanghai Stock Exchange, which is located in Pudong, was self-regulated and under municipal supervision, and became a successful center for trade.[11]

Local decision-making sometimes meant the absence of government policy directives. The Shenzhen SEZ seems initially to have been held back by a directive mandating that all foreign investors in the zone be high-technology firms. When this clause was replaced by a weaker phrase about "some technology," zone investors could more readily use the area's abundant cheap labor.[12] Fewer and weaker SEZ regulations thus allowed the zone to better match its local capacity.

While not perfect, it is likely that the Chinese system of political decentralization helped solve the country's knowledge problem. When mistakes were made, local officials could detect the problem and decide to change their conduct to solve it. More-decentralized regulation sometimes even meant no regulation, as the officials saw benefits in leaving more decisions in the hands of private actors.

Did China solve the incentive problem?

China's decentralized but authoritarian system also helped solve the incentive problem. The Chinese system of governance seems to have had a similar effect to a democratic system by making local officials accountable for the economic success of their jurisdictions. Chinese local leaders answer to the central government, which can promote them with higher positions and salaries for meeting certain economic goals, and punish them if they fail.[13]

With the Chinese reforms underway, the central government incentivized its subordinate officials to compete with each other for central-government promotions by beating each other at producing economic progress. Chinese local leaders were thus engaging in something of a tournament of economic performance with their SEZs. With their promotion and employment on the line, they were incentivized to govern in ways that improved the local economy.[14]

China was also fiscally decentralized, which gave local leaders further reasons to generate growth. In 1977, the country introduced revenue-sharing contracts between the central and local governments. The contracts stated quite clearly the share of local revenues that was attributed to the central government. While local governments did not keep all local revenue, this revenue-sharing system gave them property rights over a well-specified part of it. Similarly to commercial enterprises, they could thus plan how to use and benefit from their proceeds.[15]

Fiscal decentralization combined with the Chinese political reward system was key in solving SEZ-related incentive problems. For local policy makers, economic growth meant both higher local revenues and chances to win more political power and status. They thus had the incentive to use SEZs to attract businesses and encourage them to invest, instead of using the zones to deliver favors to cronies. As a result, the liberalized business environment the SEZs offered brought benefits that were larger than the costs of the rent-seeking and mistargeted investments related to the scheme. Because China seems to have solved both the knowledge problem and the incentive problem related to SEZs, the zones were likely an improvement for the country compared to the status quo.

Did the Chinese SEZs lead to general reform?

The next question to ask is whether the Chinese zones contributed to the country's reform process, and thus did much more than marginally improve on the status quo. Those arguing that the Chinese SEZs promoted reforms generally tend to describe them as test beds or showcases for new policies. However, these functions were not the main benefits of the Chinese zones. In what follows, I will first describe how the SEZs may have helped policy makers solve knowledge problems in their role as test beds and showcases for reforms. I will then argue that the greatest value of the SEZs lay in the way a minority power elite could use them to spur reform in the country as a whole.

The way the Chinese SEZs could work as test beds is straightforward. The SEZs served as small and confined laboratories where different reforms could be tried out. Local policy makers could test various SEZ policies to find the ones that worked best. Legal, labor, financial, and pricing policies could first be tried out in one zone, and then implemented in another. Chinese businesses could experiment with Western technology methods and see what forms of capitalism they could combine with the Chinese system.[16] One local leader could observe the success and mistakes of another, and thus become better informed about what SEZ policies work better than others.[17]

When the elites in the Communist Party could observe a policy's success, they could allow its adoption widely, independently of SEZs. In that way, particularly beneficial and applicable policies were eventually implemented countrywide.

To some extent, the SEZs also worked as showcases for capitalism. Progressive party elites could point to successful SEZs to convince skeptical powerful people in the Communist Party of their virtues and benefits. Crucially, the first experiments with SEZs showed that more influence of capitalism would not destroy the socialist society and spirit, as some had feared. Attempting to sooth such worries, the vice premier of China, Deng Xiaoping, described them as tools a socialist society can use to promote economic prosperity. As such, they would strengthen the socialist system rather than weaken it.[18]

Reform of Chinese state-owned enterprises was an important part of the journey to capitalism. The SEZs experimented with governance and incentive structures that made the enterprises more competitive. Having previously enjoyed soft budget constraints, state-owned enterprises in some SEZs saw their constraints harden, which imposed a level of market discipline on them. And while state-owned firms were previously to live up to their production quotas, they were now rewarded based on profitability and competitiveness.[19]

SEZs also experimented with privatization of state-owned firms, with the SEZ in Shenzhen becoming the first to embark on such reforms.[20] As early as 1986, Shenzhen's municipal government selected companies to become joint-stock enterprises. In 1990, it also allowed foreign companies to invest in the former state-owned enterprises, as well as for state-owned enterprises to go public.[21] As SEZs spread, more state-owned firms were converted into free enterprises throughout the country.[22]

In these ways and others, SEZs could serve as showcases for reforms. When others saw the prosperity the zones generated, they would appreciate the economic dynamism liberal policies brought.

While the Chinese SEZs did in part serve as policy test beds and showcases, they could only have contributed small improvements by performing these roles. By these mechanisms, the SEZs could only speed up a process toward reforms that would have happened anyway. Eventually, both policy makers and the general public would understand what the most beneficial policies were. Without the SEZs, this just would have taken a bit longer.

The depiction of SEZs as test beds or showcases relies on political leaders agreeing that their goal is to find policies that benefit the people. Their only disagreement can be about what those policies are. If this were the case, China would already have had the political momentum of reform. It would also likely have been more open in the 1970s than it was.

Instead of such benevolence, policy makers more likely have the incentive to pursue rent-seeking opportunities when it benefits them and promote social welfare primarily for the sake of personal gains. They will be unlikely to change their behavior just because they see that a policy is good for society at large. Therefore, whether used as test beds or showcases for reform, the SEZs could not have staked out a path the country would not otherwise have taken.

Chinese SEZs at their best

While the SEZs were hardly crucial for China's reform path in the role of policy test beds or showcases, they have many features of SEZs at their best, described in Chapter 3.

The SEZs were used by a minority of the Chinese elite to gradually change the incentive structure of other powerful officials. The first initiative for special zones came from businessmen based in Shekou in Guangdong province. They had interests in property and other commercial investments in nearby Hong Kong and wanted better conditions to conduct business in the then-British colony. To lobby for policy change, they turned to Ye Fei, the minister of transport, who granted them a special deregulated area from which they could do business in Hong Kong. The minister thus became one of the earliest proponents of SEZs among Chinese top officials. The central government opened the Shekou Industrial Zone in 1979, which facilitated joint ventures and cooperation between a Hong Kong based Chinese shipping company and foreign businesses.[23]

The secretary for the Guangdong province soon became a public supporter of the zone policy. He may have realized early on that the zones created more than opportunities for the businesses in the province. If they could promote economic growth, they would also benefit him personally. The central government soon granted Guangdong the first three Chinese SEZs, while a fourth SEZ was introduced in the Fujian province.[24]

The political pressure for SEZs thus emerged in a bottom-up fashion, with businessmen lobbying policy makers to take a positive view on the zones, and local policy makers being awarded zones by the central government.

Most policy makers did not share this interest in reforms. There were many disputes surrounding the SEZs in which anti-reformers in the central government clashed with people with interests in the prosperity of the SEZs. After the zone in Fujian was introduced, such conflicts halted any further expansion of the SEZ program for four years.[25]

At the time, the SEZs enjoyed the support of only a handful of people among the more influential officials. With time, though, more officials became zone promoters, which was manifested in 1984 in the introduction of the SEZ in Hainan together with 14 coastal zones. Following this zone expansion, the support for SEZs among the party elites started to take hold. It was also around this time that Deng Xiaoping came on board with the idea, after touring Shenzhen, Zhuhai, and Xiamen and being impressed by their progress. Others from the party elite then followed his lead in supporting the increasingly popular SEZs.[26]

Pro-reformers had to tread carefully to allow for each step in this process to be accepted. Great leaps of liberalization were politically infeasible in the rigid economic system, but the SEZs were limited enough to be introduced despite most officials' resistance to liberalizing reforms.

Pro-reformers also limited the extent to which the SEZs could include domestic businesses. Were their business environments to become superior, the zones would be a clear threat to other regions from which they might attract businesses. To prevent such a development from spurring strong opposition, pro-reformers agreed that SEZs were primarily going to aim to attract foreign investors. They also agreed that the SEZ scheme would be explicitly combined with import substitution, to please officials who benefited from protectionism.[27]

For the same reason, the fact that the SEZ system seems initially to have been insufficiently decentralized may not have been a result of ignorance about the importance of decentralization. In light of the conflict over the existence of SEZs, their limited autonomy was perhaps a necessary condition for some anti-reformers to be persuaded to support the idea. Reformist elites may thus have been forced to limit SEZ decentralization to avoid a radical deterioration of anti-reform officials' rents. Only by allowing the anti-reformers to maintain a certain amount of control could the reformist elite muster enough support for SEZs. A few years later, when SEZs were more popular, the central government could allow more decentralization of the scheme by ridding SEZ businesses of several regulations and other bureaucratic obstacles.[28]

It thus seems that the SEZs won gradual acceptance and could be increasingly liberalized as more people in the governing elite found they could benefit from the policy. It is unclear how pro-reformers convinced enough officials who were against liberalization to support the scheme so that its expansion could continue. Yet they were clearly restrained in how radical the SEZ policies could initially be. Limiting the zones' autonomy, restricting the number of domestic firms investing in them, and combining the zones with protectionism are all ways to limit the costs of anti-reformers. If they had threatened the rent-seeking elites too much, the SEZs would hardly have been allowed to spread nationwide.

The importance of decentralization

China's decentralized system did more than solve the knowledge and incentive problems. Political and fiscal decentralization was also crucial for the growing support of SEZs. Fiscal decentralization made more local leaders support reform, as well as support more reforms at the central government level.[29] With the help of the SEZs, the institutionalized decentralization helped open up the Chinese economy. Once the zones were in place, fiscal decentralization incentivized local policy makers to make them attractive for investors and beneficial for the local economy. More importantly, the benefits SEZs provided to local policy makers made them introduce the zones in the first place. This incentive structure generated the local demand for SEZs that sparked their emergence.

The locations of the initial SEZs reflect their reliance on local rather than central-government demand. Spread out along the coast, they had access to ports and other crucial transportation infrastructure. Less obviously, the locations of the first SEZs were also the sources of many emigrants from

China. These emigrants, having built up capital abroad, were readier than most to invest in China as it opened up.[30]

The SEZs were also quite far away from Beijing. That may look like a reflection of the government's plan to avoid radical economic experiments taking place on their doorstep. However, there is a reason to believe that a very different calculation was at play. Because SEZs inevitably risk attracting businesses from nearby areas, officials living off rent-seeking in nearby areas may need to be compensated for the SEZ introduction. This may be too expensive if the area boasts a lot of rent-seeking, which is likely to be the case where the central government is located. It is therefore likely that no pro-reformer found it feasible to pursue an SEZ near Beijing.

Fiscal decentralization in China provided local leaders with a trade-off between revenues from rent-seeking and local taxation. Besides money from the central government and proceeds from their local taxation, local leaders could cultivate personal ties with local businesses and earn illicit rents. In jurisdictions with sluggish growth, various forms of rent-seeking may even have been the main source of personal wealth for local officials. Encouraging rent-seeking, however, has its downside in the form of an unattractive business climate and a loss in tax revenues.

Had the Chinese system not been fiscally decentralized, this might not have mattered for local policy makers. They would, in any case, not have enjoyed the fruits of tax revenues. However, thanks to China's fiscal decentralization, more rent-seeking meant lower tax revenues for local officials. A dishonest business climate discourages investments and thus lowers the fiscal revenue. This may also mean smaller chances of promotion by the central government, when local leaders are rewarded for good economic performance. When China's local leaders could use SEZs to boost growth more than previously, the opportunity costs of rent-seeking increased further.

The same dynamic encouraged some municipalities to privatize their state-owned enterprises. While officials could earn rents by hosting state companies, forcing them to compete in a more market based manner not only made them more efficient but also created a more competitive local business climate.[31] In the case of the state-owned enterprises, the incentive to privatize was especially strong because the tax revenues from private companies were not shared with the central government, which was the case with state-owned enterprises.[32]

There was always a risk the central government would centralize the system and confiscate some of the wealth local leaders could amass. However, rather than such a risk working against economic progress, this may have been a reason for local officials to invest much of the local proceeds rather than keeping it in forms that could be easily extracted. They could "store" official proceeds in the form of investments in the region's enterprises and people. This limited the opportunity for the central government to confiscate assets from the regions and hence reverse the reform trend.[33]

The central government embarked on a fiscal recentralization effort in the beginning of the 1990s, which was formally in place in 1994. This was meant to compensate for falling revenues from state-owned companies, as they were facing new competition from private companies.[34] The reforms aimed to simplify the tax system, increase the tax share of the central government, and increase the share of tax revenue to GDP. The government succeeded in all but the latter, which meant local governments saw a noticeable decline in their official tax revenues.[35]

The recentralization incentivized local governments to increase their "informal off-budget revenues", as opposed to formal tax revenues, to shield the proceeds from the central government. With increased fiscal centralization, local elites engaged in more rent-seeking as opposed to formal taxation, as the proceeds from the latter were increasingly shared with the rest of the country.[36]

Recentralization did not, however, imply a reversion of SEZ policies. Instead, China saw the largest increase in municipalities with SEZs in the beginning of the 1990s.[37] The zones may have been a tool for local governments to shield their revenues from the central government. The SEZs, which by then had taken on a dynamic of their own, may therefore be what shielded local governments from having to pursue a reversal of the progress that Chinese decentralization helped bring about.

The Chinese SEZs fit the model of how zones can be at their very best. They could make policy makers choose to promote economic reform instead of protecting rent-seeking opportunities. Most public officials could probably not benefit from liberalization at first. If they could, a majority of the elite would have supported liberalization from the start, and the country would not have needed SEZs to enact reforms. However, thanks to the SEZs, the country did not need the majority of its ruling elite to be interested in reform in order to pursue it.

Rather than a conscious plan for national economic reform, the introduction of SEZs in China was driven by local demand to promote a better business climate in particular municipalities or provinces. Among the elite, it was a highly contested policy. Most officials were understandably reluctant to support a policy that could jeopardize their rent-seeking sources. Only when the SEZs started spreading across the country and the economic climate in China as a whole was changing did the SEZs win majority support. Like a snowy mountain shaken only slightly by isolated snow slides that eventually become strong enough to cause an avalanche, so China was reformed by isolated areas of reform that eventually turned into an avalanche of liberalization.

The self-reinforcing dynamic of China's SEZ reform

As soon as the SEZs started proliferating, they seemed to take on their own dynamic. A few years into the scheme, it would even withstand a seemingly hard blow. In 1985, a corruption scandal erupted in the young SEZ of Hainan, allowing critics to point to the reckless way in which SEZs opened the country to the world and to blame the zones for the ills of corruption. Bureaucrats and the media were also blaming the SEZs for causing "spiritual pollution". However, despite such criticism and the emerging evidence of SEZs corruption, the SEZ scheme suffered no serious consequences. The government made some cosmetic changes, with more monitoring of SEZs and retraction of some of their autonomy. By then, however, the scheme had gained so much traction that it could not be reversed.[38]

As more SEZs were introduced, more officials started to support them. As the environment changed, the opportunities to earn higher tax revenues by joining the liberalization movement increased. At the same time, it grew more difficult to foster rent-seeking through local protectionism and monopolies.

The reformers were enjoying increasing political power as more people joined their side. When all of China's provincial capitals were designated SEZs in 1992, more than half of China's municipalities became SEZ hosts. This may have been the crucial time at which the SEZs started enjoying majority support, allowing them to spread to almost all of China's municipalities by 2008.[39]

China may be the best example of SEZs at their best. A minority of politically connected people could introduce the first zone as a policy that posed only a small threat to the rent-seeking opportunities of other elites. As time went on, an increasing number of regions and cities could gain greater revenues through local liberalization than through potential rent-seeking. Between 1980 and 1985, the level of economic freedom in the country as a whole increased markedly, a trend that continued well into the new millennium.[40] With greater liberalization in the country as a whole, more policy makers could benefit from further liberalization and were thus incentivized to support SEZ expansion.

Today, China is by no means a country free from corruption, but it is at least not severe enough to prevent further economic progress. The liberalizations the government introduced have allowed for policies that promote economic growth and development that overshadow the rent-seeking still taking place. When compared to the corruption in the United States when it was at the equivalent level of development as today's China, the United States actually looks several times more corrupt.[41] Since the United States subsequently improved both institutionally and economically, corruption should not prevent China from growing in the future.

China has come a long way from isolation to openness. While few would dispute that SEZs played a role in this process, there are different views on how important they were and through what mechanism they contributed to change. The dominating story about the Chinese SEZs is that they succeeded thanks to forceful and committed leadership by Deng Xiaoping and others at the top of the Communist Party. This version of history cannot be disproven, in particular as any local initiative sanctioned by the central government would ultimately be portrayed as the latter's project. However, the theory of the central government driven SEZ program suggests that the SEZs were not crucial for the reform of the Chinese economy, as the powerful leaders pushing for change could have found other ways to accomplish it.

The description of Deng as a pivotal figure in China's reform suggests that they would never have happened without him. The theory about the emergence of a reform-minded elite suggests that change instead came about as some leaders started seeing opportunities in openness. Indeed, while China had previously traded predominantly with the Soviet Union and Eastern Europe, ruptures in those relationships meant a pivot for China towards the capitalist world. As it improved relations with the West and Japan in the 1970s, prospects for beneficial trade relations became increasingly promising.[42]

This analysis suggests instead that the SEZs played a significant role and they did so not by merely revealing the effects of liberalizing reforms. Instead, they changed the incentives of officials, making them invest in economic growth rather than in rent-seeking. As the pro-reform minority eventually became a majority, they could push for broader reforms. Only then could the Chinese rulers correctly be labeled reformist.

Not a tool to avoid reforms

A different interpretation of the Chinese SEZ scheme is that the government used it to liberalize on the margin while preserving protectionism in the rest of the country.[43] If that were the case, however, they did a poor job of it. They should certainly not have introduced such large and diversified zones, whose external effects ultimately pushed the country toward broader reforms. As we will see in the next chapter, the Dominican Republic is a much better example of how a country can stave off broader liberalization by adopting SEZs in the form of smaller industrial parks.

China's larger zones encompassed whole cities, a feature that promoted integration. The Chinese zones also affected the business climate in the country as a whole, which made it marginally more profitable for local policy makers to invest in a more welcoming and liberalized business environment. Smaller zones would hardly have generated such external effects. Given its control over the economy, it seems the Communist Party could have controlled this development differently if one of the goals of the SEZ scheme was to restrain reform.

The reform of the business climate has not been geographically even, of course. Decentralization in China, besides driving the reform process, also made China into an economy of separation between its regions, which ultimately prevented the development of a fully fledged national market. However, uneven development does not imply a central government's intentional duality. While some regions remained more protectionist than others, this was driven by a decentralized dynamic of heterogeneity, rather than the central government's imposition of policies on its regions.[44]

For other governments with potential to reform, the Chinese success story provides a cautionary tale. On the one hand, China demonstrates how SEZs can help pro-reformers in a minority to break out of a rent-seeking status quo. On the other hand, it does not give any guidance to pro-reformist central governments. SEZs are at their best only when they can change the incentives of central-government rulers from promoting protectionism to pursuing liberalizing reforms. If the government is already pursuing liberalization, the SEZs have no role in changing its incentives in that direction. Citing the Chinese case as proof that "governments" can use SEZs to promote development is therefore misleading. If a government really wants reform, it should probably consider other, less distortionary measures.

The same peculiar political circumstances that made China a great example of SEZ success may also be the reason other countries should avoid trying to copy it. There may never again be a case like China, where Chinese-style SEZs can so radically transform an illiberal system. While SEZs have the potential to do much more for a country than they are generally given credit for, they very rarely show their best side.

Notes

1 Wong and Chu 1985; Crane 1990: 62–75, 105.
2 Wang 2013: 136; Alexander 2014: 11.
3 Crane 1994; Ge 1999: 1283; Fu and Gao 2007: 22–23.
4 Xu 2011.
5 Li et al. 2000: 283.
6 Oi 1992; Xu 2011: 1109, 1111.
7 Wang 2013: 136.
8 Zeng 2011: 17.
9 Crane 1990: 55, 82–85, 101.
10 Chen 1995: 604.
11 Xu 2011: 1131.
12 White 2011: 198.
13 Oi 1992: 114; Xu 2011: 1093, 1099, 1104.
14 Id. Admittedly, producing high GDP figures on a local level also incentivizes the forging of exaggerated data (Economist 2016). By no means do I claim that the data local governments report to the central government are completely accurate. However, this does not mean local leaders lack the incentive to promote growth. To be made credible, exaggerated data need at least to be matched to some extent by real economic progress.
15 Oi 1992: 103; Li et al. 2000: 283; Chen et al. 2002: 194.
16 Wong and Chu 1985: 6.
17 Crane 1990: 91–98; Ge 1999: 1268, 1281; Cling and Letilly 2001: 7; Xu 2011: 1115.
18 Crane 1994: 94; Coase and Wang 2012.
19 Ge 1999: 1281.
20 Yeung et al. 2009: 232.
21 Yuan et al. 2010: 65, 69.
22 McKennedy 1993: 32.
23 Sit 1985: 75; Crane 1990: 26, 156.
24 Coase and Wang 2012: 60–62; Crane 1990: 27.
25 Crane 1990: 20, 28, 34.
26 Id.: 1990: 156; McKennedy 1993: 10.
27 Crane 1990: 117–22.

28 Id.: 76–79.
29 Chen et al. 2002: 196.
30 Wong and Chu 1985; 41.
31 Zhou et al. 2016: 5.
32 Qian 1999: 158.
33 Weingast et al. 1996: 69.
34 Chen et al. 2002: 196.
35 Ahmad and Richardson 2002: 6–8.
36 Chen 2004: 1002.
37 Wang 2013: 134.
38 Crane 1990: 111; McKennedy 1993: 12.
39 Wang 2013: 136; Alexander 2014.
40 During this period, the country improved in the Fraser Institute's Index of Economic Freedom from a score of 4.0 to 5.1. By 2005, China had increased its economic-freedom score to 6.3 (Economic Freedom Network 2016).
41 Ramirez 2014.
42 Wong and Chu 1985: 31.
43 Rodrik 2014: 200.
44 Naughton 1999: 32; Meyer 2008: 4.

References

Ahmad, Ehtisham, and Thomas Richardson. 2002. "Recentralization in China?" IMF Working Paper 02/168.

Alexander, Payton. 2014. "Laboratories for Capitalism: Testing the Limits of the Special Economic Zones of Mainland China Politics." MA Dissertation for the School of Social and Political Science, *University of Edinburgh*.

Chen, Xiangming. 1995. "The Evolution of Free Economic Zones and the Recent Development of Cross-National Growth Zones." *International Journal of Urban and Regional Research* 19(4): 593–621.

Chen, Kang. 2004. "Fiscal Centralization and the Form of Corruption in China." *European Journal of Political Economy* 20: 1001–1009.

Chen, Kang, Arye L. Hillman, and Qingyang Gu. 2002. "From the Helping Hand to the Grabbing Hand: Fiscal Federalism and Corruption in China." In: *China's Economy into the New Century: Structural Issues and Problems* (John Wong and Ku Ding eds.). Singapore University Press and World Scientific, Singapore, pp. 193–215.

Cling, Jean-Pierre, and Gaëlle Letilly. 2001. "Export Processing Zones: A Threatened Instrument for Global Economy Insertion?" *DIAL Working paper* DT/2001/17. Available at: http://ideas.repec.org/p/dia/wpaper/dt200117.html (accessed 29 October 2016).

Coase, Ronald and Ning Wang. 2012. *How China Became Capitalist*. Palgrave MacMillan, New York.

Crane, George T. 1990. *The Political Economy of China's Special Economic Zones*. M. E. Sharpe Inc., Armonk, New York and London, England.

Crane, George T. 1994. "Special Things in Special Ways: National Economic Identity and China's Special Economic Zones." *The Australian Journal of Chinese Affairs* 32: 71–92.

Economic Freedom Network. 2016. Data on homepage, China, Fraser Institute. Available at: http://www.freetheworld.com/countrydata.php?country=C27&x=61& y=11 (accessed 29 October 2016).

Economist, The. 2016. "Growth Targets Grossly Deceptive Plans." *The Economist,* Jan. 30, 2016. Available at: http://www.economist.com/news/china/21689628-chinas-obsession-gdp-targets-threatens-its-economy-grossly-deceptive-plans (accessed 29 October 2016).

Fu, Xiaolan, and Yuning Gao. 2007. "Export Processing Zones in China: A Survey." International Labour Organization, Geneva.

Ge, Wei, 1999. "Special Economic Zones and the Opening of the Chinese Economy: Some Lessons for Economic Liberalization." *World Development* 27(7): 1267–1285.

Li, Shaomin, Shuhe Li, and Weiying Zhang. 2000. "The Road to Capitalism: Competition and Institutional Change in China." *Journal of Comparative Economics* 28: 269–292.

McKennedy, Karen I. 1993. "An Assessment of China's Special Economic Zones." The Industrial College of the Armed Forces Report, DTIC Selected Mar. 10, 1994.

Meyer, Marshall W. 2008. "China's Second Economic Transition: Building National Markets." *Management and Organization Review* 4(1): 3–15.

Naughton, Barry. 1999. "China's Dual Trading Regimes: Implications for Growth and Reform." In: *International Trade Policy and the Pacific Rim: Proceedings of the IEA Conference Held in Sydney, Australia* (John Piggott and Alan Woodland eds.). Macmillan Press, Hampshire, UKand St Martin's Press, New York, pp. 30–55.

Oi, Jean C. 1992. "Fiscal Reform and the Economic Foundations of Local State Corporatism in China." *World Politics* 45(1): 99–126.

Qian, Yingyi. 1999. "The Process of China's Market Transition (1978–1998): The Evolutionary, Historical, and Comparative Perspective." *Journal of Institutional and Theoretical Economics* 156(1): 151–171.

Ramirez, Carlos D. 2014. "Is corruption in China 'out of control'? A comparison with the US in historical perspective." *Journal of Comparative Economics* 42(1): 76–91.

Rodrik, Dani. 2014. "When Ideas Trump Interests: Preferences, Worldviews, and Policy Innovations." *The Journal of Economic Perspectives* 28(1): 189–208.

Sit, Victor F.S. 1985. "Specials Economic Zones in China: A New Type of Export Processing Zone?" *The Developing Economies* 23(2): 69–87.

Wang, Jin. 2013. "The Economic Impact of Special Economic Zones: Evidence from Chinese Municipalities." *Journal of Development Economics* 101: 133–147.

Weingast, Barry R., Gabriella Montinola and Yingyi Qian. 1996. "Federalism, Chinese Style: The Political Basis for Economic Success." *World Politics* 48(1): 50–81.

White, Justine. 2011. "Fostering Innovation in Developing Economies through SEZs." In: *Special Economic Zones: Progress, Emerging Challenges, and Future Directions* (Thomas Farole and Gokhan Akinci eds.). The World Bank, Washington, D.C., pp. 183–205.

Wong, Kwan-Yiu, and David K.Y. Chu. 1985. *Modernization in China: the case of the Shenzhen special economic zone.* Oxford University Press, Hong Kong.

Xu, Chenggang. 2011. "The Fundamental Institutions of China's Reforms and Development." *Journal of Economic Literature* 49(4): 1076–1151.

Yeung, Yue-man, Joanna Lee, and Gordon Kee. 2009. "China's Special Economic Zones at 30." *Eurasian Geography and Economics* 50(2): 222–240.

Yuan, Yiming, Hongyi Guo, Hongfei Xu, Weiqi Li, Shanshan Luo, Haiqing Lin, and Yuan Yuan. 2010. "China's First Special Economic Zone: The Case of Shenzhen." In: *Building Engines for Growth and Competitiveness in China: Experience with Special Economic Zones and Industrial Clusters* (Douglas Zhihua Zeng ed.). The World Bank, Washington D.C, pp. 55–86.

Zeng, Douglas Zhihua. 2011. "How do Special Economic Zones and Industrial Clusters Drive China's Rapid Development?" *World Bank, Policy Research Working Paper* No. 5583.

Zhou, Yi, Canfei He, and Shengjun Zhu. 2016. "Does Creative Destruction Work for Chinese Regions?" *Growth and Change*, forthcoming. Online Early View version available at: http://onlinelibrary.wiley.com/doi/10.1111/grow.12168/full (accessed 7 November 2016).

7 Dividing the Dominican Republic[1]

The Dominican Republic has been described as an SEZ success story, with zones that have attracted investments and encouraged exports. The Dominican SEZs play a significant role in the country's economy and have a sophisticated and diverse production base.[2] However, the scheme is also criticized for failing to spread this growth and sophistication to the Dominican economy at large. The zones have become "islands of excellence" as isolated spots of development in a developing economy, with few signs of integration with the economy as a whole.[3]

After the first SEZ opened in 1969, the scheme initially grew slowly. By 1985, the Dominican Republic hosted only four SEZs, with 31,000 workers in 136 firms in total. Since then, however, the SEZ scheme has shown remarkable growth, with employment peaking at over 195,000 in 2000.[4] International liberalization of trade in textiles subsequently caused a decline that lasted until 2009.

The Dominican Republic provides a good case to understand the success and developments of SEZ schemes in other relatively small countries in the region. SEZs are a popular policy in Latin America, where exports have long benefited from natural resources, cheap labor, and geographical and political proximity to the United States.[5] Among Central American countries, SEZs generate more than 40 percent of exports and more than 4 percent of all official jobs in El Salvador, Honduras, Nicaragua, and Costa Rica. Guatemala generates almost 40 percent of its exports but less than 2 percent of employment in SEZs.[6] Guatemala's relatively low headcount is primarily due to its specialized production in such areas as pharmaceuticals and business-process outsourcing, which are less labor intensive than textile manufacturing.[7] Yet despite hosting seemingly successful SEZs, countries such as the Dominican Republic, Honduras, and Nicaragua remain quite poor as a whole.[8]

The SEZ schemes in this region thus share many features, which makes studying a representative regime useful for insights about the others as well. As we will see, the success of the Dominican scheme is no illusion, and in contrast to India, it seems better than the status quo. However, because the scheme served to avoid broader liberalization, it did not lead to general reforms, and thus falls within the middle categories of SEZ success.

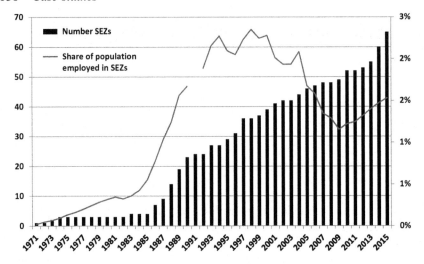

Figure 7.1 The number of EPZs (left-hand scale) and share of the population employed in the EPZs (right-hand scale)
(Sources: CNZFE 1992; 1993; 1994; 1995; 1996; 1997; 1998; 1999; 2000; 2001; 2002; 2003; 2004; 2005; 2006; 2007; 2008; 2009; 2010; 2011; 2012; 2013; 2014; 2015.)

Did the Dominican Republic solve the knowledge problem?

SEZs in the Dominican Republic are regulated by the Dominican Zone Authority, which reports to the central government. There is one legal framework for all SEZs in the country, with extra benefits for zones located near the underdeveloped region close to the border with Haiti. The Dominican system is thus not particularly decentralized. However, with a population of only 10 million people, centralization does not necessarily cause the knowledge problems that it does in India, with almost 1.3 billion people. To put this smallness in perspective, the Dominican Republic has roughly as many people as Shenzhen, which is the oldest of China's SEZs. Nevertheless, if the Dominican government were to choose the locations of all 55 zones in the country and develop them, it would surely fall prey to the knowledge problem.

Fortunately, the Dominican Republic is predominantly and increasingly relying on privately developed zones. Currently, only 15 out of 55 zones are developed by the government. This compares to 22 out of 54 zones a decade earlier.[9] The scheme has always had a mix of public and private zones. The very first Dominican SEZ was private, developed and dominated by a private sugar company.[10] The private zones tend to be highly developed, with good infrastructure and business services. The public zones, by contrast, offer more basic amenities.

Thanks to its high reliance on private zone development, the Dominican Republic seems to have solved the knowledge problem quite well. Private developers determine the location of SEZs and pay for the land they use. It is also up to them to decide what industries to invite, as the country's SEZ law does not explicitly restrict any activities, and opens SEZs to most areas of manufacturing and services.[11] SEZ locations therefore tend to reflect market conditions.

On the whole, the private zones in the Dominican Republic are well run and attractive to SEZ businesses. The public zones are simpler, and some are quite empty, with abandoned government infrastructure. Yet such failures may be compensated for by the success of the private SEZs.[12] Also, since the government mostly does not spend lavishly on fancy facilities in the public zones, misallocation of resources is limited. Because companies in public zones provide their own amenities and utilities to a large extent, some public zones are in practice more decentralized than private ones.

The knowledge problem has therefore not manifested itself as much in the Dominican Republic as it did in the more centralized system of India. And while political decentralization was crucial for China to overcome the knowledge problem, the Dominican Republic can thank the private nature of its SEZ scheme for its success.

Did the Dominican Republic solve the incentive problem?

The reliance on privately developed zones seems also to have solved the incentive problem in the Dominican Republic. The location of an SEZ is mostly determined by private investors who buy or rent the land they find most suitable. They must decide whether setting up or expanding a zone will likely be profitable. Because they will refrain from the investment if it will likely yield a loss, the incentives of these private developers are aligned with creating value.

The government, by contrast, is often biased toward locating SEZs in unattractive regions for political reasons. Dominican politicians want to develop and create jobs in the area near the border with Haiti, to alleviate poverty for the people there and discourage some of the migration of Haitians to the Dominican cities. They are therefore offering particularly attractive incentives for investors who develop zones in the border area. However, with only three zones registered near the border, it is clear that developers do not see great prospects in locating in the border region, despite extra incentives.[13] Fortunately, the government has not gone so far as to develop zones on its own where private investors dare not tread.

While the policy of developing the border area has largely failed, it is not a failure from an economic standpoint. The vast underdeveloped areas merely signal their unattractiveness. As long as no great amounts of capital are wasted in the area, these attempts are not a drain on the economy and thus not a failure.

The differences between private and public zones in the Dominican Republic illustrate the different incentives of companies and public authorities. Several private SEZs offer high-quality services to their tenant companies, including water, electricity, garbage collection, and sometimes even fire brigades and medical facilities. According to one private zone developer, the only service in the park that companies complained about was the customs administration. The zone developers were obliged to host a government bureaucrat to take care of the customs filings and provide the official with an office. The problem was that the customs official would frequently fail to show up, thus causing problems for businesses that needed to get the paperwork done for imports or exports. The presence or absence of a customs official was, alas, not under the developer's control.

Public zones may fail to utilize economies of scale through the provision of amenities to SEZ firms, but those choosing to enter public zones are more likely to do well without this provision. While public zones are simpler than private ones, they generally charge lower fees from SEZ firms. Therefore, they tend to attract companies that need to keep their costs low and are large enough to supply their own utilities and infrastructure. As a result, textile manufacturers occupy much of the public SEZ space. With the government providing such zones, it is somewhat of an irony that an official goal is to expand the SEZ scheme to include companies that rely more on highly skilled labor and less on low wages, which best describes the kind of companies more commonly found in privately developed SEZs.

Private developers have the incentive to invest in profitable zones and take on promising tenants. Before allowing them to invest, developers therefore assess the compatibility of different companies, which can help generate economies of scale through vertical integration. As an example, one Dominican SEZ developer invited both a lingerie producer and a plastic-molding company that produced the small plastic details in bras. By using their sense of market conditions and firm compatibility in this way, private developers can effectively foster dynamic zones at low costs.

Besides private development, the Dominican Republic's democratic system should also have alleviated the incentive problem. Because the country is small, there is quite a clear connection between policy making and economic development on the ground. Government officials are therefore incentivized to set the rules of the SEZ scheme, if not to enrich the economy, then at least to avoid weakening it.

This accountability may explain the government's reluctance to invest in government-funded grandiose infrastructure projects in the SEZs. With the government debt-to-GDP ratio rising fast and new taxes highly unpopular, there is little support for increasing SEZ incentives.[14] Public attention to government finances may also have prevented the government from spending too much on infrastructure in publicly developed zones.

The Dominican SEZ scheme is in no way perfect. Many private developers receive all kinds of government benefits that misdirect recourses, and the public sector is still responsible for almost 30 percent of the zones. However, several positive features of the scheme seem to have combined in a beneficial way. Overall, it seems the high reliance on private zone development in the Dominican Republic has solved both the country's knowledge and incentive problems. Being a democracy with a degree of checks and balances may further have helped the Dominican Republic to align public officials' incentives with beneficial outcomes.

Did the SEZs lead to general reform?

The Dominican SEZs are praised for increasing employment, foreign investment, exports, and diversification of production in the country. Yet they have not lived up to expectations regarding their roles as locomotives of development that would pull the rest of the economy along. There is little integration between the SEZs and the country as a whole, with the lack of backward linkages being the most prominent case in point. Scholars of the Dominican SEZs scheme have also noted a disturbing divide between an expanding and increasingly sophisticated SEZ sector and a much less sophisticated domestic economy.[15]

The SEZs have not spread and grown to encompass the country as a whole. Instead, they have remained small industrial parks that enjoy different treatment by the government than the country at large. They thus show no signs of being either experiments for reform or tools to liberalize the country as a whole.

The lack of backward linkages has long been an obvious weakness of the Dominican SEZ scheme. A survey from 1989 found no SEZ firms that used inputs from the domestic economy. Domestically produced goods were either too expensive, of too poor quality, or simply not available for purchase.[16] Data for 1996 to 2007 indicate that backward linkages remain weak.[17] As shown in the table below, among the six sectors currently dominating SEZ exports, only tobacco buys a non-trivial amount of inputs from the domestic economy. This is a natural consequence of tobacco plants growing in the Dominican Republic. The dominating sectors of textiles and medical equipment, meanwhile, buy only 3.4 percent and 0.8 percent respectively from the domestic market.

Increasing sophistication of SEZ production has likely contributed to keeping backward linkages weak. For a long time after its inception, the

Table 7.1 Share of primary material that Dominican SEZ firms in different sectors buy from domestic, non-SEZ companies.

	1996–2007 average	*2007*
Tobacco products	18.4%	20.0%
Shoes	5.7%	7.0%
Electronics	4.9%	2.4%
Jewelry	3.6%	1.3%
Textiles and apparel	3.0%	3.4%
Medical equipment	2.0%	0.8%

Source: Central Bank of the Dominican Republic.

Dominican SEZ scheme depended on cheap labor to perform simple tasks, primarily in the textile industry.[18] In 1989, textiles accounted for over 70 percent of SEZ employment.[19] Since then, the scheme has seen an increasing diversification into more-capital-intensive production that relies more on semi-skilled than low-skilled workers.

An increasing amount of technology firms, such as call centers and medical-equipment manufacturers, exemplify the trend toward more sophistication. They also show how more sophisticated industries tend to purchase less material domestically. Call centers, which function without much material input, did not report any purchases of domestic primary material between 1996 and 2007.

The Dominican medical-equipment industry emerged in the late 1980s. For this, it can thank the fate of Puerto Rico, which used to be the location of choice for medical manufacturers targeting the United States market. This changed as wages increased in Puerto Rico while the Caribbean Basin Initiative (CBI), of which the Dominican Republic was a member, made it cheaper for CBI countries to export to the United States. Producers then started to move production from Puerto Rico to countries such as the Dominican Republic. They initially kept the skill-intensive tasks on the US territory while moving the simple stages of production abroad. Gradually, though, more sophisticated tasks were trusted to the Dominicans. The first stand-alone plant, which performed both capital-intensive plastic molding and easier assembly tasks, opened in the Dominican Republic in 1994. More companies in the industry soon followed this example.

The medical equipment produced in the Dominican Republic has become increasingly sophisticated. Intravenous sets, which are simpler devices that administer solutions into patients' veins, long dominated production and still play an important role. Today, though, Dominicans also produce complex medical equipment such as biopsy needles, blood-therapy products, drainage products, and surgical sutures. Dominican-based medical-equipment manufacturers are also hiring more of their professional staff locally.

While this is a positive development, it does not bode well for backward linkages with the rest of the economy. Between 1996 and 2007, medical-equipment manufacturers purchased only an average of 2 percent of inputs domestically. In 2007, this figure was only 0.8 percent. With growing sophistication of production, it is increasingly difficult for domestic producers to meet the strict quality requirements for both components and production equipment for the US market.

Medical-equipment manufacturers are an increasingly important part of SEZ production. The SEZ sector is therefore set to be even less dependent on the domestic market for inputs. By 2015, 30 medical-equipment and pharmaceutical manufacturers were located in the Dominican Republic, together employing almost 20,000 people. The sector now generates a quarter of SEZ exports, and is thus a larger zone exporter than the clothes and textiles sector.[20]

Another important contributor to increasing SEZ sophistication is the decline of the textile industry. This began modestly in 1996, with the 1994 North American Free Trade Agreement (NAFTA), which made Mexican textiles exporters more competitive on the US consumer-goods market.

The real shock to the textile industry in the Dominican Republic came later, with the end of the Multi-Fibre Arrangement (MFA) in 2005. The MFA was an international agreement that the United States initiated in 1974 to protect its textile industry. It established a set of export quotas that determined how much and what kind of apparel each country could export. As the World Trade Organization (WTO) was formed, representatives of its member countries agreed on a gradual phase-out of the system, which finally ended in 2005. Because many of the restrictions remained until the very end, it was only in 2004 that textile investors started reacting en masse to the imminent changes. For many countries in Latin America, the MFA's abolishment meant hardship for textile producers. The winners from liberalization were found primarily in Asia, with products from China and India having the largest impact on the new world of international competition in textiles.[21]

The MFA created an artificial comparative advantage for Dominican textile producers, without which many of them would not have existed.[22] As American clothing companies looked for better deals in Asia, they stopped outsourcing to the Dominican Republic.[23] The sector started declining in 2004, with many textile producers shutting down, cutting down production, or moving out. Dominican firms in the SEZ textile industry declined from 281 to 120 between 2004 and 2010, while the textile share of SEZ exports fell to a low of 23 percent in 2010.[24]

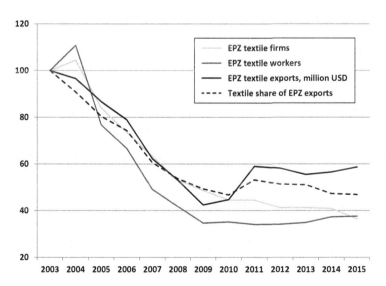

Figure 7.2 Index of the decline (2003: 100) of the free-zone textile industry.
Sources: CNZFE 2003; 2004; 2005; 2006; 2007; 2008; 2009; 2010; 2011; 2012; 2013; 2014; 2015.

While not a positive development for the Dominican Republic, the decline of textiles helped make the SEZ sector on average more sophisticated. Textiles are among the most labor-intensive forms of production in the SEZs, and the textile manufacturers that disappeared were the less advanced ones. To survive the new competition, some clothing manufacturers increased the range of tasks they performed, both in the early and late stages of production, which also increased the sector's sophistication. No longer able to compete merely on low wages, the manufacturers offered American brands full-package solutions, from design to delivery on hangers, sometimes straight to the stores around the United States. A great advantage of Dominican producers compared to those in Asia is fast delivery.[25] They can quickly send clothes samples back and forth until the customer is satisfied. For clothing brands that keep up with the trends, waiting two weeks for a ship from China just won't do.

Fewer Dominican textile firms now merely do the sewing of clothes, and if they do, this is predominantly for high-end, expensive brands for which the labor cost is less important than the quality of the work. Another growing niche is the production of personalized items such as college jackets and banners. Once the students have decided on their jacket orders, it has to be produced fast, in time for the next game or ceremony.

Increasing sophistication, both through more technologically advanced industries and upgrading within textile production, makes it increasingly hard for domestic non-SEZ firms to supply the SEZs with material. Add to this the trade protection that disincentivizes domestic firms from matching international price and quality, and the chances for more integration and backward linkages are slim.

In 1995, Larry Willmore noted that the Dominican firms outside SEZs have great potential to meet the demands of SEZ firms, if only they can increase quality and lower prices.[26] While such an observation is likely just as accurate today as it was back then, it fails to address the incentive structure that prevents this change. While the SEZ firms live in a tariff-free world, the country's domestic firms still benefit from a substantial amount of trade protection. They thus enjoy higher prices for their goods on the domestic market than the SEZs might offer them. They also have no particular incentive to produce the types of products that the SEZ firms import.

Domestic companies are also reluctant to export themselves. The Dominican export-promotion agency (CEI-RD) has the task of promoting Dominican exports by training people at domestic non-SEZ businesses to compete internationally by becoming exporters. However, representatives at the agency tell of much reluctance among domestic firms to make the investments needed. They are too comfortable with their situation, the people at the agency say, to venture outside the domestic market. It is easy to explain this reluctance in light of the incentive that trade protection gives. They do not have a reason to upgrade their production when they might just as well stay on the home market.[27]

In the absence of any good deals from domestic producers, SEZ firms stick with the cheaper and higher-quality products available on the international market. As SEZ firms become detached from domestic producers, they do not need the domestic firms to keep up with international standards. For all these reasons, we should not be surprised that the Dominican SEZ scheme is lacking integration via backward linkages.

The minimal external effects of the SEZ scheme are also reflected in the lack of any obvious connection between SEZ growth and improvement in the rest of the economy. While the SEZ sector began its ascent in the 1980s, the rest of the economy was stagnating and the government was asking for loans from the IMF.[28] In 1986, as the zones were taking off, 18 percent of Dominicans were classified as poor. By 1990, this figure had risen above 20 percent. Throughout the 1980s and 1990s, unemployment stayed stubbornly high between 19 percent and 25 percent.[29] While production in the SEZs became increasingly sophisticated, little such development was seen in the country as a whole. In 2014, among the non-SEZ workforce, 62 percent was devoted to agriculture, trade, and simple kinds of services, all sectors with generally low productivity.[30]

The Dominican SEZs function as islands of prosperity in a sea of backwardness. Rather than promoting growth in the country as a whole, the SEZs have, if anything, grown partly at its expense. Although American investors long dominated the scheme, there are now more SEZ firms based on Dominican than American capital.[31] Growing domestic participation is perceived as a positive trend but it implies that capital is being relocated from other parts of the country, where it may have been used more efficiently.[32]

While these observations do not mean that the zones have been negative for the economy, they suggest that they will not promote reforms in the country as a whole. In addition, the whole structure of the SEZ scheme prevents it from serving as a driver of reforms. The Dominican SEZs are export processing zones, which means they are limited in size and do not host any residents. As a result, they generate few external effects that could change the incentive structure of local governments without SEZs. Because the legal framework is the same for all SEZs, local policy makers cannot experiment with SEZ policies to use the zones as test beds or showcases for reform. The regime thus lacks the political decentralization that would allow local leaders to design SEZs with policies that match local conditions and that may have external effects.

Finally, there are no major reforms in the country that could be attributed to the SEZ scheme. The conclusion must be that the SEZs in the Dominican Republic have not led to countrywide reforms.

How the SEZs helped the government avoid liberalization

The positive side of the Dominican SEZ scheme is that it looks better than its protectionist status quo. It does not seem to have been introduced by wildly misinformed or corrupt officials aiming to milk it for rents or to dole out favors to cronies. On the other hand, it has also not led to economy-wide liberalizing reforms. No external effects were created by the zones that changed the country as a whole. What, then, was the political motivation behind the scheme?

To understand why they came about, we need to examine the political economy considerations of SEZ decision-makers at the time. As we will see, the Dominican SEZ experience is a good example of how policy makers can use SEZs for rent-seeking purposes in a way that is not necessarily corrupt. A look at the political situation as they were introduced will illustrate this point.

Beginning in the 1930s, the Dominican Republic was ruled by the military strongman and dictator Rafael Trujillo. He held de facto power for three decades until his assassination in 1961. During this time, Trujillo used his powerful position to gain control and influence over much of the Dominican economy. He was the country's main investor and owned many of the buildings in the capital of Santo Domingo. Toward the end of his life, Trujillo controlled more than 80 percent of the country's industrial production. He also imposed high trade barriers on particular goods and favored the sugar industry, where he also made big investments.

The dictator's distortive policies put Dominican manufacturing at a disadvantage that discouraged production in the sector. Manufacturing grew slower in the Dominican Republic than in other Latin American countries as a result, which kept the country dependent on agricultural crops for its exports. There was therefore no Dominican exporting sector with an interest in tariff-free imports that would sway politics away for protectionism. As long as the country was kept poor, moreover, the Dominican people did not have much capacity to consume imported goods. All powerful interests were on the side of protectionism, allowing Trujillo to nurture his crony relationships by doling out such favors as tariff exemptions to individual companies.[33]

A few years after Trujillo's death, Joaquin Balaguer became president, in part with the help of the United States, whose army occupied the country for a period. While not a reformist, Balaguer benefited the country by stepping away from some of Trujillo's destructive policies. He, like Trujillo, cultivated rent-seeking arrangements between the government and business, but spread his favors more widely than the sugar industry. Balaguer also abolished requirements that domestic production must use Dominican raw material.[34] These policies, together with US foreign aid and higher sugar prices, all contributed to higher economic growth in the country.[35]

As the Dominicans got wealthier, they demanded more imported goods, which threatened the consumer base of import-substitution industries. The animosity over trade policies could begin. Import-substituting sectors that had not previously demanded much protection started pressuring the government to install more solid barriers. Balaguer obliged. While he did not use trade protectionism to target favored businesses as much as Trujillo, he made the country's import-substituting regime more institutionalized and systematic.[36]

Balaguer soon met resistance to the increasing protectionism. Import-substituting industrialization, which had prevailed in Latin America for so long, was increasingly unpopular. People now recognized trade liberalization and export-led growth as the path to economic development. When the United States government put pressure on Balaguer's administration to liberalize, the president could not simply refuse. Balaguer owed his position to the United States, which helped him assume power to prevent any communist factions from ruling in the Dominican Republic. The United States was also the Dominicans' greatest trading partner and donor of development aid. Balaguer was also being pressed by critics at home to reform the economy and lower trade barriers. While he sought to please these critics, he also knew he needed the support of import-substituting industries. Liberalization would therefore have severely damaged him politically.[37]

Balaguer's solution to this dilemma was to launch SEZs. In 1968, he introduced a law that divided the economy into different sectors that would enjoy different benefits.[38] On the one hand, import-substitution companies were granted solid protection against imports. For the first time, the tariff scheme became both substantial and systematic, which allowed the protected firms to monopolize the domestic market. On the other hand, companies that invested in an SEZ and exported their goods would receive tariff and tax exemptions. This allowed Gulf & Western of the Americas, a sugar producer, to set up the first SEZ in 1969. The next SEZ, run by the government, opened in 1973. More zones soon emerged in the North around the second city of Santiago. They were predominantly privately developed and attracted many exporting manufacturers that relied on imports for their production.[39]

Out of the two kinds of benefits the president offered, trade protection was considered the most valuable and was quickly claimed by the politically connected bourgeoisie based around Santo Domingo in the South. The people in the periphery simply had to make do with the less attractive fiscal incentives. Many of the early SEZs were therefore formed far away from the capital.[40]

Balaguer used the SEZ policy in a way that carefully preserved the protection of import-substituting companies, while also pleasing his pro-trade critics. The United States, while not happy about this half-measure, nevertheless ended up accepting the new regime.[41] The political economy of the Dominican SEZ scheme is thus best described by the framework laid out in Chapter 4. A government may use SEZs to avoid reform, so as to maximize its rents without necessarily using them as vehicles for corruption.

It is no wonder the Dominican SEZs did not lead to general reforms. First of all, this was never their purpose. Their role was to divide the economy between SEZ firms and the rest, allowing the government to promote exports while still protecting its import-substituting industries. Also, through a central government initiative, the SEZs were imposed in a top-down manner to please different sectors with different benefits. It was not driven by local interests. Finally, the scheme discourages backward linkages with its tariff exemptions, thus limiting any external effects.

Short of promoting reforms, the best the SEZ scheme could do was to marginally improve the country's trade policies. This it likely did, since the

SEZ scheme seems to have been an improvement on the status quo, thanks to its mitigation of the knowledge and incentive problems.

However, before concluding SEZs were beneficial for the economy, another question must be answered. Even if SEZs are better than the status quo, they may not be superior to the situation that would have prevailed in their absence. What would Balaguer have done if the SEZ option had not been available to him in the late 1960s? He might have been forced to pursue broader liberalization, in which case the SEZs were not a good thing for the country. However, the pressure on him from domestic companies may also have been so great that he would never have considered broader liberalization. In that case, Balaguer might have found a less beneficial way out of the situation than the SEZ regime. Whether we deem the Dominican SEZ scheme a good thing for the country must therefore depend on our necessarily speculative guesses about the counterfactual political scenario.

Why the Dominican SEZs persist

Since the SEZs were introduced, no Dominican government has had a reason to abolish them. Without the SEZs, they would either have to liberalize the economy and lose support and rents from the protected industries, or return to protectionism. Since the latter option would result in loud opposition from trading partners and domestic media none of these alternatives dominate the choice of staying with the current regime.

One reason no government will abolish the SEZs and revert to protectionism is the political importance of the SEZ exporters. An important step in this regard was taken in 1988, when the Dominican Republic had only 14 zones. The SEZ investors then managed to grab six seats on the board of the national SEZ authority. One of their demands was a change to the allocation of MFA export quotas, which the agency handed out at the time in a corrupt and unpredictable manner. The SEZ investors pushed through that the quota distribution would thenceforth be based on previous export performance. This effectively shielded the incumbents from new entrants into the zones.[42]

This political victory for the SEZ investors was perhaps also what established their influence as a lobbying group. That same year, SEZ companies organized to form ADOZONA (La Asociación Dominicana de Zonas Francas), which became the main lobbying organization to promote SEZ interests.[43] The organization helped make the public case for the SEZ regime and pushed for more benefits to SEZ firms. Because of this advocacy, the government knew it would face vocal criticism if it weakened SEZ benefits. Therefore, when the government reformed the tax system to make it less discriminatory, it spared the SEZs from any changes.[44]

The government's commitment to support the SEZs became particularly evident in the wake of the textile downturn that started around 2004 with the end of the MFA. The SEZ textile industry lost over 100,000 of its workers in a few years' time, with only 40,500 left by 2011. The sector thus became the source of rapidly rising unemployment. A reasonable lesson from this decline might have been that the Dominican Republic does not have a real comparative advantage in textiles and that the country may be better off with a smaller or differently focused SEZ regime.

The politically savvy response was instead to preserve the SEZ regime in its current form. Around 2007–8, the Dominican government offered subsidized loans to textile companies in SEZs and wage subsidies to all SEZ firms. The policy makers also sought to absorb laid-off textile workers by offering SEZ incentives to all companies in the textile, clothing, leather, and shoe-production businesses, regardless of their location.[45] While some claim the measures did little to stem the decline, the political signal was that the government was eager to maintain the size and employment of the regime.

Current administrations are still balancing the interests of import-substituting firms and the exporting sector. The difference from the 1960s, though, is that the exporters have become economically and politically important with an efficient lobbying organization. No longer are the benefits of import-substitution firms necessarily seen as more attractive.

In its current form, the Dominican SEZs will continue to benefit the economy only at the margin. They provide needed breathing room for the country's exporters and a regime that international investors accept. However, no pro-trade interests have an incentive to use them as tools for reform. The SEZ investors already have the market access and fiscal benefits they want. The incentive for the Dominican government, meanwhile, is to keep the new status quo. It has nothing to gain from changing a system divided between a successful and growing SEZ sector and a lagging domestic economy.

Notes

1 The reader might note that my observations of the Dominican SEZ scheme contain fewer references than in the case studies of India and China. The reason is that many of my observations stem from my own field research, which includes around 50 interviews with SEZ policy makers, institutions, developers, SEZ business-people, and Dominican academics. I promised my interviewees anonymity to secure frank conversations.
2 Willmore 1996: 21; Adozona 2012; Farole 2012.
3 Kaplinsky 1993: 1857; Farole 2012: 17; Sánchez-Ancochea 2012.
4 CNZFE 2016a.
5 Jenkins et al. 1998; Farole and Kweka 2011: 1; Farole 2012: 2.
6 Farole 2012: 4.
7 Id.: 12. The Dominican Republic's zone authority presents numbers of exports and workers per sector that gives a hint of the varying labor intensity. While one worker in the textile industry generated less than 30 thousand dollars in exports in 2015, the equivalent figure for a worker in the medical and pharmaceuticals sector was almost 70 thousand dollars (CNZFE 2015: 33, 49). Among these countries, the Dominican Republic and Costa Rica have the most diversified SEZ production (Farole 2012: 2).
8 McCallum 2011: 10; Sánchez-Ancochea 2012.
9 CNZFE 2003; 2013.
10 Schrank 2003a: 96.

11 CNZFE Law 890 of 1990.
12 There is one source of possible misguided investments in the private zones as well. Because bodies such as the International Finance Corporation (IFC) of the World Bank offer subsidized loans, zone developers are sometimes encouraged to take on larger and riskier project than warranted. However, if these resources are wasted, the burden does not fall on the Dominican economy.
13 Zone locations are easily gauged on the map of SEZs provided by the Dominican zone authority (CNZFE 2016b).
14 The unpopularity of raised taxes was manifested in protests that erupted when the government raised the VAT to stem the government deficit (*Economist* 2012).
15 Kaplinsky 1993: 1857–9; World Bank 2000: 2; Burgaud and Farole 2011: 177; Sánchez-Ancochea 2012.
16 Rhee et al. 1990: 32.
17 After 2007, the system for the SEZ firms to report to the central bank changed, and any compiled data after 2007 were not obtainable at the time of writing.
18 Kaplinsky 1993; Willmore 1995; Godínez and Máttar 2008: 27; Burgaud and Farole 2011: 163; Sánchez-Ancochea 2012.
19 Kaplinsky 1993: 1856.
20 CNZFE 2015; Dominican Republic Central Bank data (compiled for the author, not for distribution).
21 Hartlyn 1998: 140; Waglé 2005; Burgaud and Farole 2011: 177.
22 Mortimore 2003: 23, 26.
23 Waglé 2005.
24 CNZFE 2004; 2010.
25 Some textile manufacturers also mention the advantage of US companies enjoying the reliability of working with a people with whom they are familiar.
26 Willmore 1995: 533.
27 Schrank 2005a: 55; Burgaud and Farole 2011: 178.
28 Betances 1995: 129; Black 1986: 143.
29 Hartlyn 1998: 143–44.
30 Central Bank 2014; Sánchez-Ancochea 2012: 222.
31 CNZFE 2015: 23.
32 Kaplinsky 1993: 1856.
33 Haggerty 1989; Betances 1995: 107; Pons 2010: 362–65.
34 Pons 1990: 561; Betances 1995: 120; Schrank 2003a: 95.
35 Black 1986: 44, 63; Pons 2010: 399.
36 Fiallo 1973: 162; Hartlyn 1998: 104; Schrank 2003b: 423–4.
37 Nanda 1966; Betances 1995: 118; Hartlyn 1998: 105; Schrank 2003a: 95; Schrank 2003b: 423; Pons 2010: 398, 402.
38 A 1955 law allowed for their creation, but was not adequate to lead to the introduction of any SEZs.
39 Haggerty 1989; Betances 1995: 121; Schrank 2005a: 46–47; Schrank 2005b.
40 Schrank 2003a: 97.
41 Id.: 95.
42 Schrank 2003a: 105.
43 Adozona 2016.
44 WTO 1996: xiii.
45 National Congress 2007.

References

Adozona. 2012. "Impacto Económico y Social de las Zonas Francas: Una Visión de 360 Grados." *ADOZONA* – la Asociación Dominicana de Zonas Francas.

Available at: http://www.adozona.org/serve/listfile_download.aspx?id=1139&num=1 (accessed 29 October 2015).

Adozona. 2016. "About Us." *Adozona Homepage*, available at: http://www.adozona. org/app/en/somos.aspx (accessed 29 October 2016).

Betances, Emilio. 1995. *State and Society in the Dominican Republic*. Westview Press, Boulder, CO.

Black, Jan Knippers. 1986. *The Dominican Republic: Politics and Development in an Unsovereign State*. Allen & Unwin, Boston.

Burgaud, Jean-Marie, and Thomas Farole. 2011. "When Trade Preferences and Tax Breaks are No Longer Enough: The Challenge of Adjustment in the Dominican Republic's Free Zones." In: *Special Economic Zones: Progress, Emerging Challenges, and Future Directions* (Thomas Farole and Gokhan Akinci eds.). The World Bank, Washington, D.C., pp. 159–181.

Central Bank. 2014. "National Account Statistics and the National Survey of Labor Force." *Banco Central* Available at: http://www.bancentral.gov.do (accessed 29 October 2016).

CNZFE (National Free Zones Council) Law 890 of 1990. Available at: http://www. cnzfe.gob.do/transparencia/index.php/base-legal (accessed 29 October 2016).

CNZFE (National Free Zones Council). CNZFE 1992; 1993; 1994; 1995; 1996; 1997; 1998; 1999; 2000; 2001; 2002; 2003; 2004; 2005; 2006; 2007; 2008; 2009; 2010; 2011; 2012; 2013; 2014; 2015. Yearly statistical publications. Available at: http://www.cnzfe. gob.do/transparencia/index.php/estadisticas/informe-estadisticos-anuales (accessed 29 October 2016).

CNZFE (National Free Zones Council). 2016a. Yearly statistical publications. Available at: http://www.cnzfe.gob.do/transparencia/index.php/estadisticas/informe-estadisticos-anuales

CNZFE (National Free Zones Council). 2016b. Map of SEZ sites available at: http:// www.cnzfe.gob.do/transparencia/index.php/estadisticas/mapa-del-sector-zonas-francas (accessed 29 October 2016).

Economist, The. 2012. "The Dominican Republic: A rum do." *The Economist*, Nov. 24, 2012. Available at: http://www.economist.com/news/americas/21567090-new-president-faces-tax-revolt-rum-do (accessed 29 October 2016).

Farole, Thomas. 2012. "Competitiveness and Regional Integration in Central America: The Role of Special Economic Zones." *World Bank memo*, Washington DC.

Farole, Tom, and Josaphat Kweka. 2011. "Institutional Best Practices for Special Economic Zones: An Application to Tanzania." *World Bank, Africa Trade Policy Notes*, Note #25.

Fiallo, Fabio Rafael. 1973. "Alternativas de política industrial en la República Dominicana." *Trimestre Económico* 159–172.

Godínez, Victor, and Jorge Máttar. 2008. "La República Dominicana en 2030: Hacia una nación cohesionada." Mexico, DF: *Economic Commission for Latin America and the Caribbean (CEPAL)*.

Haggerty, Richard A. 1989. "Dominican Republic: A Country Study." *The Library of Congress* Federal Research Division of the Library of Congress, Washington D.C. Available at: http://countrystudies.us/dominican-republic (accessed 29 October 2016).

Hartlyn, Jonathan. 1998. *The Struggle for Democratic Politics in the Dominican Republic*. University of North Carolina Press, Chapel Hill, NC.

Jenkins, Mauricio, Felipe Larrain, and Gerardo Esquivel. 1998. "Export Processing Zones in Central America." *Harvard Institute for International Development Working Paper* 646.

Kaplinsky, Raphael. 1993. "Export Processing Zones in the Dominican Republic: Transforming Manufactures into Commodities." *World Development* 21(11): 1851–1865.

McCallum, Jamie K. 2011. "Export Processing Zones: Comparative Data from China, Honduras, Nicaragua and South Africa." *International Labour Organization, Working Paper* No. 21, March 2011.

Mortimore, Michael. 2003. "Illusory Competitiveness: The Apparel Assembly Model of the Caribbean Basin." *United Nations University, Discussion Paper Series*, No. 2003-2011.

Nanda, Ved P. 1966. "United States Action in the 1965 Dominican Crisis: Impact on World Order – Part II." *Denver Law Journal* 44: 225–274.

National Congress (Congreso Nacional). 2007. Law 56–07 (Ley No. PI-56–07). Available at: https://www.dgii.gov.do/legislacion/leyesTributarias/Documents/56-07. pdf (accessed 29 October 2016).

Pons, Frank Moya. 1990. "Import-Substitution Industrialization Policies in the Dominican Republic, 1925–1961." *Hispanic American Historical Review* 70(4): 539–577.

Pons, Frank Moya. 2010. *The Dominican Republic: A National History.* 3rd ed. Markus Wiener Publishers, Princeton.

Rhee, Yung Whee, Katharina Katterbach, and Janette White. 1990. "Free Trade Zones in Export Strategies." *World Bank Industry and Energy Department, PRE, Industry Series Paper* No. 36.

Sánchez-Ancochea, Diego. 2012. "A Fast Herd and a Slow Tortoise?" *Studies in Comparative International Development* 47(2): 208–230.

Schrank, Andrew. 2003a. "Luring, Learning, and Lobbying: The Limits to Capital Mobility in the Dominican Republic." *Studies in Comparative International Development* 37(4): 89–116.

Schrank, Andrew. 2003b. "Foreign Investors, 'Flying Geese,' and the Limits to Export-Led Industrialization in the Dominican Republic." *Theory and Society* 32(4): 415–443.

Schrank, Andrew. 2005a. "Entrepreneurship, Export Diversification, and Economic Reform: The Birth of a Developmental Community in the Dominican Republic." *Comparative Politics* 38(1): 43–62.

Schrank, Andrew. 2005b "Peasants, Planters, and the Predatory State Export Diversification in the Dominican Republic, 1970–2000." *Research in Rural Sociology and Development* 10: 353.

Waglé, Swarnim. 2005. "International Trade in Textiles and Clothing and Development Policy Options: After the Full Implementation of the WTO Agreement on Textiles and Clothing (ATC) on 1 January 2005." *UNDP Center in Colombo*, Policy Paper.

Willmore, Larry. 1995. "Export Processing Zones in the Dominican Republic: A Comment on Kaplinsky." *World Development* 23(3): 529–535.

Willmore, Larry. 1996. "Export Processing in the Caribbean: Lessons from Four Case Studies." *United Nations Economic Comission for Latin America and the Caribbean*, Working Paper 42. Available at: http://archivo.cepal.org/pdfs/1996/S9600501.pdf (accessed 29 October 2016).

World Bank. 2000. *Dominican Republic: Social and Structural Policy Review*, Vol. 2, Report No. 20192. Mar. 23, 2000.

WTO (World Trade Organization). 1996. "Trade Policy Review: Dominican Republic." *Report by the Secretariat*, WT/TPR/S/11. Jan. 3, 1996.

Part III

The political economy of future SEZs

8 Implications for SEZ policy makers

The political economy discussion of SEZs lends itself to a variety of policy implications for the different actors involved in zone planning and development. In what follows, I will first discuss how outside advisors on SEZs may deal with the fact that the policy sometimes does more harm than good. I will then lay out advice useful to a government attempting to preserve its rents by dividing the economy through the use of SEZs. Giving such advice can be beneficial if the political alternative to the SEZs is more protectionism. Finally, I discuss useful tactics for a political minority elite hoping to use SEZs as steps toward broader economic reforms.

When to deal with the knowledge and incentive problems

It should be clear by now that the benefits of SEZs are highly contextual, as are the policy implications to draw from this book. It may seem that the political economy analyses imply that you should never give policy advice to SEZ policy makers. Officials will not act on useful advice anyway but will rather pursue the SEZ policies that benefit them, regardless of the welfare effects. As conveyed in Chapter 4, government officials are likely to be pursuing rents when they introduce SEZs. They may want the zones to grow, but they do not care about resources wasted along the way.

This implies that policy makers would be asking an outside economist how to implement SEZs only as a way to legitimize the policy, make it credible to outside observers, or probe the possibilities for outside funding by pursuing some popular political goal with the SEZ scheme. Nevertheless, economic advice on SEZs can be beneficial to the country as a whole if it seems the scheme, despite being driven by rent-seeking motives, would be on net positive for the economy. In that case, an outside advisor would do the country a favor by helping the government alleviate its knowledge and incentive problems associated with the SEZs.

The existence of the knowledge and incentive problems is not an argument against policy making generally. In the SEZ context, it is true that policy makers and bureaucrats have the incentive to use zones as rent-seeking tools and that they have knowledge problems that cause wasteful spending and misguided subsidies. However, as we have seen, there are ways to solve these problems so that an SEZ scheme can become good enough to benefit an economy.

The only time outside advisors should help a government solve the knowledge and incentive problems is when they believe a functioning SEZ scheme will actually help the economy. If, for instance, the introduction of SEZs is driven by reform-minded local elites, as discussed in Chapter 3, their incentives are likely aligned with benefiting the economy as a whole because profit generating SEZs will benefit them personally. In this context, SEZs can be beneficial if the local elites find ways to tackle the knowledge problem and safeguard against incentive problems within the local government bureaucracy.

It is worth recalling that reform-minded elites do not have a more altruistic motivation for introducing SEZs than policy-makers who seek to preserve a rent-seeking government. The difference is that their best source of revenue is the tax payments they can collect from new SEZ investors, rather than rents that they obtain through protectionist policies. They therefore want to promote successful SEZs and weaken the power of their opposing coalitions, as a way to increase their personal power and wealth.

Not all local policy makers are created equal, of course. Some will pursue SEZs for rent-seeking purposes, such as using public funds to provide infrastructure contracts to their friends and family. The fact that local elites are pushing for SEZs is therefore not enough for the policy to create the kind of reform process discussed in Chapter 3. An SEZ advisor should try to assess whether the officials can best benefit from the revenues stemming from the economic growth the SEZs generate. If so, they could use the zones in a way that transforms the economy, rather than just liberalizing it on the margin.

Once an advisor has determined that the local elites are reform-minded, there is some useful advice to give them. First, they need to consider what tactic to employ to spur the kind of liberalization avalanche explored in Chapter 3. They must detect which powerful government officials are more moderate and thus susceptible to smaller amounts of kickbacks in exchange for SEZ support. They also need to ponder what kickbacks are feasible. Money may be an expensive and dangerous way to exchange favors. A better offer might come in the form of promises to support other policies that moderate anti-reformers favor.

For each local policy maker who is granted an SEZ, the next step is to make it work. With lower revenues from rent-seeking, taxes and other legitimate revenues from SEZs must sufficiently compensate the local official for the SEZ introduction to be worth the work, expenses, and risks involved in going against the majority of the power elite.

SEZ reformers can therefore not afford to fall prey to the knowledge and incentive problems discussed in Chapter 2. As previously observed, the knowledge problem is more easily solved in a decentralized system. With a better understanding of local market conditions, local policy makers governing SEZs thus have that advantage from the start. To avoid the knowledge problem, though, they should still refrain from micromanaging the activities in the zones and determining their locations. Even better, they can privatize zone development, knowing that private investors have better market knowledge than policy makers do.

The local elites must also avoid the incentive problem. As they are seeking to profit from higher tax revenues from SEZ firms, they do not have the incentive to make the zones unprofitable by showering them with public resources. However, the SEZs can still succumb to the incentive problem because of the motivations of the people in the local government bureaucracy. The elites therefore need to avoid introducing a system that allows for bribe extraction throughout the bureaucratic process.

One way to avoid low-level corruption is to simplify the bureaucracy by making the process of SEZ registration and development simple and transparent. Another way is to limit the public resources devoted to developing the SEZs. A local government might not be able to concentrate as many resources in a zone as a central government can. Nevertheless, even local policy makers should consider privatizing the system to the largest extent possible by making private developers responsible for the zone infrastructure. If the local government does not invest capital in the zones, SEZ developers are less dependent on the approval of local bureaucrats to pursue projects. They then have less incentive to lobby the bureaucrats, which means fewer opportunities for extracting rents.

While reform-minded local elites can benefit from genuine SEZ success, a government using SEZs to avoid broader reforms needs very different, if any, advice. A consultant advising such a government on SEZs should give advice only if the SEZ scheme is likely to benefit the economy. If it seems the government will pursue broader reforms in the absence of SEZs, helping them to create a functioning SEZ scheme is doing the country a disfavor.

Recall that it is also possible that, in the absence of SEZs, the government will find ways to avoid any liberalization by bribing and subsidizing pro-reformist interest groups. If this is the most likely alternative scenario, an SEZ advisor can benefit the country by helping the government use SEZs to create a dual economy, divided between exporters and trade-protected firms. We should therefore explore what advice might help a government preserve protectionism through SEZs.

A government using SEZs to avoid reforms must grant sufficient trade liberalization to satisfy the interests that are opting for the change it wants to avoid. The goal should be to make the SEZs sufficiently satisfying for liberalization advocates, so that they choose not to pressure the government for further change. In countries such as the Dominican Republic, for example, the SEZ scheme encompasses such a large share of the country's importing exporters that those outside of the SEZs are probably not powerful enough to pursue broader liberalization.

For an SEZ scheme to be politically sustainable, policy makers must make sure SEZ exporters find tariff exemptions, tax breaks, and other incentives sufficient so that they will not push for general liberalization. It is also important that the government limit the incentives to fiscal benefits. Regulatory changes risk serving as catalysts for broader reforms that the government wants to avoid.

The government should prevent any leakage of goods, technologies, or policies from the SEZs, to maintain a clear separation between SEZ companies and the rest of the economy. Import-substitution firms must be shielded from the threat of competing goods from SEZ companies. If they do not find the trade protectionism valuable, they do not have an incentive to lobby for it, as the government wants them to.

Governments often prevent SEZ goods from entering the domestic market by requiring SEZ firms to export their products. However, such rules are sometimes breached. SEZs have been found to serve as vehicles for smuggling of goods into the domestic market, and the control system in place is sometimes inadequate to spot such breaches.[1]

Even if the government succeeds in policing against smuggling through SEZs, foreign exporters can still take market share from domestic companies. In the Philippines, for instance, the garment imports of zone firms ended up competing with domestic garment firms for contracts with textile manufacturers in the zones.[2] If it seems some zone firms are likely to abandon their domestic suppliers, the government may need to offer protected domestic firms subsidies as compensation.

Governments seeking to prevent SEZ leakage that could threaten import-substituting firms should be careful about what kind of zones they introduce. In particular, they should avoid SEZs that include residential areas. If SEZs become real communities or even cities, they can threaten domestic non-SEZ industries and influence policy making in other parts of the country. Because people must be able to travel freely in and out of such SEZ communities, the risk of smuggling into the domestic market also increases.

It can be hard to control the dynamic growth of large, diversified, and integrated SEZs, like those seen in China. Without clearly defined limits, they may spread to consume a large part of the country, which puts increasing competitive pressure on import-substituting firms. Governments seeking to avoid reform should therefore opt for smaller industrial parks, such as export processing zones (EPZs). These can be clearly limited by walls and fences, which prevent both zone growth and goods leakage. Their lack of residential building also limits their growth when located in a city. While EPZs in rural areas are not limited for this reason, any integration with communities is prevented by their isolation.

The benefits of the smallness of EPZs do not imply that single-factory zones would offer an even better model. First of all, single-factory zones are less efficient in dividing the economy. Each firm must obtain its own zone status, which imposes costs on the government. Exporting companies may also perceive the single-factory zones as too constrained a model to really benefit them. They and other promoters of reform are likely to keep pushing for further liberalization if tariff exemptions are offered only through individual concessions.

Second, single-factory zones are harder to monitor for leakages than EPZs. As with larger SEZs, single-factory zones often cannot practically function with a fence around them. Many single-factory zones locate in city centers and must integrate with their surroundings to function like normal companies. If located outside the city, they may have a fence, but it is still impractical for the government to devote resources to controlling all goods coming out of them. Hundreds of single companies spread out across the country are much more difficult for the government to monitor than hundreds of firms located in an EPZ. An SEZ scheme like that in Ghana, for instance, which relies on single-factory zones for over 80 percent of SEZ exports, would work poorly to divide the economy.[3] Such a setup is therefore more likely to serve as a vehicle for rent-seeking in a more direct exchange of give and take between the government and SEZ firms.

Single-factory zones are best used as a supplementary tool for a government seeking to divide the economy into exporters and import-substituting firms. A government may introduce EPZs as a default but allow single-factory zones as a way to target specific exporting sectors that cannot benefit from the EPZ model. These might, for instance, be farmers who need to import machinery, or large factories such as food-packaging plants.

These are all pieces of advice an SEZ consultant may give to a government as long as it seems like the SEZs will be a net benefit for the country. Even if the motive of the government is to avoid broader reforms, the SEZs can provide marginal improvements if they present the best political alternative. The most important, as well as the hardest, assessment a consultant must make is therefore what kind of counterpart he or she is dealing with. That is the topic for the next section.

Meeting with the SEZ planners

A high-ranking representative of a government in a developing country calls a trade expert at the World Bank in Washington, DC. The government officials have decided to introduce SEZs, which they believe can help industrialize the country. They have read about the success of the Chinese SEZs and believe similar zones can spur development in their country as well by opening it up to trade and diversifying the economy.

A couple of months later, a delegation from the World Bank sits across the table from the government representatives. The government officials explain that they now have a law allowing SEZs and that they need help with zone implementation. What is the blueprint for SEZs, they ask, what are the best practices, and how can they make them grow fast by attracting investors? The officials assure the World Bank economists that the whole government stands unified in backing the policy. Combined with the expertise of the World Bank, the scheme therefore has great potential for success.

The World Bank economists, having read this book on the political economy of SEZs, ponder their response. If the whole government really is behind the SEZs, it may well be introducing them as a way to safeguard trade protection and hence the rents they collect from import-substituting companies. If they really are interested in opening up to trade, why do it in a piecemeal fashion? If economic development is the ultimate goal, there are surely more general reforms the government can pursue that do not risk causing costly resource reallocations.

The World Bank delegates conclude that the government is probably misguided in its exaggerated hope in SEZs. It does not realize that, economically, SEZs are a second-best policy, and one that risks being vitiated by knowledge and incentive problems. Therefore, the delegation determines that the best advice is to explore other alternatives before implementing SEZs. The delegates explain that broader reforms in labor and product markets, combined with trade liberalization, are a more promising way to go.

If the government officials are really pursuing economic development, they should welcome that advice and realize they were misinformed about the promise of SEZs. When they heard about other countries' successful SEZ schemes, they perceived them as an efficient way to spur economic development. They did not understand that the news articles about seemingly successful SEZs did not consider their costs. The government delegation can then leave the meeting elated by the new insight and convinced that a more holistic way toward economic reform will be more beneficial.

However, rather than being grateful, the government delegates respond with indignation at the suggestion that their SEZ plans are misguided. They invited the trade experts to tell them how to implement zones, not to dissuade them from doing so. Insults soon start flying at the World Bank economists, hinting at Western arrogance and neo-colonialism.

The government officials' staunch insistence on the preeminence of SEZs should ring alarm bells for the foreign delegation. They may want SEZs so badly because they are such an effective way to preserve protectionism. All they really want from the World Bank is a stamp of approval for the scheme to signal their allegedly pro-trade position. Had they thought that SEZs were the best tool for economic development, they would have listened as the World Bank delegation came with different proposals. Realizing their real motives, the World Bank delegation walks out.

However, there are two reasons the World Bank experts may be mistaken in walking out. First, although the government officials are likely to use SEZs to preserve protectionism and avoid reform, the zones may still be better than their alternative. The World Bank delegates should inquire about the status of protectionism in the country and find out what political factions have the upper hand in disputes over liberalization. If the pro-liberalization camp is weak, it is unlikely reforms would come about in the absence of SEZs, and the zones may therefore be the best option.

The second reason the World Bank delegates might not want to walk out is because the government delegation may in fact represent a pro-reformist minority of the governing elite that is seeking to use SEZs to obtain liberalization through gradual change in the country. In that case, broader reforms are likely out of reach, and SEZs may be the best tool they have to achieve positive change.

It might not be obvious to the World Bank economists whether the people across the table are in a minority position in government. Even if they enjoy the backing of powerful ministers and even the head of state, they may represent a minority in terms of real political power. Interest groups and lower-level officials are sometimes powerful enough to come together and obstruct reforms. Unions might hold a tight grip over trade, transport, and monopolized sectors, for instance. If the president were to introduce broad reforms, powerful interest groups outside government might swiftly impeach the president and reverse the new policies. Even with the official support of the government, therefore, the officials may function as a power minority.

To find out whether the government delegates constitute a minority, the World Bank delegation can ask about the political situation in the country and about resistance to broader reforms. It is a good sign if government representatives start complaining about the political obstacles to reform that force them to turn to such piecemeal policies as SEZs. Reform resistance tells the World Bank economists that the SEZs are likely the best possible policy the reforming officials can pursue. With luck, the zones might even launch a process toward increasing liberalization in the country.

Any outside observer or consultant should ponder the political economy of SEZs before offering advice. If it seems broader reforms are politically feasible, there is reason to be skeptical if the government insists on the superiority of SEZs. If, by contrast, SEZs are proposed as a way to create pockets of liberalization in the face of reform resistance, advice on better SEZ implementation can actually benefit the country.

There is thus not one consistent policy implication for outside consultants. They will always be presented with motivation about the welfare of the people, but the policy-makers will always have their own interests at heart. Whether the SEZ scheme will be beneficial depends on how aligned those interests are with benefiting the economy as a whole. This, in turn, depends on how the policy-makers will exploit the zones for their own advantage and what might be the policy alternative.

Notes

1 FATF 2010: 17, 19.
2 Ofreneo 2009: 545.
3 Farole 2010: 11.

References

Farole, Thomas. 2010. "Case Studies of Special Economic Zones: Ghana." *World Bank memo*, The World Bank, Washington, D.C.

FATF (Financial Action Task Force). 2010. "Money Laundering Vulnerabilities of Free Trade Zones." (2010). *FATF* Available at: http://www.fatf-gafi.org/media/fatf/documents/reports/ML%20vulnerabilities%20of%20Free%20Trade%20Zones.pdf (accessed 29 October 2016).

Ofreneo, Rene E. 2009. "Development Choices for Philippine Textiles and Garments in the Post-MFA Era." *Journal of Contemporary Asia* 39(4): 543–561.

9 The changing world of SEZs

Throughout the decades since the first modern SEZ was introduced, several forces have been pushing governments away from older zone models and toward models that seem to incorporate many political economy insights that numerous failed SEZs have provided. This induces hope for a world free of the political economy problems plaguing SEZs today, and where SEZs can play an increasingly important role in economic development.

The modern SEZ is said to have been born in 1956 with the export processing zone at Shannon International Airport in Ireland. While SEZs have come in many shapes and sizes since then, they have primarily served to spur manufacturing and to attract trade-related activities such as warehousing and shipping. Then as now, SEZs focus on assembly manufacturing, primarily in apparel, textiles, electronics, and electrical goods. Many zones rely on low-cost labor and attract foreign investors with fiscal incentives that reduce their costs further.[1]

This model best describes the export processing zone (EPZ) version of SEZs. Indeed, so closely identified have EPZs become with the SEZ concept that much scholarly work on zones deals only with EPZs. A well-cited World Bank survey on the topic from 1992 counts only export processing zones. It also notes that the Chinese SEZs constitute a different arrangement from EPZs, while China also has plenty of EPZs.[2] Chinese-style SEZs are thus treated as an exceptional case and are set apart from EPZs. Because EPZs are more numerous, they have been of primary interest for most studies. Today, new SEZ regimes are emerging in Africa, and there, too, most countries aim for the traditional EPZ model of zones.[3]

Because diversified and rules-based SEZs offer more promising zone models than the classical EPZs, zone researchers and policy makers alike should imminently shift their focus. While the SEZ model of cheap labor combined with fiscal incentives will likely remain dominant for some time, there are reasons to believe in a very different future for the world's zones.

First, EPZs no longer provide an easy way for poorer countries to promote exports and employment. The EPZ model has benefited from the revolution of globalization that followed dramatic price drops in goods transport. FDI from developed countries became increasingly important for exports and employment in poorer countries. Also, along with higher global wealth, it seemed an economic law that the share of trade in world GDP would be constantly rising. This changed with the new millennium. Between 2001 and 2015, the value of trade to GDP barely increased at all.[4]

Because EPZs spread along with the rise of global value chains, the zones are commonly seen as contributors to this progress. Yet it is more likely that EPZs could spread thanks to this global development rather than the other way around. EPZs may not have been crucial for countries finding their place in new global value chains. More likely, they played but a marginal role as governments competed with each other to attract foreign capital.[5]

As countries progress, the low-cost model becomes less sustainable. Much growth has come about as people have moved from the countryside to take up jobs in industry in the cities. Because new workers have only low-pay alternatives, wages can remain low as long as this dynamic is in progress. However, as the marginal worker from the countryside demands ever-higher pay to move, companies must raise their wages regardless of whether they are trying to attract people from the countryside or from other urban companies.[6]

The dilemma of wealth causing a loss in competitiveness is commonly referred to as the middle-income trap. This term is misleading, as it refers to rising wages, and hence wealth, as some kind of a problem. Higher wealth does, however, imply that policies such as EPZs become increasingly obsolete. They may have the appearance of a growth-promoting policy while wages are low enough for foreign investors to choose the country in general. Once they have picked a country, they would rather invest in a zone offering fiscal benefits than anywhere else. But as countries develop toward more economic diversity and reliance on services and human-capital-intensive production, EPZs can no longer play this role. As such, they may no longer be attractive even politically.

A second reason EPZs are increasingly obsolete is because of the changing nature of world trade. After people started using the steam engine for transportation, lower transport costs drove the trade revolution. This allowed multinational companies to locate their production complexes in other countries, from where they could inexpensively ship the goods to the consumers in the developed world. Since the 1980s, transportation costs have remained basically stagnant, while communication costs have fallen significantly instead. This means multinationals no longer need to concentrate their whole supply chain in one country, but can coordinate supply chains extending over many countries.[7]

Lower cost of communication means EPZs are losing strength in their role as promoters of agglomeration and economic development. To understand their role in agglomeration, we should first note that industrial clusters were a natural part of the rise of trade in the 20th century. They formed in different parts of the world thanks to lower transportation costs that made exporting across the world feasible. In this context, EPZs often provided attractive locations for the producing exporters that benefited from economies of scale. The EPZ country supplied labor and fiscal benefits, and the country could industrialize in the sense of hosting a whole industrial process.

As long as communication costs were high, it was better to keep several stages in the supply chain in one location. As a result, physical proximity between firms was important, which encouraged agglomeration. This was true regardless of whether the companies integrated vertically, by being part of the same supply chain, or horizontally, by producing similar goods and sharing a labor force and market for inputs.[8]

Despite often hosting clusters, it is unclear to what extent EPZs actually contributed to cluster formation. In some cases, government efforts certainly seem to have been misplaced. In Pakistan, for instance, the government has had EPZs since 1989.[9] However, while most of the government-sanctioned zones remained more or less stagnant with little impact on the economy, industrial clusters emerged elsewhere, driven by market fundamentals and coordinated through social networks.[10] Pakistan may be an outlier in seeing more clusters growing outside of its SEZs than within them. However, even when fiscal incentives in SEZs have determined the locations of cluster, those clusters would likely have come about also in the zones' absence.

The lower cost of communication since the 1980s changed the role of agglomerations. Coordinating dispersed and complex production chains became significantly cheaper, which diluted the rationale for cluster formation. With better communication, the steps in a production chain can be spread out over several countries, with each production plant integrating with its suppliers, customers, or the company headquarters in other countries, rather than with geographically proximate firms.[11] Thanks to this development, the role of the old EPZs in cluster formation is increasingly obsolete. The zones can provide benefits to production plants that specialize in a specific part of a supply chain. However, these plants gain little from the proximity to other firms.

The international unbundling of supply chains also makes it harder for EPZs to promote economic development in their host countries. Even less than the exports of the traditional EPZ model, exporting goods after adding only small value will not contribute much to a country's industrialization. A multinational company investing in or outsourcing to a country has little incentive to integrate its operations in the countries where it is based. Technology transfers therefore become unlikely. With better communication, companies can also better control against leakage of intellectual capital.

When plants in the same supply chain are spread out over several countries, it also becomes easier to move them between countries offering the lowest costs. This further weakens the potency of EPZs in contributing to a country's industrialization. If, for instance, molding a particular component in a radio becomes cheaper in another country, the company can move that production stage without worrying about this obstructing the supply chain as a whole.

In addition to the lower cost of communication, cheaper technology also makes entering global value chains less important as a step toward indus-trialization. When technology increasingly substitutes for cheap labor, people need to add skills and sophistication, either to perform more complicated tasks or to work effectively with the new technology. As jobs in manufacturing become increasingly sophisticated, they will be both fewer and less likely to be outsourced to developing countries. Manufacturing may thus not be the safe road to industrialization it has been so far.

When low wages cease to be a ticket to enter into international production networks, SEZs need to change if they are to ride the globalization waves of the future. Similarly to the development in the Dominican Republic, zone production will have to become more sophisticated. As we have seen, though, the problem with increasingly sophisticated SEZ industries is that they generally fail to promote countrywide economic development. Thus, regardless of what kind of jobs a government seeks to foster through SEZ implementation, these kinds of zones, industrial parks where businesses enjoy fiscal benefits, will not be able to give jobs to massive amounts of low-skilled people.

The role of the World Trade Organization

The traditional SEZ model is also threatened by the organization tasked with promoting global free trade. With the birth of the WTO, two major policy shifts have shaken the world of SEZs. One is the end of the Multi-Fibre Arrangement during the period 1995–2004. As we saw in the case of the Dominican Republic, this meant the death of many typical zone businesses, as the space of low-wage cost competition was opened up to previously disfavored Asian countries.

The MFA served to protect textile manufacturing in industrialized countries from the competition of emerging markets. Because it created such a patchwork of bilateral trade quotas, its final abolition generated both winners and losers. Bangladesh, India, Pakistan, and Vietnam saw employment in the apparel sector rise between 2004 and 2008. Mexico, Honduras, Morocco, and Sri Lanka saw opposite trends.[12]

The full effect of the imposition and abolishment of the MFA is hard to discern because many of the supply chains the MFA encouraged may have emerged in its absence as well. Bangladesh however is one country that can thank the MFA for the opportunity to develop its industry in ready-made garments. Lacking the technology and know-how, Bangladesh was not a textile exporter at the time the MFA came into place. As a result, the United States did not impose textile quotas on the country. Entrepreneurial Korean investors, limited by the quotas imposed on them at home, then started investing in Bangladesh. By training Bangladeshi workers in Korea, they laid the foundations for a domestically viable textile industry in Bangladesh. It was also the Korean investors, with their experience of SEZs from home, who convinced the government of Bangladesh to introduce a similar system to encourage their investments in the form of a "Special Bonded Warehouse System."[13]

Once the United States imposed textile quotas on Bangladesh in 1985, the country had already become a player on the textile market. While the country exported almost no garments at the time the MFA was introduced in the 1970s, the sector constituted 76 percent of exports by 2005 and more than 80 percent in 2014. Although the industry in Bangladesh shrank as a result of the US quotas, many textile exporters remained, and benefited from relatively less restrictive import quotas compared to such competing countries as Korea, China, Hong Kong, and Japan.[14]

With the MFA quotas removed, it seems the textile industry in Bangladesh has not been much hurt by the increasing competition. This may be due to the export restrictions on China that the United States insisted on as the MFA expired. However, it may well signify the fundamental competitiveness in textiles that companies in Bangladesh established, much thanks to the Korean investors. The country has since attracted many foreign investors to its garment industry, and has used its SEZs to a large extent in this pursuit.[15]

Sri Lanka had a similar experience to Bangladesh. There, foreign investors proliferated with the MFA, in search of unexploited export quotas. As the quotas were removed, Sri Lankan apparel manufacturers could no longer secure a share of their main markets, the United States and the European Union. However, despite the challenges from new competition that they faced with the end of the MFA, Bangladesh and Sri Lanka have both managed to preserve their apparel industries at a healthy size.[16]

With the MFA, the Philippines also saw an influx of foreign investors, who were taking advantage of its quotas in garment exports. Compared to China, Indochina, and Bangladesh, the Philippine labor was relatively expensive. Yet thanks to the export quotas, the Philippines could secure a market share.[17] Indonesia did not have enough domestic investors to exploit its entire MFA quota. It ended up attracting investors from South Korea, Hong Kong, and Taiwan.[18]

As the MFA was abolished, apparel manufacturing languished in several countries. Mexico has enjoyed a particularly privileged access to the US market since the signing in 1994 of the North America Free Trade Agreement (NAFTA). The Mexican maquiladoras, which are free zones established along the border with the United States, enjoyed their greatest upswing after joining NAFTA, although the role of the agreement in their success is disputed.[19] With the end of the MFA, previously restricted competition from Asian countries emerged, which left many Mexican textile producers struggling.[20]

Malaysia also benefited from the MFA and saw its industry challenged with its abolition. Similarly to the case of the Dominican Republic, many textile manufacturers in Malaysia had to become more sophisticated to stay in business.[21]

In many of these countries, the textile sectors in the SEZs could ride on the artificial competitiveness the MFA provided. As the quota system was abolished, many SEZ schemes were put under strain. Countries such as Malaysia, the Philippines, Indonesia, and Thailand all benefited from the MFA quotas and used SEZs to attract manufacturing investment. After the end of the MFA, they have all seen their textile industries shrink.[22] However, in those countries, as in the Dominican Republic, SEZ schemes have generally remained intact after the end of the MFA, despite the severe blow to textile exports.

The end of the MFA revealed how dependent many countries had become on the artificial competitiveness the textile quotas created. Because their SEZs host much of the textile production, they came under severe pressure as the MFA ended. On the bright side, though, the end of the MFA encouraged the development of more-sustainable SEZ models that do not rely as much on low-cost competition through fiscal incentives and cheap labor. Abolishing the quotas means the truly cheap countries were allowed to compete on that margin, while leaving others to compete on higher quality.

Today, the WTO is posing another threat to the traditional EPZ model. Ever since the founding year of the organization in 1994, the WTO has banned export subsidies for its members. According to the Agreement on Subsidies and Countervailing Measures (SCM), governments are prohibited from giving subsidies to companies on the basis of export performance that causes "injury to the domestic industry of another Member."[23] They also cannot subsidize companies for using domestic goods as inputs.[24]

It might seem that SEZs are a way to get around the subsidy prohibition. After all, SEZ firms receive benefits on the basis of their zone status rather than their exports. The government can have one provision that all SEZ firms must export and another provision granting benefits to SEZ firms. However, the similarity between export subsidies and SEZ benefits on the basis of export requirements is simply too obvious. The WTO therefore correctly sees SEZ schemes with export requirements as de facto export subsidies, even in the absence of any explicit export subsidies. The organization rules an arrangement a prohibited subsidy if the benefits would not have been granted in the absence of export performance.[25] This inevitably includes EPZs whose companies are required to export their goods.

There is no one unified sanction against a country engaging in export subsidies. If a country is found breaching the agreement and refuses to change, the country filing the claim has the right to impose retaliatory measures, such as import tariffs on the guilty country.[26]

Subsidies do not have to come in the form of direct tax benefits to count. The concept also includes government provided goods and services beyond just general infrastructure.[27] A country with SEZs could therefore be implicated even if the zones do not offer fiscal benefits, but lower the costs of its exporters in other ways. Since SEZ schemes primarily rely on fiscal incentives, furthermore, most of them risk being accused of breaching the WTO agreement.

No rule lacks exceptions, though. Countries are exempt from the export-subsidy ban if they have a GDP below $1,000 per capita, in 1990 US dollars.[28] Other countries that were not quite as poor enjoyed several years of respite. Later on, several countries managed to negotiate additional postponements of their deadlines. Finally, the WTO put its foot down and declared that all countries above the $1,000 threshold must comply with the rules by December 2015. This includes countries such as the Dominican Republic, India, Indonesia, the Philippines, and Sri Lanka.[29]

The subsidy ban is thus pushing several countries to reform their export-focused SEZ schemes. To comply, governments try primarily to avoid discriminating between exporters and importers when doling out their subsidies. In theory, one way is to offer generous subsidies in the form of tariff and tax breaks to all companies in the country, whether they are exporters or not. However, that is highly undesirable or even infeasible for many governments since granting SEZ benefits to all businesses can erode their tax base.

Granting benefits to everyone might be feasible if the government determines that all companies, whether exporters or not, still pay taxes and tariffs that are somewhere between the normal rates and those currently imposed on SEZ firms. However, governments might worry that many current SEZ firms would leave in the face of higher tax payments.

Another way to avoid subsidizing exports is to remove the export requirements on SEZ companies. Non-exporting companies could then import material tariff free and sell their products on the domestic market. However, that would open the floodgates to tariff-free imports entering the country's domestic market. In the absence of export requirements, SEZ firms could simply import goods, add only marginal value, and then sell them domestically. That would obviously not be in the interest of governments using SEZs to benefit exporters while still protecting import-substituting industries.

Another problem with abolishing the export requirements is that if any company could obtain SEZ status, it would make little sense for importing companies to stay outside the zones. Since many companies import at least something, this would potentially place a large share of the economy under the SEZ umbrella. Governments would then lose the tax revenues from all those new SEZ companies. They would also lose the rents from several import-substituting industries, which would no longer benefit from lobbying for higher tariffs.

One option to avoid illegitimate subsidies is, of course, to abolish subsidies altogether. However, that would risk wiping out a big part of a country's exporting industry and foreign investments. Any government presumably wants to avoid the resulting job losses and the lost elections, demonstrations, and violent uprisings that might result.

It seems as though countries trying to reform their SEZ schemes are choosing different combinations of these admittedly politically unpalatable options. Both Vietnam and Malaysia have taken steps toward lower SEZ benefits by reducing the incentives for new SEZ investors. It is not quite clear how far they need to go in this direction to comply with the subsidy ban. China is pursuing a combination of broader SEZ inclusion and lower SEZ benefits. Starting in 2013, Chinese SEZ firms pay the same 25 percent corporate rate as other investors. They previously enjoyed a 10 percent rate, as opposed to 30 percent for the non-SEZ economy.[30] Thus far, though, China is keeping some of its incentives to companies that export.[31] Mauritius has a similar approach. It officially phased out its export oriented SEZ scheme in 2006, thus depriving exporters of their privileges.[32] In what may serve as a compensation for this change, the country introduced a 15 percent flat tax on all companies in the country in 2007, thus lowering the previous top business tax of 25 percent.[33] The Dominican Republic simply abolished the requirement that SEZ firms need to exports. At the same time, it started requiring SEZ firms to pay an extra tax on anything they sell on the domestic market.[34]

Some countries are avoiding the uncomfortable task of adjusting their tax and tariff rates by employing another way of offering benefits to traditional SEZ industries. One example of this is Costa Rica, which is defining a new category of processing companies that does not depend on their exports from the country. It is also basing more of its fiscal benefits on investors' location in impoverished and deprived areas.[35]

Not surprisingly, companies receiving subsidies on new terms that are not defined by exports tend to be the very firms that would take advantage of privileges for SEZ exporters. In small and developing countries, it is often easy to distinguish between goods that can be sold domestically and those that can only be exported. Much of the apparel produced in developing countries' SEZs, for instance, is exclusively targeted at markets in developed countries, where people can pay a price that covers production costs. Advanced medical equipment also lacks any substantial domestic market in small or poor countries. The same is true with many other kinds of traditional SEZ goods. And even if domestic consumers exist for the same kinds of goods, the domestically produced ones are too expensive for domestic consumers. SEZ workers in the Dominican Republic and Honduras make thousands of nice sweaters, pants, and pieces of underwear, while the clothes they wear are more likely made in China.

Thanks to the natural separation between domestic and foreign markets, a government can designate its export industries as belonging to new categories of firms and give subsidies on that basis without risking much leakage into the economy. The main leakage might come from damaged or defective products that producers decide to sell cheaply on the domestic market, but most brands have control systems to prevent such trade as a way of safeguarding their reputation.

Another way to single out exporters for SEZ benefits is to use the criterion of the size of a company's investment. In smaller countries, only multinational exporters can make large investments since no domestic consumer market exists for any large-scale production. A country with many such companies in its SEZs can therefore give subsidies to them without explicitly imposing export requirements. Investment requirements are part of the reforms in both El Salvador and Costa Rica (the latter of which has also designated strategic sectors eligible for tax benefits).[36] When joining the WTO in 2012, Russia also had to remove its export requirements for its SEZs but only the previous year, it imposed a $500 million investment requirement in the auto sector.[37]

As countries probe these various ways to preserve benefits for their exporters, they seem to be doing their best to maintain the structure of the SEZ regimes the WTO is requiring them to reform. Such actions reflect how important it is to governments to maintain a way to divide the economy into exporters enjoying tariff and tax relief, and import-substituting industries still protected by tariffs. If a government cannot use SEZs with export requirements, it will look for second-best options, such as strategic sectors and investment requirements, to accomplish the same thing. As long as such export-requirement proxies are available, governments can keep avoiding moving toward more liberalized or less distortive regimes.

Despite its implicit loopholes, the WTO ban on export requirements is inevitably stirring up the world of SEZs. As a result, the ban is likely to promote the natural path toward SEZs that are less reliant on fiscal benefits and more focused on regulatory and legal reforms. After the abolishment of the MFA, the enforcement of the subsidy ban is thus the second big driver of change in the world's SEZs regime stemming from the intergovernmental politics of international trade. It will unlikely be the last.

Future threats

Both the end of the global quota system and the introduction of restrictions on export subsidies caused a lot of disruption in the world of SEZs. In the long run, however, these reforms will likely foster a more efficient international allocation of capital. While this may be obvious in the case of textile quotas, making sure countries do not use SEZ benefits to discriminate between their exporters and non-exporters should also wipe out internal distortions, which ultimately would make the global economy more efficient as a whole.

Future threats to SEZs may be less benign for SEZ host countries. Their most obvious source comes from the use of FDI and capital flows for political means, which prevents economic activity from emerging where it is most warranted. Intergovernmental cooperation, through the WTO in particular, strives to prevent countries from using protectionist measures against each other. When cooperation breaks down, we see such restrictions appear in companies' ability to trade across borders, as they face import bans and other trade sanctions.

Nationalistic sentiments breed calls for nationalistic economic policies. With the increasing popularity of nationalistic politicians in many parts of the Western world, there will likely be more calls for policies that keep the jobs at home. The free flow of FDI may thus be constrained. This hinders companies from investing and expanding where they can be most profitable and also makes it harder for developing countries trying to attract foreign investors with their SEZs.

Capital controls are also playing an increasingly important role in international politics and cooperation, despite previously being disdained for hampering efficient resource allocation. The IMF has, since 2012, signaled its support for capital controls when warranted. A 2013 staff paper warned about the risks to China of opening its capital account, as free flows of capital might not only cause large inflows but also disruptive outflows.[38] After China saw large capital outflows in 2015 and 2016, the calls for tighter capital controls grew.[39] Such events further increase the risk of future acceptance and institutionalization of restrictions on capital movements.

To a large extent, SEZs rely on the flow of capital across national borders. When these are stymied, zones instead need to rely on domestic capital for their growth. The more domestic capital an SEZ regime hosts, the larger the risk that it falls prey to the political economy problems discussed in this book while failing to generate the positive dynamic effects that can lead to radically beneficial changes. If resources are merely moved from one part of the country to another, the risk is overwhelming that the losses will be larger than the gains. There is also more scope for rent-seeking since government officials can more easily extract rents from domestic firms, for whom it is harder to leave the country if they do not like the rent-seeking system.

When SEZs need to rely on domestic investors, it is also hard to imagine they could ever generate a countrywide liberalization driven by a reformist majority facing a predominantly rent-seeking elite. If a pro-reform minority introduces an SEZ in a country without foreign capital inflows, it risks causing a larger decrease in rent-seeking revenues for elites in other areas than the increase in new tax revenues for the SEZ's host. If so, the pro-reformers would be unable to pay off anti-reformers with the SEZ proceeds to get them to support the zone project.

With luck, these developing perspectives on international policy will revert to more open and market-friendly attitudes. If they do, there is reason to believe SEZs have a long future, with much potential to bring economic prosperity in many countries. However, it is also likely that tomorrow's SEZs will look very different than the traditional industrial-zone models that have dominated their history. This book concludes with a discussion of the future of SEZs.

The zones of the future

The zone concept has traveled far during its lifetime, from freeports to industrial parks to all-encompassing SEZs. Judging by the interest in zones today, it seems likely they are only at the beginning of their development, with ample opportunities for changes and improvement in the future.

After the great success of the Chinese SEZs, more countries have pledged their faith to larger and more-diversified zones, rather than the limited industrial parks exemplified by the traditional export processing zones. While many governments have political incentives to preserve more limited and isolated SEZ models, other regimes see profit opportunities in allowing SEZs to become larger, more diversified, and thus more economically beneficial.

SEZs are more effective when they include, or even rely on, regulatory reforms rather than fiscal incentives. A focus on rules will also make the SEZ model a likelier contributor to international economic efficiency, as opposed to the opposite. When SEZ regimes compete on being the cheapest alternative by offering fiscal benefits, they can rightly be blamed for misallocating resources both between and within countries. By contrast, competition between zones on the basis of the quality of their rules will likely increase global prosperity, by encouraging more business friendly and efficient public services.[40]

With the old industrial-park model of SEZs becoming obsolete and the WTO making it increasingly difficult to benefit exporters for political gains, the development is underway toward new forms of SEZs set to revolutionize the zone concept.

One type of change has to do with the sort of production and economic activity that SEZs foster. Most of the old SEZs aimed at establishing manufacturing industries in non-industrialized countries. Today, governments use SEZs to go further. Korea is using the zone model to promote human-capital formation by attracting foreign universities to set up campuses in the Incheon Free Economic Zone. Russia is investing in zones targeted at areas such as research and tourism.[41] The government of Ghana is supporting a $10 billion project called Hope City. The construction of this future high-tech city and IT hub has yet to begin.[42] Meanwhile, there are initiatives to launch so-called Eco-Industrial Parks, focused on various ecological and sustainable practices.[43]

Targeting more-advanced sectors may seem like the obvious path to the SEZs of the future. However, the political economy lesson to draw from past experience is that zone success relies on the institutional context of SEZs rather than the ability of policy makers to pick the right industries. Governments need to create environments for bottom-up development where investors are driven to invest in the most beneficial sectors by incentives that align their interests with engaging in wealth-increasing activities. For SEZs to be truly beneficial, they must solve political problems rather than economic ones. Thus, rather than seeking the optimal fiscal benefits, governments should focus on the rules and institutional setups of SEZs.

Some newer SEZ projects do have the potential to change the rules and institutions businesses face. China, the SEZ pioneer, is taking significant steps in this direction. It introduced the Shanghai Free Trade Pilot Zone (SFTPZ) in 2013, without offering it any preferential treatment. The zone is instead meant to experiment with new forms of administration. Among the reforms is the opening up of financial and other service sectors, the convertibility of the Renminbi, and broader market access for international investors.[44]

Another zone project focused on rules and institutions is an area the king of Saudi Arabia announced in 2005, called King Abdullah Economic City. This megaproject, with a size of Washington DC, aims primarily at economic diversification and job creation for the country's young population. Importantly, the city is to be completely privately developed, which may make it the largest privately developed zone in the world.

There are however worrying signs that the project may end up costing the Saudi government dearly. The project's finances deteriorated after the 2008 financial crisis, whereby the government stepped in and lent out money. If the city project blows up, the Saudi government might not get all its money back.

In this context, it is not a good sign that it seems the expensive buildings in the city are being erected before the legal framework is established.

If all goes well, though, the city has the potential to change the country's political economy. As with the early SEZs of China, people doing business in the new Saudi Arabian city zone will enjoy freedoms that people do not practice in the rest of the country. In addition to increased economic freedom, there will be greater personal freedom in the city. The religious police, which oversee proper Muslim conduct, will not be permitted there. Women and men are to be able to work and co-mingle quite freely, thus alleviating a separation that hampers much entrepreneurship today. Women will be able to dress more freely, while still being prohibited from driving. The new city might therefore, like the first SEZs of China, set in train a cascade of new oases of freedom in Saudi Arabia as local policy makers find they can benefit from similar reforms. This could change the country as a whole for the better.[45]

Another potentially radical SEZ project is located in Lagos, Nigeria. There, land is being reclaimed to establish Eko Atlantic City, projected to be a new, modern hub of opportunities in Africa's largest country. While many rules will likely improve with the zone, here too the government's commitment to the project risks creating a burden rather than a benefit for the Nigerian tax payers. With so much at stake, policy makers will have an incentive to funnel more resources to the city than optimal to make sure businesses come once it is built. The government will likely also need to find ways to isolate zone investors from such scourges of the Nigerian economy as corruption, political interference, and nepotism. It is nevertheless promising that much of the planning and development of the Nigerian city will be privately managed. Private investors will also administer the city's security, electricity, and water supply.[46]

Another example of an island of independent rule-making is found in Dubai, in the United Arab Emirates. The sharia laws governing the country make business hard for financial investors. The rulers of Dubai have therefore granted the Dubai International Financial Center the status of an independent jurisdiction, with its own non-sharia laws. Parties doing business in the finance center can agree on their own statutes as long as they do not clash with the rules of the financial center itself. Ultimately, if parties cannot agree, they are to revert to the "laws of England and Wales."[47]

Much of the growth of Dubai's financial center in the past decade can surely be attributed to this access to better rules for financial investors than those governing the country as a whole. The wealth creation this implies may well outweigh any infrastructure cost the government has contributed.

Sri Lanka is pursuing a similar strategy to Dubai in its development of a financial center. Plans are afoot there to introduce several new laws meant to make the financial zone attractive for investors.[48]

To be truly promising, the SEZs of the future will likely need to be more radical in their institutional emphasis. They will need to rely heavily on better rules and policies rather than merely including the institutional aspect as a complement to fiscal benefits to attract investors.[49]

The most successful SEZs may therefore still only be on the drawing table. The economist Paul Romer has promoted the idea of "charter cities." These are zones that would emulate or import the institutions of more-developed countries as a way to function better and become more prosperous.[50] With better rules, the thinking is, people could lift themselves out of poverty by unleashing the power of their creativity being hampered by the constraints bad institutions impose.

The concept of islands with Western rules in a sea of institutional under-development has been tested in various forms before. One historic example of this is the system of extraterritoriality in China, initially imposed on it by the British and Americans in the 1840s. It allowed the foreigners from numerous countries to be exempt from Chinese laws and instead be submitted to their own domestic laws.

The foreigners were more comfortable living and working in China because they felt safer living under their own judicial system, not least when it came to rules regarding property rights. They could even feel freer in the Chinese system than at home because their foreign status shielded them from many of their home regulations. Extraterritoriality in China likely increased the incentive for foreigners to do business in China, although it was also seen as preventing the country from opening up to trade, investments, and residency of foreigners.[51]

While the charter-city concept rightly emphasizes the adoption of better policies and institutions, the question is whether it entails the right process to find and implement the right institutions. The institutions of already-prosperous countries may not promote progress in less developed countries if they do not fit with the norms and cultures of those societies. Introducing other countries' institutions also imposes a problem in itself by possibly threatening the notion of a country's sovereignty. Even if the institutions are fundamentally compatible with the local culture, they may be rejected and disrespected on this basis.

A parallel, albeit radical, example of institutional transfer is the story of Fordlandia, mentioned in the prologue. This was a town established by Henry Ford in the Brazilian jungle as a production spot for the rubber used in tires, hoses, and other parts of the Ford cars. To create an American working environment for the indigenous workers, Ford not only built American-looking neighborhoods and facilities such as mess halls and churches in the jungle. He also prohibited alcohol, mandated an American diet, and offered only Western forms of entertainment, including golf during the day and American square dance in the evenings.

Alas, rather than generating a Western work ethic and Western efficiency, his workers complained about working conditions, the food, which tended to rot in the humid heat, and of being deprived of consuming alcohol. Eventually, the workers rebelled. As the Ford family abandoned the project, it was clear that the American institutions and way of life had not served to replicate the positive side of Western business culture.[52]

While no new plans are afoot to create a modern Fordlandia, Ford's project in the Brazilian jungle serves as a cautionary tale of how foreign institutions can clash with the local culture in dramatic and destructive ways. The stigma of colonialism and the power of patriotism also make people reluctant to allow a higher authority to impose its rules on them. Institutions are more likely to stick and become efficient if they can at least partially develop endogenously.

Honduras may be the country that has come furthest in instituting zones with an emphasis on endogenously enhanced institutions. A 2013 Honduran law allows the creation of so-called ZEDEs (*zonas de empleo y desarrollo* – employment and economic-development zones). These zones would be self-governing, with independent courts, police, prosecution, and prisons. They would also set their own immigration rules and control their own transportation systems.

Honduras criminal law is still to apply in the zones, though only under the administration of zone officers. As for the rest of the legal system, the ZEDE law expressly requires that the zone's courts operate independently of national ones and in the common-law tradition. Such a regime might create spaces in Honduras with a better institutional environment than that prevailing in the country as a whole.

The Honduran initiative also has important fiscal components, such as tariff-free imports for businesses investing in the zones. However, at least on the basis of the law in place, the government would not be obliged to provide the infrastructure and buildings needed to attract foreign businesses. Instead of providing resources to the zones, the government is actually to receive 12 percent of the taxes ZEDEs collect. The idea is that the improved rules will increase the prosperity in the zones to the extent that they can provide the rest of the country with direct benefits without that depriving the zones of their attractiveness to investors.[53]

The central part that rules and institutions play in these new initiatives is promising. These projects also have the potential to create entire communities and cities of development, which, like the SEZs of China, are much more diversified and dynamic than conventional industrial parks. So far, only smaller SEZs have been privately developed and managed. However, with more experimentation with different rules in city-sized SEZs, even such large zones might flourish thanks to private ownership and development. In many places, governments may thus cease to be the go-to developer of new communities. The attractiveness of this extraterritorial feature of rule-based SEZs has even spurred a movement to create floating cities on the ocean, away from the legal frameworks of any nation-state.[54] Even if governments do not introduce independent SEZs, the demand for spaces with better rules may be so strong that they emerge without government involvement.

The biggest threat to privately developed city zones is host governments exceeding their limited role as hosts. Based on the history of SEZs, the worry should not be primarily that the government will step in and raise the fees or taxes zone investors must pay, or even confiscate attractive and successful companies and other resources. Once a government has endorsed a zone project, it seems the political imperative is instead to make sure to keep it alive and thriving.

Governments pose a larger threat to the success of new SEZ initiatives in their tendency to deploy their fiscal powers to help attract zone investors. Once SEZs start growing, policy makers have an incentive to control their development and claim credit for their growth. They might therefore choose to devote resources to the zones and impose directives on them beyond their original mandate. While more public resources increase the chance for superficial success for the zones and private cities, they also mute the signal that profits and losses send to zone developers about the net benefit of a project. They therefore diminish the chance that the zones will be drivers of countrywide economic development.

The ultimate test for new, rules-based city zones will therefore be whether governments will tweak their institutional frameworks to transform them into more traditional SEZs. To truly benefit their host countries, zones need better-working rules that are free from the old patterns of nepotism and that can work unhindered by a country's networks of corruption. The political economy dilemma is that this kind of development is unlikely to provide specific accomplishments that policy makers can claim credit for achieving.

If policy makers and practitioners stick to such radical reforms as different judicial and political systems, tomorrow's zone projects should be able to claim genuine success. Perhaps by necessity, many governments will increasingly also choose to rely on the private sector to provide for the SEZs and also acknowledge the limits of the old industrial-park model.

The political economy of SEZs teaches many lessons of how zone schemes can go wrong. Yet while many mistakes have been made throughout the history of SEZs, there is reason to be optimistic about the future. If done right, tomorrow's SEZs offer the chance to improve the lives of millions of people.

Notes

1 Wong and Chu 1985: 2; FIAS 2008.
2 World Bank 1992: 8.
3 Farole 2011; Farole and Moberg 2014.
4 Constantinescu et al. 2015: 8.
5 Subramanian and Kessler 2013.
6 Eichengreen 2011.
7 Baldwin 2011; 2012.
8 Baldwin 2012.
9 FIAS 2008: 65.
10 Nadvi 1992: 19; Nadvi 1998; CSF 2007: 63.
11 Baldwin 2012.
12 Acevedo and Robertson 2011.
13 Rhee and Belot 1990: 3–18; Ahmed 2009.

14 Id.; Hasan et al. 2016: 40, 46.
15 Id.
16 Kelegama 2009.
17 Ofreneo 2009.
18 Thee 2009.
19 Truett and Truett 2007.
20 Ofreneo 2009: 553.
21 Rasiah 2009.
22 Rasiah and Ofreneo 2009: 504.
23 WTO 2016: Article 3.1(a), Article 5(a).
24 Id.: Article 3.1(b).
25 Waters 2013: 502.
26 WTO 2016: Article 4.10.
27 Id.: Article 1.1(iii).
28 Id.: Annex VII; Waters 2013: 484.
29 USTR and Commerce 2010: 25.
30 Defever and Riaño 2016: 9.
31 Id.: 10.
32 WTO 2014.
33 IMF 2008.
34 National Congress 2011.
35 Farole 2012: 6.
36 Waters 2013:509–11.
37 O'Neal 2014: 411; United States Trade Representative 2014: 45.
38 Ostry et al. 2012; Bayoumi and Ohnsorge 2013.
39 Wheatley and Donnan 2016; Giles 2016.
40 Bell 2012.
41 Rybakov 2009.
42 BBC News 2013; Swali Africa 2015; Vourlias 2015.
43 Kechichian and Jeong 2016.
44 Hu 2016.
45 Moser et al. 2015; *Economist* 2016; Kane 2016.
46 Africa Research Online 2013; Oduntan 2015; Eko Atlantic 2016; Uroko 2016
47 DIFC Law No. 3 of 2004.
48 Jayasekera 2016.
49 *Economist* 2015.
50 Romer 2010.
51 Foreign Policy Association 1925; Loring 1925; Turner 1929; Thomas 1943.
52 Grandin 2009.
53 Gazeta 2013.
54 Seasteading Institute 2016.

References

Acevedo, Gladys Lopez, and Raymond Robertson. 2011. "Sewing Success: Employment and Wage Effects of the end of the Multi-fibre Arrangement (MFA)." *Volume I: Main Report.* The World Bank, Washington D.C.

Africa Research Online. 2013. "Nigeria: Africa's First 'Smart City'." *Africa Research Online*, Mar. 19, 2013. Available at: https://africaresearchonline.wordpress.com/2013/03/19/nigeria-africas-first-smart-city/ (accessed 29 October 2016).

Ahmed, Nazneen. 2009. "Sustaining Ready-Made Garment Exports from Bangladesh." *Journal of Contemporary Asia* 39(4): 597–618.

Baldwin, Richard. 2011. "Trade and Industrialisation After Globalisation's 2nd Unbundling: How Building and Joining a Supply Chain are Different and Why It Matters." *National Bureau of Economic Research*, No. w17716.

Baldwin, Richard. 2012. "Global Supply Chains: Why They Emerged, Why They Matter, and Where They Are Going." *SSRN* Available at: http://ssrn.com/abstract= 2153484 (accessed 29 October 2016).

Bayoumi, Tamim, and Franziska Ohnsorge. 2013. "Do Inflows or Outflows Dominate? Global implications of capital account liberalization in China." *International Monetary Fund Working Paper* No. 13–189.

BBC News. 2013. "Ghana's John Mahama Launches Hope City Project." *BBC News*, Mar. 4, 2013. Available at: http://www.bbc.com/news/world-africa-21658149 (accessed 29 October 2016).

Bell, Tom W. 2012. "Principles of Contracts for Governing Services." *Griffith Law Review* 21: 472.

Constantinescu, Cristina, Aaditya Mattoo, and Michele Ruta. 2015. "The Global Trade Slowdown: Cyclical or Structural?" *The World Bank, Policy Research Working Paper* 7158. Available at: http://documents.worldbank.org/curated/en/ 991561468127799318/pdf/WPS7158-REPLACEMENT-The-Global-Trade-Slowdown-Cyclical-or-Structural.pdf (accessed 29 October 2016).

CSF (Competitiveness Support Fund). 2007. "Special Economic Zone Benchmarking and Policy Action Plan." *CSF*May 31, 2007.

Defever, Fabrice, and Alejandro Riaño. 2016. "Protectionism through Exporting: Subsidies with Export: Share Requirements in China." *CEP Discussion Paper* No 1431.

DIFC Law No. 3 of 2004. Law on the Application of Civil and Commercial Laws in the DIFC, art. 8(2)(e), (making provision for the laws of England and Wales the default in the absence of other rules specifically applicable or chosen by the parties). Available at: https://www.difc.ae/files/9214/5448/9184/Law_on_the_Application_of_Civil_and_ Commercial_Laws_in_the_DIFC_DIFC_Law_No._3_oF_2004.pdf (accessed 29 October 2016).

Economist, The. 2015. Special Economic Zones: Political Priority, Economic Gamble." *The Economist*, Apr. 4, 2015. Available at: http://www.economist.com/news/fina nce-and-economics/21647630-free-trade-zones-are-more-popular-everwith-politicia ns-if-not (accessed 29 October 2016).

Economist, The. 2016. "Saudi Arabia's Financial Hub: Castles in the Air." *The Economist*Jan. 30, 2016. Available at: http://www.economist.com/news/middle-east-and-a frica/21689615-if-you-build-it-they-may-not-come-castles-air (accessed 29 October 2016).

Eichengreen, Barry. 2011. "Escaping the Middle-Income Trap." Proceedings-Economic Policy Symposium-Jackson Hole. Federal Reserve Bank of Kansas City.

EkoAtlantic. 2016. "About Eko Atlantic." *Eko Homepage*. Available at: http://www. ekoatlantic.com/about-us/ (accessed 29 October 2016).

Farole, Thomas. 2011. *Special Economic Zones in Africa: Comparing Performance and Learning from Global Experience.* The World Bank, Washington, D.C.

Farole, Thomas. 2012. "Competitiveness and Regional Integration in Central America: The Role of Special Economic Zones." World Bank memo, The World Bank, Washington D.C.

Farole, Thomas, and Lotta Moberg. 2014. "It Worked in China, so Why not in Africa? The Political Economy Challenge of Special Economic Zones." UNU-WIDER

Working Paper 152/2014. Available at: https://www.wider.unu.edu/publication/it-wor ked-china-so-why-not-africa (accessed 29 October 2016).

FIAS (The World Bank's Facility for Investment Climate Advisory Services). 2008. *Special Economic Zones: Performance, Lessons Learned, and Implications for Zone Development*. World Bank Group, Washington, D.C.

Foreign Policy Association. 1925. "Extraterritoriality in China." *Editorial Information Service*, Series 1925–1926, No. 6, Dec. 18, 1925. Available at: https://archive.org/ stream/ExtraterritorialityInChina/B0007678_djvu.txt (accessed 29 October 2016).

Gazeta, La. 2013. "Poder Legislativo: Decreto No. 35–2013.". Sep. 6, 2013. *La Gazeta* (Official Journal of the Republic of Honduras).

Giles, Chris. 2016. "Kuroda Calls for China to Tighten Capital Controls." *The Financial Times*, Jan. 23, 2016. Available at: http://www.ft.com/intl/cms/s/0/03395bdc-c1c4-11e5-808f-8231cd71622e.html (accessed 29 October 2016).

Grandin, Greg. 2009. *Fordlandia: The Rise and Fall of Henry Ford's Forgotten Jungle City*. Macmillan.

Hasan, K. M. Faridul, Md. Shipan Mia, Md. Mostafizur Rahman, A. N. M. Ahmed Ullah, and Muhammad Shariat Ullah. 2016. "Role of Textile and Clothing Indus-tries in the Growth and Development of Trade & Business Strategies of Bangladesh in the Global Economy." *International Journal of Textile Science* 5(3): 39–48.

Hu, Jiaxiang. 2016. "A Small Difference in Wording, but a Big Difference in Rule-Making: A Retrospective and Prospective View on the Development of China's Economic Zones." In: *Finance, Rule of Law and Development in Asia* (Jiaxing Hu, Matthias Vanhullebusch, and Andrew Harding eds.). International Law E-Books Online, Collection 2016. Brill | Nijhoff, Leiden, The Netherlands, pp. 137–167.

IMF Country Report No. 08/238. 2008. Mauritius: 2008 Article IV Consultation—Staff Report; Staff Statement; Public Information Notice on the Executive Board Discussion; and Statement by the Executive Director for Mauritius." Available at: https://www.imf.org/external/pubs/ft/scr/2008/cr08238.pdf (accessed November 3, 2016).

Jayasekera, Sandun A. 2016. "Port City to Become Int'l Financial Center Soon." *Daily Mirror* (Sri Lanka), June 30, 2016.

Kane, Frank. 2016. "King Abdullah Economic City Chief Champions Cause of a Red Sea Metropolis." *The National*, Jan. 26, 2016. Available at: http://www.thenational. ae/business/economy/king-abdullah-economic-city-chief-champions-cause-of-a-red-sea-metropolis#full (accessed 29 October 2016).

Kechichian, Etienne, and Mi Hoon Jeong. 2016. "Mainstreaming Eco-Industrial Parks." World Bank. Available at: https://openknowledge.worldbank.org/handle/ 10986/24921 (accessed 29 October 2016).

Kelegama, Saman. 2009. "Ready-Made Garment Exports from Sri Lanka." *Journal of Contemporary Asia* 39(4): 579–596.

Loring, Charles. 1925. "American Extraterritoriality in China." *Minnesota Law Review* 10: 407.

Moser, Sarah, Marian Swain, and Mohammed H. Alkhabbaz. 2015. "King Abdullah Economic City: Engineering Saudi Arabia's post-oil future." *Cities* 45: 71–80.

Nadvi, Khalid. 1992. "Flexible Specialisation, Industrial Districts and Employment in Pakistan." *International Labour Organization working paper* No. 288872.

Nadvi, Khalid. 1998. "Knowing Me, Knowing You: Social Networks in the Surgical Instrument Cluster of Sialkot, Pakistan." Institute of Development Studies, University of Sussex, Sussex, UK.

National Congress (Congreso Nacional). 2011. Law 139-1 (Ley 139-11). Available at: http://www.poderjudicial.gob.do/documentos/PDF/novedades/Novedad_Ley_No_ 139-11.pdf (accessed November 3, 2016).

Oduntan, Gbenga. 2015. "Why Nigeria's Plans for a Dream Eldorado City are not Radical Enough." *CNN*, Aug. 10, 2015. Available at: http://www.cnn.com/2015/08/ 10/africa/eko-atlantic-gbenga-oduntan-conversation/ (29 October 2016).

Ofreneo, Rene E. 2009. "Development Choices for Philippine Textiles and Garments in the Post-MFA Era." *Journal of Contemporary Asia* 39(4): 543–561.

O'Neal, Molly. 2014. "Russia in WTO: Interests, Policy Autonomy, and Deliberations." *Eurasian Geography and Economics* 55(4): 404–421.

Ostry, Jonathan, Atish Ghosh, and Anton Korinek. 2012. "Multilateral Aspects of Managing the Capital Account." *International Monetary Fund Staff Discussion Note* No. 12/10.

Rasiah, Rajah. 2009. "Malaysia's Textile and Garment Firms at the Crossroads." *Journal of Contemporary Asia* 39(4): 530–542.

Rasiah, Rajah, and Rene E. Ofreneo. 2009. "Introduction: The Dynamics of Textile and Garment Manufacturing in Asia." *Journal of Contemporary Asia* 39(4): 501–511.

Rhee, Yung Whee, and Therese Belot. 1990. "Export Catalysts in Low-income Countries: A Review of Eleven Success Stories." *The World Bank*The World Bank, Washington, D.C.

Romer, Paul. 2010. "Technologies, Rules, and Progress: The Case for Charter Cities." *The Center for Global Development Essay*, Mar. 2010. Available at: www.cgdev.org/ content/publications/detail/1423916 (accessed 29 October 2016).

Rybakov, Leonid. 2009. "Special Economic Zones: Foreign direct investment boosts Russian economy." *Telegraph*, Apr. 24, 2009.

SeasteadingInstitute. 2016. Homepage, available at: http://www.seasteading.org/ (accessed 29 October 2016).

Subramanian, Arvind, and Martin Kessler. 2013. "The Hyperglobalization of Trade and its Future." *Peterson Institute for International Economics Working Paper* 13–16.

Swali Africa. 2015. "Is Ghana's Hope City a Reality or Fantasy?" *Swali Africa*, Nov. 7, 2015. Available at: http://blog.swaliafrica.com/is-ghanas-hope-city-a-reality-or-fantasy/ (accessed 29 October 2016).

Thee, Kian Wie. 2009. "The Development of Labour-Intensive Garment Manufacturing in Indonesia." *Journal of Contemporary Asia* 39(4): 562–578.

Thomas, Elbert D.Thomas. 1943. "Extraterritoriality in China." United States Senate Document No. 102, 78th Congress, 1st Session. United States Government Printing Office, Washington, D.C.

Truett, Lila J., and Dale B. Truett. 2007. "NAFTA and the Maquiladoras: Boon or Bane?" *Contemporary Economic Policy* 25(3): 374–386.

Turner, Skinner. 1929. "Extraterritoriality in China." *British Year Book of International Law* 10: 56.

United States Trade Representative. 2014. "Report on Russia's Implementation of the WTO Agreement." *Report*, Dec. 2014.

Uroko, Chuka. 2016. "ESLA, Orlean Lead Ambitious Residential Towers Developments in Eko Atlantic City… 1,000 Apartments Expected from First Set of Towers." *Eko Atlantic*, Mar. 15, 2016. Available at: http://www.ekoatlantic.com/latestnews/esla-orlean-lead-ambitious-residential-towers-developments-eko-atlantic-city-1000-apartm ents-expected-first-set-towers/ (accessed 29 October 2016).

USTR (U.S. Trade Representative) and Commerce (U.S. Department of Commerce). 2010. "Subsidies Enforcement: Annual Report to the Congress." *Joint Report*, Feb. 2010. Available at: http://ia.ita.doc.gov/esel/reports/seo2010/seo-annual-report-2010. pdf (accessed 29 October 2016).

Waters, James J. 2013. "Achieving World Trade Organization Compliance for Export Processing Zones while Maintaining Economic Competitiveness for Developing Countries." *Duke Law Journal* 63: 481.

Wheatley, Jonathan, and Shawn Donnan. 2016. "Capital Controls No Longer Taboo as Emerging Markets Battle Flight." *The Financial Times*, Jan. 27, 2016. Available at: http://www.ft.com/intl/cms/s/0/36cfcc66-c41b-11e5-808f-8231cd71622e.html#axzz3z W2gkWZL (accessed 29 October 2016).

Vourlias, Christopher. 2015. "Lowered Expectations for Ghana's Hope City?" *Aljazeera America*, Apr. 19, 2015. Available at: http://america.aljazeera.com/articles/2015/4/19/ lowered-expectations-for-ghanas-hope-city.html (accessed 29 October 2016).

Wong, Kwan-Yiu, and David K.Y. Chu. 1985. *Modernization in China: the case of the Shenzhen special economic zone*. Oxford University Press, Hong Kong.

World Bank. 1992. *Export Processing Zones*. The World Bank, Washington, D.C.

WTO (World Trade Organization). 2014. "Trade Policy Review Body, Trade policy review: Report by the secretariat: Mauritius." WT/TPR/S/304, (14-5196). Available at: https://www.wto.org/english/tratop_e/tpr_e/tp404_e.htm (accessed November 3, 2016).

WTO (World Trade Organization). 2016. "Uruguay Round Agreement: Agreement on Subsidies and Countervailing Measures." *WTO* Available at: https://www.wto.org/ english/docs_e/legal_e/24-scm_01_e.htm (accessed 29 October 2016).

Conclusion

At first glance, SEZs look like the optimal development policy. They have numerous obvious benefits and seem less costly than foreign aid and most industrial policies. They encourage market actors to invest, expand, and employ people.

The hidden side of SEZs is a plethora of market distortions, rent-seeking, and expensive vote-winning schemes by politicians. When taking these downsides into account, the disappointing conclusion is that countries are sometimes better off without them. This is particularly so for poor countries with badly designed institutions that encourage rent-seeking or distort the government's decision-making.

However, when looking deeper into the political economy of SEZs, it becomes clear they can also have powerful political effects, which are rarely mentioned in the literature on SEZs. In the right context, SEZs can align the incentives of powerful elites with the development of the economy as a whole. They can disrupt systems of protectionism. They can generate processes yielding more zones that ultimately change policies and the business environment in the rest of the economy.

Through their dynamic and political impact, SEZs have benefited people in ways we cannot always detect afterward. I used the example of China to illustrate some of these effects because the country provides the most illustrative case of an SEZ scheme spurring both economic and political reform. However, several other countries may also enjoy a better policy climate today than they would have in the absence of their SEZs.

The political impact of SEZs is hard to discern through regular economic analysis. You should not conclude too quickly that a developing country's SEZs were useless simply because they failed to take off or grew only slowly due to bitter opposition from the establishment. The political economy side of such a story may be that the SEZs succeeded where no other policy could, in slowly but steadily breaking through a powerful wall of reform resistance until most policy makers found that they could benefit from the openness the zones provided.

While the hidden success stories about SEZs offer reasons to be sanguine about the past, there is an even greater reason to be optimistic about the future. Some may believe that SEZs have already completed their role in most countries, which are stuck in the middle-income trap and can no longer use zones to boost manufacturing exports. In fact, SEZs are transforming into much more promising models with more potential to serve as the policy catalysts that made some of them especially beneficial in the past.

In building the zones of the future, this book offers some guidance for SEZ practitioners to what makes SEZs truly successful:

- Promote private zones with limited government investments
- Avoid centralized planning of zone locations and industries
- Make zones special through institutional and policy reforms rather than fiscal incentives
- Make zones large enough so that the dynamics of institutional and policy reforms can play out

By no means is this a comprehensive list and as has been discussed, an SEZ practitioner may also need to discard some of the best zone models depending on what is politically feasible.

We may think of the time since the first modern SEZ as a half-century test ride of a vehicle during which the concept was not fully developed into what it should be but occasionally still managed to steer quite right. The ancient Greeks made the island of Delos into a free harbor, and Ireland later applied the same concept. Fordlandia, in the Brazilian jungle, tried changing the rules and institutions in a confined space, similar to some zones and cities currently under development in Saudi Arabia, Honduras, and elsewhere.

In the future, SEZs will likely be larger, more diversified, and more focused on regulatory and legislative reforms rather than fiscal incentives. This will make them more dynamic, less expensive, more conducive to natural market developments, and therefore more likely to improve on a country's economy.

For anyone interested in policies for economic development, SEZs are a policy to watch. We just need to remember that behind the façade of export performance, investment figures, and employment data lie political economy dynamics, which are the true determinants of whether an SEZ scheme will really be a success. Only by understanding these hidden sides of SEZs can we ensure that the zones will serve as the development policy they are meant to be.

Index

Taylor & Francis eBooks

Helping you to choose the right eBooks for your Library

Add Routledge titles to your library's digital collection today. Taylor and Francis ebooks contains over 50,000 titles in the Humanities, Social Sciences, Behavioural Sciences, Built Environment and Law.

Choose from a range of subject packages or create your own!

Benefits for you
» Free MARC records
» COUNTER-compliant usage statistics
» Flexible purchase and pricing options
» All titles DRM-free.

Benefits for your user
» Off-site, anytime access via Athens or referring URL
» Print or copy pages or chapters
» Full content search
» Bookmark, highlight and annotate text
» Access to thousands of pages of quality research at the click of a button.

| REQUEST YOUR **FREE** INSTITUTIONAL TRIAL TODAY | **Free Trials Available** We offer free trials to qualifying academic, corporate and government customers. |

eCollections – Choose from over 30 subject eCollections, including:

Archaeology	Language Learning
Architecture	Law
Asian Studies	Literature
Business & Management	Media & Communication
Classical Studies	Middle East Studies
Construction	Music
Creative & Media Arts	Philosophy
Criminology & Criminal Justice	Planning
Economics	Politics
Education	Psychology & Mental Health
Energy	Religion
Engineering	Security
English Language & Linguistics	Social Work
Environment & Sustainability	Sociology
Geography	Sport
Health Studies	Theatre & Performance
History	Tourism, Hospitality & Events

For more information, pricing enquiries or to order a free trial, please contact your local sales team:
www.tandfebooks.com/page/sales

 Routledge
Taylor & Francis Group

The home of
Routledge books

www.tandfebooks.com

Printed in the United States
by Baker & Taylor Publisher Services